JOHN LEE "SONNY BOY" WILLIAMSON

Roots of American Music
Folk, Americana, Blues, and Country

June Skinner Sawyers, series editor

In recent decades American roots music has experienced a revival in popular performance and critical attention. Rowman & Littlefield's series Roots of American Music: Folk, Americana, Blues, and Country seeks to explore the origins of these musical genres as integral parts of cultural experience and shared musical history. With dynamic biographies of musicians responsible for enduring traditions in these genres, the series introduces accessible scholarship to expose the significance of these musicians to a wide audience. Stylistic and cultural investigations into the genres provide contextual anchors for broader understanding of trends which continue to influence music today. Just like the musical traditions investigated, this series looks to music's past in order to understand its future. The series welcomes projects which seek to explore the reaches of folk, Americana, blues, and country traditions as they were formed in the past and as they continue to evolve in the contemporary music scene.

Titles in the Series

John Lee "Sonny Boy" Williamson: The Blues Harmonica of Chicago's Bronzeville by Mitsutoshi Inaba (2016)

JOHN LEE "SONNY BOY" WILLIAMSON

The Blues Harmonica of Chicago's Bronzeville

Mitsutoshi Inaba

ROWMAN & LITTLEFIELD
Lanham • Boulder • New York • London

Published by Rowman & Littlefield
A wholly owned subsidiary of The Rowman & Littlefield Publishing Group, Inc.
4501 Forbes Boulevard, Suite 200, Lanham, Maryland 20706
www.rowman.com

Unit A, Whitacre Mews, 26-34 Stannary Street, London SE11 4AB

British Library Cataloguing in Publication Information Available

Library of Congress Cataloging-in-Publication Data

Name: Inaba, Mitsutoshi, 1964–, author.
Title: John Lee "Sonny Boy" Williamson ; the blues harmonica of Chicago's Bronzeville / Mitsutoshi
    Inaba.
Description: Lanham : Rowman & Littlefield, 2016. | Series: Roots of American music: folk,
    Americana, blues, and country | Includes bibliographical references and index.
Identifiers: LCCN 2016010945 | ISBN 9781442254428 (hardcover : alk. paper)
Subjects: LCSH: Williamson, Sonny Boy, 1914–1948. | Harmonica players—United States—Biogra-
    phy. | Blues musicians—United States—Biography. | Blues (Music)—Illinois—Chicago—His-
    tory and criticism.
Classification: LCC ML419.W53 I53 2016 | DDC 788.8/21643092—dc23 LC record available at
    http://lccn.loc.gov/2016010945

Printed in the United States of America

For everyone who taught me the beauty of black music
and to love the blues

* * *

For Pam and Aria

CONTENTS

SERIES FOREWORD

This volume is the first book in a series called Roots of American Music: Folk, Americana, Blues, and Country. Each book in the series examines the influences on and of the music from a cultural context. Moreover, the books are written by authors who are knowledgeable and authoritative in their field, but who still are able to communicate to the general reader. The series examines the body of work by particular artists in folk, Americana, blues, and country, and their offshoots; explores the various influences and roots of these artists, both major as well as lesser-known artists who warrant closer examination; and studies musical trends within these genres in an attempt to understand, and reveal, their histori-cal influences.

The first title in the series, *John Lee "Sonny Boy" Williamson: The Blues Harmonica of Chicago's Bronzeville* by Mitsutoshi Inaba, offers an in-depth exploration of this singular bluesman's life and career with an emphasis on the recording sessions that began in 1937 and ended with his untimely and tragic death at the age of thirty-four in 1948. His lyrics were original and idiosyncratic. They included biographical and personal refer-ences as well as sharp observations of life as he knew it and lived it.

John Lee "Sonny Boy" Williamson was a highly influential harmonica player credited with turning the blues harp from an accompanying instru-ment into a versatile solo instrument. He was also one of the first harmon-ica players to introduce amplification, an important cultural moment that anticipated the careers of subsequent generations of bluesmen and, later, rock 'n' rollers. With the possible exception of Little Walter, no harmonica player was as important a figure within the blues tradition. His playing technique was widely imitated as was his distinctive voice: a tongue-tied, lisping style of singing. Along with Big Bill Broonzy, Arthur "Big Boy" Crudup, and Tampa Red, among others, he helped create the celebrated Bluebird Beat, a mixture of older black blues with newer swing rhythms, featuring electric guitar, harmonica, piano, and drums. For these and other reasons, he has often been called "the father of the modern blues harp."

A prolific songwriter, his compositions include "Blue Bird Blues," "Early in the Morning," "Decoration Blues," "Hoodoo Hoodoo" (Hoodoo Man Blues), "Mellow Chick Swing," "Polly Put Your Kettle On," and many more. But his first recording, "Good Morning, School Girl," remains his best-known work, and quickly became a blues standard as well as a favorite of later rhythm and blues and rock 'n' roll bands.

Despite his fame, surprisingly little has been written about Sonny Boy Williamson. To fill that gap, Mitsutoshi Inaba offers a close reading of Williamson's lyrics, placing them in a historical perspective while also examining the important role he played in the Chicago blues tradition, specifically, and the broader blues tradition, generally. It is both a cultural study—of a man, his art, and his times—but also a historical study of America writ large as seen through the perspective of a seminal figure in the early Chicago blues scene during the first half of the twentieth century: an African American musician who truly helped create the Sound of Bronzeville.

June Sawyers
Series Editor

ACKNOWLEDGMENTS

This is my second book, but it never was easy. Not only was writing a book in a second language a lot of work, but learning about African American folk culture is quite a profound task, especially for a total alien like me, who was born in Japan in the mid-1960s. The more I learn, the less I know. But as with my book on Willie Dixon, many people kindly offered me help and guidance with their hands, feet, voices, and thoughts beyond simply bridging cultural differences.

This work started as a collaboration with Jim O'Neal, cofounder of *Living Blues*. After I conducted research in Chicago and started writing the manuscript, Jim contracted a serious medical condition. When he got better, he became very busy with *Mississippi Blues Trail* so I took over the project. He generously provided me with his unpublished interview with T. W. Utley, Sonny Boy's half brother, and Fred Utley, Sonny Boy's uncle. Thank you, Jim.

This work would have not been developed without the cooperation of the Jackson-Madison County Library in Jackson, Tennessee. Jackson is Sonny Boy's birthplace, and this is where he started to play harmonica. I would like to express my most sincere appreciation to librarians Michael Baker and Jack Wood.

I would like to thank Vera Davis of the Black Metropolis Research Consortium for funding my research in Chicago. For their research assistance in Chicago, I thank Linda Evans of the Chicago History Museum, Suzanne Flandreau of the Center for Black Music Research, and Roger Williams of the Harold Washington Library. Also in Chicago, I conducted interviews with Billy Boy Arnold, Joe Filisko, and Bob Koester. Your voices are the most valuable in this work. Thank you.

For their contributions in obtaining information, inspiration, constructive criticisms, networks, and warm friendship, I thank Sumito "Ariyo" Ariyoshi, Dr. David Evans, Dr. Bill Ferris, Dr. Greg Hansen, Laurence Hoffman, Kit Michaels Sensei, Shoji Naito, and Jas Obrecht. And Dr. Adam Gussow, thank you very much for a nice blurb on the back cover.

I would like to thank Dr. David Guest of Austin Peay State University for funding copyright fees.

My very special gratitude is extended to the editors and staff members at Rowman & Littlefield—Bennett Graff, June Sawyers, Natalie Mandziuk, Monica Savaglia, and Kellie Hagan in editorial acquisitions and production; Dustin Watson in cover design; Jacqline Barnes in publicity; and Jared Hughes in marketing. Thanks for your patience with me.

Most of all, I would like to thank my parents, Terumi and Shuko Inaba. Your encouragement, understanding, and constant support are greatly appreciated.

And to my wife, Pam, and daughter, Aria—you two are very good listeners to my story, my true inspiration, and my most faithful supporters. I don't know how to thank you. There will be more.

PERMISSIONS

"Bluebird Blues," "Dealing with the Devil," and "Sonny Boy's Jump"

Words and music by Willie Williamson
  Copyright © 1970 by Arc Music Corp.
  Copyright renewed
  This arrangement copyright © 2016 by Arc Music Corp.
  All rights administered by BMG Rights Management (U.S.) LLC
  All rights reserved, used by permission
  Reprinted by permission of Hal Leonard Corporation

"Decoration Day"

Words and music by Sonny Boy Williamson

"Good Morning Little Schoolgirl:

"Deep Down in the Jungle," "Early in the Morning," and "Sunny Land"

"Mellow Chick Swing"

Advertisements of Club Georgia: August 16, 1947, and September 13, 1947

INTRODUCTION

His popularity started in the 1930s . . . and he was one of the guys who kept recording during the war. That was a pretty good indication to see how popular he was.—Bob Koester, Delmark Records and Jazz Record Mart[1]

One truly amazing characteristic of [Sonny Boy] Williamson's music is that in it, one hears not only the past . . . but also the future.— Lawrence Hoffman, *Living Blues*[2]

John Lee "Sonny Boy" Williamson (1914–1948) was one of the most popular blues artists in the late 1930s and 1940s. With Big Bill Broonzy, Tampa Red, Roosevelt Sykes, and Washboard Sam, Sonny Boy recorded for Bluebird Records, a subsidiary of RCA Victor Records. The music they created was called the Bluebird Beat, which occupied the blues record market until it was taken over by the next generation of Chicago blues with artists such as Muddy Waters, Little Walter, and Howlin' Wolf. Sonny Boy recorded more than 120 sides for the Bluebird and RCA Victor labels and played harmonica accompaniment on many more blues records by his label mates. With his innovative performing style, Sonny Boy was one of the artists who formed the foundation of the electric Chicago blues.

In the history of blues harmonica, before Little Walter there was Sonny Boy Williamson. As detailed in this book, he popularized the harmonica performing style of quickly switching between voice and instrument. He also standardized harmonica performing techniques that became quite common for many musicians—producing loud and crunchy sounds from a tiny instrument to both compete and collaborate with other instruments in a band. In this way, Sonny Boy was one of the musicians who changed the role of harmonica from a complementary to a lead instrument in a blues band. What's more, he was one of the harmonica players who introduced amplification.

Sonny Boy Williamson came from a long lineage of blues harmonica—beginning with a dusty, countrified style to a sharp, urbanized style spiced with the music of Louis Jordan. As quoted by Lawrence Hoffman at the beginning of the chapter, Sonny Boy's music shows both the past and the future of harmonica performance. He was a student of the musical tradition of West Tennessee. By jamming with the musicians of the Jackson-Brownsville blues community—Sleepy John Estes, Yank Rachell, and Hammie Nixon—Sonny Boy polished his musicianship. He learned harmonica directly from Hammie Nixon and absorbed influences from such artists as Noah Lewis, who recorded mainly in Memphis. This was the past.

Sonny Boy established his professional career in St. Louis before moving to the South Side of Chicago. With influences from swing to jump blues, he crafted a sound of his own—the sound of Bronzeville. The performing style he established anticipated the future of blues harmonica performance. He influenced many musicians—Little Walter, Junior Wells, Billy Boy Arnold, and Snooky Pryor. Like Aleck/Alex "Rice" Miller, better known as Sonny Boy Williamson II, some artists even took their nicknames from Sonny Boy.

Sonny Boy was also an influential singer. His lisping, gabbling vocal style—he crammed many words into short phrases—was widely imitated. He was also a prolific songwriter. His compositions made the Chicago blues repertoire rich—"Good Morning, School Girl," "Blue Bird Blues," "Early in the Morning," "Decoration Blues," "Hoodoo Hoodoo" (Hoodoo Man Blues), "Mellow Chick Swing," "Polly Put Your Kettle On," and many more.

But life was not very easy for him. He was constantly battling against alcohol. At the peak of popularity and just after forming his new musical style, Sonny Boy was murdered while on his way home from his regular venue. He was only thirty-four years old. Many people believed that he was stabbed in the head with an ice pick. Because the case remains unsolved to this day, there are many different stories about his death, and we still hear new theories.

* * *

This book describes the music and life of Sonny Boy Williamson, a bluesman who transformed harmonica performance practice from West Tennessee to a blueprint of postwar electric Chicago blues.

This is not the first book written about Sonny Boy. A German blues enthusiast, Wolfgang Lorenz, published *Bluebird Blues* in 1986. While I relied on Lorenz's book to some extent, especially for transcriptions of lyrics, my book still adds much to the literature. To begin with, this is the first book about Sonny Boy written in English. Moreover, one of its most unique features is the commentary by Joe Filisko on Sonny Boy's harmonica techniques. The Hohner harmonica company describes Filisko, a Chicago-based harmonica player, as "the world's foremost authority on the diatonic harmonica."[3] Filisko has thoroughly studied Sonny Boy's style, and he has shared his profound observations with me: I learned harmonica myself in order to write this book. Although I need far more time to achieve the artistry of Sonny Boy and Filisko, my experience helped me recognize the complicated nature of this tiny instrument—its many restrictions and benefits—as well as Sonny Boy's own techniques. With my training as an ethnomusicologist over the years, as well as daily practice on the instrument, I could better analyze Sonny Boy's performances and illustrate my analysis with musical notations.

For this biography, I obtained primary sources, including two unpublished interviews with Sonny Boy's family members—Sonny Boy's half brother, Thomas W. Utley, and Sonny Boy's uncle, Fred Utley. Both were interviewed by Michael Baker, a librarian at the Jackson-Madison County Library, and Jim O'Neal, an acclaimed blues historian and cofounder of *Living Blues* magazine. When Baker and O'Neal interviewed them in 1992 and 1997, respectively, they had difficulties adequately expressing themselves because of their age. However, they still provided significant information about Sonny Boy's development and the music scene of the times. Thomas Utley even talked about Sonny Boy's actual relationship with Rice Miller—the second Sonny Boy Williamson.

In addition, I conducted interviews with Billy Boy Arnold and Bob Koester. Billy Boy is the sole surviving harmonica player who took lessons directly from Sonny Boy. Though Billy Boy's story has been published previously, the inclusion of his interview helps us understand Sonny Boy as a living human being. Billy Boy also provided important information about Sonny Boy's musical gear—his amplifier.

Bob Koester, the owner of the Chicago-based independent label Delmark Records and a shop called the Jazz Record Mart, is a well-known historian of Chicago blues.[4] He spoke to me about the Windy City's music scene in the 1940s at the time Sonny Boy was performing. Though Koester did not have a direct relationship with Sonny Boy, he was familiar with Lester Melrose, who worked for Bluebird Records and owned Wabash Music, publisher of Sonny Boy's compositions.

In addition to the primary sources, a recent release of a genealogy database and assistance from the librarians at Jackson-Madison County Library gave me access to Sonny Boy's vital records—including two marriage licenses, a divorce file, and a regional slave schedule that listed Sonny Boy's possible ancestors. Of equal importance, the coroner's inquest that I obtained from the Cook County Medical Examiner in Chicago reveals the details of his death. I also conducted extensive media research about the murder case. Surprisingly, his death was not reported as a murder in any printed sources, including the *Chicago Defender*, a leading black newspaper.

* * *

The first chapter deals with Sonny Boy's childhood and youth in Jackson, Tennessee, as this second generation descendant of slavery prepared to be a harmonica wizard by schooling in the Jackson-Brownsville blues circle. The second chapter discusses his career in St. Louis and his early recordings in Aurora, Illinois, from 1937 to 1938. The third chapter is about his recording career in Chicago from 1939 to 1947. All the recordings are discussed in historical order. While the music discussed in chapter 2 is mainly a continuation of the musical tradition in West Tennessee, chapter 3 shows how it changed drastically to urban blues, and the fourth chapter describes its full maturation of his unique sound—the sound of Chicago's Bronzeville. The fifth chapter covers Sonny Boy's last days when he reunited with his old schoolteacher and gave harmonica lessons to Billy Boy Arnold. Also in this chapter, Sonny Boy's death and its aftermath are fully explored. The epilogue discusses posthumous events. While he had been forgotten for years in his own country, Sonny Boy's name appeared in European dictionaries and periodicals; European jazz musicians regarded his work highly. In 1989, a casual conversation with the Jackson-Madison County Library staff members—"some kind of old bluesman was buried somewhere near here"—developed into a redis-covery project of the long-gone local hero. This chapter also addresses the controversy regarding Sonny Boy's copyrights. The appendix lists his recording sessions as a leader and a sideman, respectively.

The musical notations that support my musical analysis are based on my listening to the available recordings. I limit myself to showing the core ingredients of his harmonica techniques. While maintaining accura-cy as much as possible, I avoided complicated notations with expressions of slight pitch bends and subtle rhythmic nuances. For greater details of his performance, readers should turn directly to the recordings them-selves.

The transcriptions of lyrics are also based on listening to recordings. As stated at the beginning of this chapter, Wolfgang Lorenz's book in-cludes transcriptions of Sonny Boy's songs in their entirety, which was very helpful, but I have corrected some sections when I found discrepan-cies. The lyric transcriptions follow standard English practice, but I also observe obvious and characteristic vernacular variations; for example, *flyin'* instead of *flying*, and *oughta* instead of *ought to.*

The discussion includes Sonny Boy's sideman work with such artists as Yank Rachell, Big Joe Williams, and Robert Lee McCoy; in fact, his collaborations with Yank and Big Joe are highly impressive. But not all of their recordings are in my scope, unless their songs are related to Sonny Boy's. In addition, many artists made Sonny Boy's compositions part of their repertoire, although, again, detailed analyses of these record-ings are not my focus.

* * *

The original intention of this work was just to explore Sonny Boy's harmonica—the musical tradition in West Tennessee in the 1930s and its development in Chicago in the 1940s. However, as I discovered sources (such as a slave schedule), it grew beyond just the study of music. To repeat: this work is not just about the history of music. A second-genera-tion descendant of slaves with a harmonica and a creative mind became an influential wizard of the instrument. Coming up from a southern town to Chicago, he came to represent the sound of the urban community—the sound of Bronzeville. He inspired many others even after he was brutally murdered, and the mainstream African American media of the time did not seem to care. This is a cultural study consisting of a collection of memories of the bluesman as told by his family members and close associates—direct and indirect students of his artistry. But this is also a unique American story. In my mind, it is a microcosm of American history.

1

LEARNING THE BLUES

Jackson, Tennessee: 1914–1937

John Lee Curtis Williamson was born in Britton Lane near a small town called Denmark in southwest Madison County, Tennessee, on March 30, 1914. According to the 1910 U.S. Census, the population of Madison County was 39,357: 23,184 European Americans; 16,167 African Americans; and 16 from various Asian countries (including India, China, and Japan).[1] Cotton was the main revenue source in the county—an average of 26,000 bales were produced annually before the government's acreage reduction program that started in 1933.[2] Jackson, the largest city—named after the seventh U.S. president, Andrew Jackson—was known as "the Hub City of the West" with four railway systems that radiated to all parts of the nation: the Gulf, Mobile and Northern; the Illinois Central; the Mobile and Ohio; and the Nashville, Chattanooga, and St. Louis. Today Jackson is best known as the home of the famed railroad engineer Casey Jones.

John Lee Curtis's parents were Nancy Jane Utley[3] and Raphael "Rafe" Williamson. One of the most important Sonny Boy sources was Emma Bruce Ross, who was also his fourth-grade homeroom teacher at Blair's Chapel Christian Methodist Episcopal Church in Madison County. According to Ross, Sonny Boy's parents were descendants of slaves, John and Eliza Williamson and Elijah and Millie Tyson Utley.[4] They lived on farms in the old District No. 3, southwest of Denmark and fourteen miles southwest from Jackson.

The community heritage revival project at the Jackson-Madison County Library has revealed much of Sonny Boy's genealogy. The 1860 Slave Schedule of this area includes four slave owners named William-son—Caroline, Rebecca, Anthony, and Lewis—and one Utley, Daniel. A total of thirty-eight slaves are recorded for the Williamsons and fifteen for Utley. After the Emancipation Proclamation in January 1863, they were allotted lands for sharecropping and settled around the area. In the antique map published in 1877, "Mrs. A. S. Williamson," "N. William-sons," and "D. B. Utley" are marked in the same district, though it is possible that the ex-slaves who acquired the names of Williamson and Utley had moved to different districts. In the same map, at least five Williamsons are identified in District No. 6 (north of No. 3), and W. L. Utley is found in No. 4 (east of No. 3).

Nancy Utley was born on February 15, 1894. When she was eighteen, she fell in love with the youngest son of the Williamsons, Rafe, who was two or three years older.[5] They filed a marriage license on June 21, 1913.[6] In the same year, they eloped from the South to Cairo, Illinois, where they lived with Rafe's sister. Though not much is known about Rafe, some sources say he was a guitar player.[7] About a year after their marriage, however, Rafe died suddenly, when Nancy was pregnant with her first son, John Lee Curtis. After he was born, Nancy returned home to Jackson where she met her new husband, Willie Utley (no relation). The public record shows they filed a marriage license on June 10, 1918.[8] Their son Thomas W. (he went by T. W. or T.) was born on February 15 of the following year.

It is not known when John Lee Curtis's grandmother gave him the nickname "Sonny Boy."[9] Emma Bruce Ross remembered him fondly: "He was polite and generous to a fault. I can remember his eyes. They were clear and sparkling as he looked into yours. He was always a leader and acted as a spokesman for his friends and relations."[10]

During Christmas 1925, when he was eleven years old, a life-changing event occurred. Nancy presented him with a harmonica as a gift. T. W. remembered, "a Marine Band harp. That was the best harp."[11] "[My brother was] real proud [of it]."[12]

The harmonica was perhaps the most prevalent musical instrument in the nineteenth and the early twentieth centuries in the United States. German instrument maker Matthias Hohner, who succeeded in mass pro-duction of the harmonica, sent samples to his cousins, who had immigrated to the United States. The harmonica soon became a popular novelty. During the Civil War, many soldiers on both sides carried one, and new immigrants and peddlers helped spread the instrument all over the country. Reportedly more than half of the ten million instruments that Hohner manufactured were exported to the United States every year.[13] In 1896, Hohner developed a ten-hole diatonic Marine Band harmonica, which was named after the U.S. Marines. The price then was twenty-five cents. A promotion poster from the mid-1920s reads, "Get behind a Hohner harmonica for real music and fun! The world's best harmonica 50 cents up."[14] Thus, this affordable, handy, and playable instrument was accessible to many people: it was often used to play familiar tunes as well as to imitate the sounds of everyday life, from the whistle of trains to the cries of babies.

According to Sonny Boy's schoolmate Clenton Bobbitt, Nancy purchased the Hohner Marine Band harmonica at Woolworth's or Kress in downtown Jackson.[15] Bobbitt said, "Everybody wanted to hear him [Sonny Boy] blow that harp."[16] T. W. remembered Sonny Boy was always playing it if he was not helping on the farm.[17] It is not difficult to imagine that the harmonica was his treasure and one of the very few escapes that he had from hard manual labor. But Sonny Boy's harmonica also got him into trouble. One time on the way to Blair's Chapel Church, while the brothers were busy playing a tune, they lost sight of their mother, who had to wait for them before crossing the deep creek: "We got way behind. . . . And he was [still] blowing the harp. She caught him to hit [spank]."[18] Playing the harmonica was not always welcome, especially in a church setting. Sonny Boy was a member of the gospel quartet of Blair's Chapel Church, the Four Lambs Jubilee from Jackson, Tennessee,[19] but in his household—as was the case in many others of the rural South—playing church songs on harmonica was considered taboo. T. W. said, "Of course we done not [sic] blowing church songs. . . . [We were] blowing harp."[20] "She'd take a harp away from him. If we're playing church songs, she talked to us."[21]

Though his mother sometimes had reservations about the gift that she gave to her son, Sonny Boy certainly had no qualms: he spent many hours practicing on it. Sonny Boy and a guitarist friend—his name has been lost to history—offered to play music at family picnics on Mount Pinson Road.[22] He formed a musical group with five other schoolmates and performed during recess. Emma Bruce Ross remembered his enthusiasm and offered instruments to his friends: "He showed talent and business spunk when he gathered school mates and began a group that met under a big oak tree out at Blair's Chapel School. They would perform during early recess, making music until bell time. . . . Often I would get harps for the other five who could only afford ten cent harps."[23] Around the same time, Sonny Boy started to write his own songs, including "Good Morning, School Girl."

Sonny Boy had an outgoing personality and made friends easily. One of them was a railroad agent who helped him and his brother. This was T. W.'s fond memory:

> He had a friend, [a] railroad agent here in Jackson. And we wanted [to go] from here to Mississippi. Now here, a car to Mississippi, it changed in here. And the guy who knowed [*sic*] pulling off the train was going to the highway. And the railroad agent told [us] "he goin' to the highway [that is] too far from here. When I do kind of like this [beckoning], you come on over here. You can get on over."[24]

Guitarist/vocalist Homesick James remembered Sonny Boy as a delivery boy.

> I remember he'd come around on his bicycle about '31, '32 or '33. He was riding a bicycle in Jackson, Tennessee, for a guy named Trevor Jones, T. J. Furniture Store. He was a delivery boy running around for him, going round after people who owed him money. Then Sonny Boy used to come 'round with a note telling you to pay your bills and stuff like that. I used to play all round there with Sonny Boy every time I'd go down there for the weekend.[25]

By the age of sixteen (circa 1930), Sonny Boy's harmonica techniques became good enough for him to play with the more proficient local musicians. Three artists were particularly important for Sonny Boy's development: guitarist/vocalist "Sleepy" John Estes, his partner mandolinist/guitarist/vocalist James "Yank" Rachell, and another of Estes's musician friends, harmonica and jug player Hammie Nixon. At the time all of them were based in Brownsville, Tennessee, but they often traveled to Jackson, only twenty-five miles away; Memphis and Arkansas were also their territory. But there were many other musicians around the area, though they would not become as famous. T. W. remembered, "Some playing guitars, some playing fiddles. Bill Seaton, Camel Lee, and Eddie Pannell

[Parnell]. Eddie played the twelve-strings guitar. That's the best twelve-string I ever saw. He was good with it, too."[26]

"Sleepy" John Adam Estes, the most prominent of the Brownsville-Jackson blues community, was born in Ripley, Tennessee, on January 25, 1899,[27] although he was raised in Brownsville. When he was a teenager, he lost sight in his right eye due to an accident—his friend threw a rock at him during a baseball game. He eventually became totally blind. He learned to play the guitar and performed for local social gatherings in Brownsville and Jackson, for which he often teamed up with Yank and Hammie. In 1929, Sleepy John with Yank and pianist Jab Jones recorded for RCA Victor Records. One of the cuts from this session was "Divin' Duck Blues," which contains one of the most famous blues lines: "If the river was whiskey, and I was a diving duck."[28] He was blessed with an easily recognizable tenor voice—he had a highly emotional vocal style, often characterized as "crying." As the legend goes, he was nicknamed "Sleepy" because he had an ability to sleep standing up.[29]

Blues mandolin player Yank Rachell was born on March 16, 1910, in Brownsville. According to his own words, he traded his family's pig for a mandolin.[30] He learned mandolin from a local musician, Hambone Willie Newbern, who premiered "Roll and Tumble Blues" in 1929, better known today as "Rolling and Tumbling," the "Delta National Anthem."[31] They performed for local house parties. Sometimes Newbern played the guitar and Rachell played the mandolin, and sometimes they would switch instruments. One day Sleepy John Estes, after hearing good things about Yank, sat in on one of his performances. Yank remembered, "So we got to playin' together, and I told him I played mandolin too. He said, 'You can? I can't play no mandolin.' So the next night I brought my mandolin. And he went to playin' behind me and I'm playin' the mandolin. Then we team [sic] up. Play [sic] together forty years, I and Sleepy John."[32]

Sometime in 1933, when Yank played in Jackson, he got to know Sonny Boy. Yank remembered how they became acquainted: "He'd follow me around on his bike. 'Let me play with you. Let me play with you.' I looked at him; I said, 'Alright. Next time.' So I went over there one evening. People giving a dance out there in the country. From Jackson, I carried Sonny Boy out there with me. He got down and go to playing that harp and singing."[33] Now Sonny Boy was brought into the Brownsville-Jackson blues circle. He, Yank, and Sleepy John jammed together around the area. And through them, Sonny Boy met Hammie Nixon. Hammie was born in Brownsville on January 22, 1908. Hammie learned harmonica from Noah Lewis—of Cannon's Jug Stompers—who hailed from Henning. They met in Brownsville as well. Hammie also played kazoo, jug, and guitar. Sometime in the mid-1920s, he joined Sleepy John and Yank. Although Hammie remained mainly an accompanist for most of his career, he was an important figure to Sonny Boy and helped him master his harmonica techniques.

In February 1934, Yank Rachell was invited to a recording session in New York City. Because Yank felt Sonny Boy was not yet good enough to record, he only took his guitarist partner Dan Smith along with him; for this session, they cut twenty titles, including "Blue and Worried Woman" and "Gravel Road Woman."[34] After they returned from New York, Smith was robbed in a nightclub in Jackson and killed. Yank, who lost his musical partner, started to hook up with Sonny Boy. Around this same time Yank got married. He worked on a dairy farm while raising four children. It was not easy for him to be on the road all the time. Sonny Boy also had to help his family's farm.[35] Sleepy John, on the other hand, liked to travel. He teamed up with Hammie, and they had their first recording session with Decca Records in Chicago in July 1935.[36] Subsequently, Yank had more opportunities to jam around with Sonny Boy. Yank remembered:

> Then I started playin' with Sonny Boy, and John and Hammie were playin' together. Me and Sonny Boy played together a long time but me and John would go back to playin' together. We never did quit playin' together. But when he wasn't [sic] 'round, I played with Sonny Boy 'cause John didn't stay in one place. He [would be] here today and tomorrow he may be in Chicago, or anywhere. I couldn't do that. I was workin'.[37]

Although, for practical reasons, Yank and Sonny Boy could not play with Sleepy John, they were still close. Yank recollected, "They were good friends, John and Sonny Boy. They were different kinds of people, but I got along with all of 'em. They knowed me and I knowed them [sic]. So, I knowed Sonny Boy [sic] way; I knowed Sleepy John [sic] way. Sonny Boy alright [sic]. You get too much whiskey in him, he'd act up sometime. But we never had no trouble. I and him didn't."[38]

Yank continued: "He [Sonny Boy] [would] catch the bus and come to Brownsville. Stay two or three nights, and next time I catch the bus to Jackson and stay with him two or three nights."[39] To Yank and Sonny Boy, playing music at social gatherings was a much more fun and lucrative business, especially compared with the types of manual labor they were accustomed to doing. But sometimes they got into trouble with customers. Yank recalled, "I went out to play with Sonny Boy one night. Went to a man's house, went playin' there. Man's wife got stuck on him [Sonny Boy]. Run us all away from there; we left."[40]

* * *

Through playing with skilled musicians of the community—they were recording artists—Sonny Boy Williamson was receiving an excellent music education. As Yank Rachell said, "We train [*sic*] a lot of guys, brought up under us."[41] Sleepy John, Yank, and Hammie mentored many musicians in the Brownsville-Jackson area, including guitarist/vocalist Son Bonds, who recorded as Brownsville Son Bonds with Hammie Nixon; guitarist/vocalist "Jackson" Joe Williams (not to be confused with "Big" Joe Williams from Crawford, Mississippi); and guitarist/vocalist Charlie Pickett. Homesick James was also under their wings.

Sonny Boy studied composition, harmonica performance, and arrangement under his mentors. According to T. W., Sonny Boy was interested in Sleepy John particularly because he could write songs. "Sleepy John put out records . . . ten or fifteen years before Sonny Boy started. He's gon' out and found . . . made a lot of songs. That's when Sonny Boy started paying attention to him."[42] There are indications that Sonny Boy was influenced by Sleepy John's particular compositional style—"localizing the lyrics," one of the common blues writing techniques.[43] Sleepy John often included actual names of streets and people that he was familiar with in his lyrics. For example, in "Brownsville Blues" (1938), he uses a local car mechanic named Vasser Williams on Durhamville Road near Ripley—where Sleepy John was born—for sexual allusions.

["Brownsville Blues" Verse 3]
Now my generator is bad, and you know my lights done stopped,
Now my generator is bad, and you know my lights done stopped,
And I reckon I'd better take it over to Durnhamville,
     and I'm going to stop at Vasser Williams' shop.[44]

Similarly, Sonny Boy often localized lyrics. For example, in "Blue Bird Blues," recorded in his debut session in May 1937, he sings:

> ["Blue Bird Blues" Verse 2]
> Now bluebird when you get to Jackson,
>   I want you to fly down on Shannon Street,
> Now bluebird when you get to Jackson,
>   I want you to fly down on Shannon Street,
> Well, that I don't want you to stop flyin'
>   until you find Miss Lacey Bell for me.

Bob Riesman, Big Bill Broonzy's biographer, writes, "His [Sonny Boy's] songwriting reinforced the personal connection a listener might feel with him, as he would often describe his hometown of Jackson in terms that could, as has been observed, make it feel like everybody's hometown."[45] Shannon Street was the street in Jackson near where he lived after his second marriage to Lacey Bell Davidson in 1937. On this street there were house bars called "goodtime houses" for social gatherings. Fred Utley, Sonny Boy's uncle, remembered, "Goodtime Houses! On Shannon full of them."[46] The street exists to this day—although not the goodtime houses.

"Personalizing the lyrics"[47] is another compositional technique that Sleepy John shared with Sonny Boy. As Sleepy John's girlfriends inspired his "Black Mattie Blues" in 1929 and "Vernita Blues" in 1935, Sonny Boy's best-known song, "Good Morning, School Girl" in 1937, is also about the girl he fell in love with.

> ["Good Morning, School Girl" Verse 1]
> Hello, little school girl,
> Good mornin', little school girl,
> Can I go home with, can I go home with you?
> Now, you can tell yo' mother an' yo' father, um,
> That Sonny Boy's a little school boy too.

T. W. recalled that Sonny Boy composed this song when he was twelve or thirteen years old. "He wanted to go to see her there . . . and of course he was singing blues and playing harp. . . . [Her] daddy watched him and told her she couldn't date him. He wanted her to be in a house. That's when he made that song 'Good Morning, School Girl' back in the first '30s."[48] Although Sonny Boy wrote this song before he started to perform with Sleepy John Estes and Yank Rachell, biographical songwriting with personalized lyrics became the core of his compositions. For instance, as we will see, many of his songs are about liquor. Alcohol was a persistent problem—he once admitted that he started playing blues and drinking at the same time, after he had been rejected by the parents of a girl he was in love with. In an interview with Alan Lomax in 1947, Sonny Boy stated:

> I used to have a sweet little girl. . . . We used to go to school together. We grew up together. In another words, I wanted to love her. . . . Her father found I wasn't a right boyfriend. And so they turned me down, and then I just got to sitting down thinking, you understand, and then I thought of a song, and I started to drinkin', and I started to singin', that's the way.[49]

Sonny Boy also learned to rework existing songs. In fact, the music of "Good Morning, School Girl" is loosely based on "Back and Side Blues" by Son Bonds with Hammie Nixon on harmonica, recorded in 1934. Yank explained, "Everybody wrote their [*sic*] own songs and played them their own way. Then some other guy come along and play them his way. I borrowed some that way myself."[50] Yank also said, "Most of Sonny Boy's songs I wrote them, me and him together."[51] Although this statement contains an element of exaggeration, there are songs that Sonny Boy apparently reworked by Yank and Sleepy John. For example, Sonny Boy's "Skinny Woman" (1937) is a derivative of Yank's "Gravel Road Woman" (1934). Sonny Boy sings Yank's first verse almost exactly verbatim, while the next four verses are his own. Sonny Boy's "Western Union Man" (1941) is based on Sleepy John's "Mailman Blues" (1940). Sonny Boy changed the words here and there and he even personalized the lyrics by adding his wife's name, but the similarities between the two are obvious. Sleepy John's "Little Laura Blues" (1940) inspired Sonny Boy's "She Was a Dreamer" (1941). We will examine these songs in the following chapters.

T. W. remembered Sonny Boy's songwriting methods: "He would sit down and listen to a song. . . . He would stop and straighten it out. If he created a song, two, three verses of it, he called it. That's same as the church song. He set [*sic*] church songs."[52] Sonny Boy became quite a prolific composer; he made more than 120 recordings in eleven years—from 1937 to 1947.

Another musical education Sonny Boy received was, of course, in harmonica performance. Memphis, which is not far from the Brownsville-Jackson area, was a center of harmonica techniques. Sonny Boy, in fact, was part of the Memphis harmonica tradition that dated back from roughly 1925 to 1930, and included such musicians as Noah Lewis, Will Shade, Jed Davenport, Hammie Nixon, and Walter Horton.[53] Though Sonny Boy did not visit Memphis very often, Jackson was a place for Memphis musicians to stop, and Sonny Boy sat in on their performances. T. W. remembered his brother sat in with a jug band named the Lost Dance Troupe from Memphis.[54] They performed at "different places on the corner mostly. [If there were] no clubs back here, then [they would play] in a house somewhere and in the woods somewhere."[55]

By 1930, Sonny Boy's harmonica techniques had matured enough for him to play with the local—and recording—artists. More likely by this time he had learned the cross harp technique (second position), which was a standard method in the blues community by the end of the 1920s. Cross harp refers to playing the diatonic harmonica in a key a fourth below its intended key; for example, playing a C harmonica in the key of G. One of the main characteristics of the harmonica is that in the lower register it is easier to manipulate the sound by drawing as opposed to the upper by blowing. That is, playing the harmonica in a cross harp position places important notes of the scale on the draw side of the instrument; this side is where most of the bends are, making the sound bluesy and expressive. For instance, a flatted seventh on the blues scale is achieved by natural draw, while a flatted third is also acquired by bending or choking.

Many artists around the Memphis area used this technique—one of the most familiar examples is "Chicksaw Special" created by Noah Lewis in 1929, which mimics the sound of a train.[56] It is not surprising that Sonny Boy learned cross harp by hearing the records of these musicians or by actually seeing them perform.

Hammie Nixon said that Sonny Boy needed help to reach the next level—choking, which is also known as bending technique:

> He [Sonny Boy] used to live right there (Jackson) and really got his schooling from us. We had what you call a fish fry, and a lot of people would be there. We played there whenever the man could catch us. Sonny Boy, he wanted to learn them blues, you know, and I learned [taught] him how to really choke them harmonicas. He started to play, but he couldn't choke one. Soon, he be helping us, getting in with us.[57]

Besides the choking technique, Hammie also helped Sonny Boy with writing phrases. Lawrence Hoffman, a contributing writer for the *Living Blues* magazine, pointed out, "as John Lee Williamson absorbed the style of Hammie Nixon, [he leaned] more heavily on the melodic side, discarding much of the chordal work."[58] Their recordings show that one of the phrases Sonny Boy learned from Hammie was a fill between vocal phrases. For example, Hammie plays a succession of triplets—most of the notes here are played by choking. An almost identical phrase is heard in "Down South Blues" (recording time 0"10-0"14, indicated in figure 1.1) and "Hobo Jungle Blues" (recording time 0"09-0"14, indicated in figure 1.2), both of which were recorded with Sleepy John in 1935 and 1937, respectively. Sonny Boy used applications of Hammie's fill in "Good Morning, School Girl" in 1937 (recording time 0"11-0"15, indicated in figure 1.3).

Figure 1.1. "Down South Blues," fill.

Figure 1.2. "Hobo Jungle Blues."

[Subdivisions of Hammie Nixon's fill phrase]

Figure 1.3. "Good Morning, School Girl," fills.

In addition, another possible technique Hammie shared with Sonny Boy is a phrase combined with dirty notes—that is, playing multiple notes at the same time—and bending as well. Figure 1.4 shows the introductory phrase for "Down South Blues." Figure 1.5 shows Sonny Boy's application of the similar phrase for the introduction of "Good Morning, School Girl." Figure 1.5 is also an example of choking. In this case, he uses the technique for the last note of the measure as the resting point.

Chicago-based harmonica player Joe Filisko observes that Sonny Boy acquired much of the basic blues harp techniques from Hammie:

Sonny Boy probably got his basic playing foundation and blueprint from Hammie. Hammie was quite accomplished at getting a seamless sound by working the inhaling notes and their corresponding bends. The result was a very potent and smooth blues sound not broken up by too many changes of breathing direction which can result in the blues having a more folk-like sound to it. Sonny Boy seems to have picked this up from Hammie along with his song repertoire.[59]

Figure 1.4. "Down South Blues," introduction.

[Same material for the fill between vocal phrases]

Figure 1.5. "Good Morning, School Girl," introduction.

On the other hand, there is an important difference between Hammie Nixon's style and Sonny Boy's. Nixon has a more free floating style while Sonny Boy uses a rigid phrasing scheme. He probably learned how to arrange music, especially from Yank Rachell, by playing a short recurring riff that gives a characteristic unity to a composition, as heard in Rachell's mandolin lick for Estes's "Divin' Duck Blues" (figure 1.6) heard in the recording time 0"37-0"45.

Similar to Yank's accompaniment, the repetition of a clearly articulated phrase is a highly noticeable trait in Sonny Boy's work. For example, the introductory phrase for "Good Morning, School Girl" (recording time 0"11-0"15, indicated in measures 5–6 of figure 1.7) is also used for the response phrase for the vocal and for the interlude. In this song, he is singing and playing response phrases with his own harmonica; in other words, he is playing the instrumental punctuation while singing. This is how he brought his instrument to the musical foreground.

Figure 1.6. "Divin' Duck Blues," mandolin fill.

Figure 1.7. "Good Morning, School Girl," vocal and response fill.

* * *

This chapter outlined Sonny Boy Williamson's childhood and youth. It also described the musical education he received from local musicians. As we have observed, he was a student of the Jackson-Brownsville blues tradition and absorbed Memphis-derived harmonica techniques. In the following chapter, we will closely examine how Sonny Boy Williamson changed the role of blues harmonica, giving it a new and elevated position within the blues tradition.

2

REACHING NEW HEIGHTS

St. Louis and Aurora, Illinois, 1937–1938

John Lee "Sonny Boy" Williamson's recording career can be divided into two periods according to the locations: 1937–1938 in Aurora, Illinois, and 1939–1948 in Chicago.

By 1934, Sonny Boy established his performing style. He was ready to be more than a local musician in Jackson, Tennessee. First he went to St. Louis and forged important business relationships. As he was developing his career in the St. Louis blues circle, he signed a recording contract with Bluebird Records, a subsidiary of RCA Victor. This chapter describes his first five Bluebird sessions, all held in Aurora.

* * *

During the 1920s and 1930s, St. Louis was one of the most important cities for the development of urban blues. Together with East St. Louis, Illinois, on the other bank of the Mississippi River, St. Louis was a dominant industrial center with stockyards, steel mills, and a major railhead. And it was an important communication center, too. Many African Americans migrated from the southern states to St. Louis. The African American population in St. Louis rose from 44,000 in 1910 to 109,000 in 1940, and many of them lived in the ghetto around the neighborhood known as Deep Morgan.[1]

Along with the massive number of African American immigrants, St. Louis was flourishing with musicians. For example, acclaimed guitarist/vocalist Lonnie Johnson moved from New Orleans to St. Louis, where he and his brother found work on steamboats on the Mississippi River, playing in the jazz bands. In 1925, Johnson, who won the weekly blues contest at the Booker T. Washington Theater, signed a recording contract with Okeh Records. Johnson soon became the most influential and commercially in-demand guitarist of blues and jazz recordings—he performed and recorded with Louis Armstrong, Duke Ellington, Bessie Smith, and Texas Alexander, among others.[2] Johnson's single-string, flat-picking soloing influenced many St. Louis–based guitar players, including Clifford Gibson, Charley Jordan, Jaydee Short, Henry Spaulding, and Henry Townsend.[3]

There were mainly two distinctive styles of St. Louis blues: women singers with hard nasal voices, represented by Alice Moore, Streamline Mae (St. Louis Bessie Mae Smith), and Lillian Miller, and male vocalists who used a slow, chorded-bass piano style—often embellished with a guitar—and flavored by strong melancholy feelings, such as Roosevelt Sykes, Peetie Wheatstraw, Walter Davis, Henry Brown, Pinetop Sparks, and Eddie Miller.[4] Sykes, Wheatstraw, and Davis were the most popular among them. From 1934 to 1942, approximately 500 sides were cut by St. Louis–based blues pianists, but 70 percent were by Sykes, Wheatstraw, and Davis combined.[5] In addition, many musicians settled in St. Louis or at least passed through for brief periods, including Dr. Clayton, Honeyboy Edwards, Son House, Robert Johnson, Robert Lockwood Jr., Muddy Waters, Robert Nighthawk (Robert Lee McCoy), St. Louis Jimmy Oden, Speckled Red, Jimmy Rogers, Johnny Shines, Bukka White, Big Joe Williams, and Sonny Boy Williamson. Historians typically refer to them as Chicago bluesmen, but St. Louis is often where the critical process of urbanization and ensemble development took place for bluesmen from Arkansas, Tennessee, and Mississippi.

Sonny Boy made important professional relationships when he was developing his career; they included Lester Melrose, Walter Davis, Big Joe Williams, and Eli Oberstein.

Lester Melrose was born in Olney, Illinois, in 1891. He and his brother co-owned a music store in Chicago. As he entered the recording business in the mid-1920s, he became a talent scout and producer—then called an A&R (artist and repertoire) man. The record companies hired independent A&R men like Melrose to produce sessions, and the artists often had publishing contracts with these producers. In 1928, the Hokum Boys, a blues duo of guitarist/vocalist Tampa Red and pianist/vocalist

Georgia Tom Dorsey, one of Melrose's discoveries, enjoyed a great success with "It's Tight Like That" on Paramount Records. In the mid-1930s, Columbia Records and its Vocalion and Okeh subsidiaries, and Bluebird Records, a subsidiary of RCA Victor, heavily relied on Melrose's ability to find new talent.

Melrose was responsible for popularizing the "Bluebird Beat," a blues performing style that was designed for the tastes of audiences living in a new citified environment. The Bluebird Beat—"a mixture of older black blues and vaudeville styles and material with the newer swing rhythms"[6] —usually featured guitar (sometimes even electric), harmonica, and piano; the ensemble was often accentuated by the addition of bass, drums, or washboard. From the mid-1930s to the late 1940s, the Bluebird Beat nearly dominated the blues record market with such artists as Big Bill Broonzy, Arthur "Big Boy" Crudup, Jazz Gillum, Memphis Minnie, Tampa Red, Washboard Sam, Big Maceo, Bukka White, and Big Joe Williams. Sonny Boy Williamson was one of the most popular of the genre.

Melrose heralded two practices that have been standardized in the popular recording business. He liked to use the same musicians as accompanists in his recordings in order to ensure a consistent quality in both musical style and the actual sound—the musicians mentioned previously played on each other's sessions. Such a production strategy has come to be called a house sound or a house band—like Chess in the 1950s or early (classic) Motown and Stax/Volt in the 1960s. A particular record label is recognized for its signature sounds.

Melrose's most profitable domain, though, was in music publishing. As a founder of Wabash Music, he established an in-house music publishing system. And as a co-owner of the songs written by his musicians, he received royalties until copyrights expired.[7] In some cases, he just bought out songs by paying fees to songwriters on the spot. Many writers chose this way to grab immediate cash, though there are numerous instances where they were no longer entitled to receive a royalty share when the songs became popular.

Melrose encouraged his artists to compose new songs. While making variations of preexisting songs was still a common practice in blues recordings, songs had to be original to be copyrighted; however, writers often copyrighted songs based on previous hits and claimed them as their original compositions.[8] Sonny Boy Williamson as a composer was not an exception, as will be described later in the chapter.

While Lester Melrose was based in Chicago, pianist/vocalist Walter Davis in St. Louis worked as a talent scout under Melrose. Davis was born on March 1, 1912, in Grenada, Mississippi. In 1925, when he was thirteen years old, he moved to St. Louis. In 1930, he claimed he recorded for Paramount as a novice pianist, but those sides were unreleased. In the same year, he made a contract with RCA Victor. Subsequently "M&O Blues" from the first session became an instant hit. In this recording as well as other cuts from the same session, Davis's label mate Roosevelt Sykes played the piano under the pseudonym Willie Kelly. As the legend goes, Davis was too nervous to accompany himself.[9] Until 1935, Sykes-Kelly was always the pianist for Davis's session, which guitarist Henry Townsend often joined as well.

Walter Davis was a prolific songwriter. He recorded approximately 180 cuts before he had a stroke; he then became a minister in 1952. Davis is known for his dark, gloomy voice, sometimes referred to as a funereal vocal style. He also had a quite idiosyncratic piano style as heard in "Think You Need a Shot" in 1936. While his left hand only plays the basic pulse of slow four-four time with one note, his right hand moves around the keys in a jerky way. Then he inserts minor chords in phrases. As will be discussed later, when he played at Sonny Boy's session, he maintained this same peculiar musical style.

"Sonny Boy got so good, we went recording. We went to St. Louis and we met Walter Davis. And he met [*sic*] us playing with Lester Melrose. We played some and Lester Melrose wanted us to record for him," said Yank Rachell, Sonny Boy's mentor.[10] But it is not clear when they went to St. Louis and how they met Walter Davis. As mentioned earlier, Sonny Boy had established his performing style by 1934, but he did not actually record until May 1937. Yank Rachell also had a long time span between his last New York session in February 1934 and his first Bluebird session with Lester Melrose in 1938.

There are two missing pieces in this picture—guitarist/vocalist Big Joe Williams and Eli Oberstein, an A&R man who had worked for Bluebird Records before Melrose.

"Big" Joe Lee Williams was born on October 16, 1903, in Crawford, Mississippi. He had a long career until his death in Macon, Mississippi, in 1982. As a youth, he traveled around the South, playing at levee and lumber camps. He was another musician who polished his musical skills in St. Louis—the train through Crawford ended in St. Louis. Here he became a close friend of Walter Davis.[11] Sonny Boy became acquainted with Davis more likely through Big Joe Williams.

On February 25, 1935, Big Joe had his debut session with Bluebird Records. In his second session on October 31 in the same year, he cut "Baby Please Don't Go," still a blues classic. He is known for his rugged vocal and rough playing style, using a nine-stringed guitar.

Big Joe got a recording contract through an agreement with Eli Oberstein (1902–1960). Oberstein originally worked for the Columbia Records' subsidy Okeh label, but he switched to RCA Victor. Here he launched its new budget label Bluebird, which became very successful during the Great Depression. Bluebird had a wide range of artists. Besides bluesmen like Big Joe Williams, country musicians such as Fiddlin' John Carson and the Allen Brothers were on the label. But the most popular artists were the dance bands of Glenn Miller and Artie Shaw, both of whom Oberstein brought to the label. Moreover, Oberstein was one of the first A&R men to make business deals with songwriters in order to receive royalty shares.[12] Lester Melrose possibly acquired knowledge of music publishing from Oberstein. On the other hand, it is said that Oberstein pioneered a music business practice that later came to be called payola, the illegal practice of payment by record companies for the broadcast of recordings on radio.[13]

Sonny Boy was introduced to Eli Oberstein through Big Joe Williams sometime in 1935 or 1936. About a decade later in 1948, just before Sonny Boy died, Billy Boy Arnold visited him. Billy Boy asked Sonny Boy how he got his record deals: "I asked him how to get famous . . . 'Who got you over the record?' He said, 'Eli Oberstein.' I just remembered a few years ago when somebody mentioned that name. I said, 'that's the name Sonny Boy called.' But I know there was Lester Melrose. Eli Oberstein wasn't running the blues with Victor anymore."[14] In 1936, Oberstein was suddenly fired from RCA with no explanation. Big Joe said, "Me and Walter Davis and Sonny Boy both [*sic*] was sold from this Jewish fellow Oberstein and was sold to Lester Melrose."[15]

* * *

Between 1934 (or 1935) and 1937, Sonny Boy and Yank Rachell went back and forth from West Tennessee to St. Louis. Although St. Louis was an important place to pursue their performing careers, they did not settle there. Yank worked for a dairy farm in Brownsville, as mentioned earlier. For Sonny Boy, marriage was a plausible reason to maintain a base in Jackson. He married a maid named Sallie Lee Hunt, though their relationship only lasted about three and a half years. They got married on June 14, 1933, and filed for divorce on January 11, 1937.[16] Sonny Boy's half brother T. W. remembered, "She left him. Then she died."[17] According to the Chancery Court minute record, "the defendant, Sallie Lee Hunt Williamson, has committed adultery with one Acey Collier, in Jackson, Tennessee, after their said marriage."[18]

When Sonny Boy was in St. Louis, he lodged at his uncle Fred Utley's house. Fred said Sonny Boy stopped at his house even after he started to record in Chicago: "He'd stay as long as he wanted to. And he would stay awhile. Whenever he'd get ready to make records he always'd come through St. Louis, stay a few days, then out for Chicago. When he'd leave Chicago, come back to St. Louis all the time."[19] As Sonny Boy made connections with St. Louis musicians, their homes also became good places to stay. Henry Townsend, a vocalist/guitarist living in St. Louis, recalled, "John Lee Williamson came through St. Louis quite often then. . . . I was, I guess, pretty much a safe haven when he went to St. Louis. He'd just come on in and I'd be unaware of it, but he knew he had a place to settle himself."[20]

* * *

On May 5, 1937, John Lee "Sonny Boy" Williamson made his debut recording session for Bluebird Records. How he made contact with Lester Melrose is not exactly known, but Yank Rachell explained how typically a recording session was arranged: "Well, we're living down South. So he [Melrose] sent Walter Davis down there every spring to pick up me and Sonny Boy, and we'd go to Chicago and record. We were staying with Tampa Red."[21] "We said, 'Well, Big Bill [Broonzy] and them gonna record.' Say 'Let's [sic] us go and record too. We gonna put out something that they ain't got.' Something like that, y'know."[22] In spring or early summer, Lester Melrose sent Walter Davis to West Tennessee to see if any artists had enough material for recording. Davis made a deal with Sonny Boy while Yank passed on it. As mentioned earlier in the chapter, Yank's first Bluebird session was held in June 1938, in which Sonny Boy also participated.

Another possible reason for Sonny Boy's first session is that music journalist Dave Clark, who was a Jackson native and contributing writer for *DownBeat*—he is known as the first African American writer for the magazine—took Sonny Boy to Chicago.[23] Again, with the exception of 1941, the recording took place in Aurora, a town located approximately forty miles from Chicago: Clark reported that a producer by the name of Alar [*sic*] Green in Jackson and Sonny Boy was a member of the group.[24]

Whatever the case, Sonny Boy's debut session was held in the Sky Room, the ballroom on the top floor of the Leland Hotel in downtown Aurora.[25] Although Aurora is close to St. Louis geographically, it is not known specifically why the Leland Hotel was chosen for the recording site, but Sonny Boy's label mates Tampa Red and Washboard Sam also recorded there in 1937.[26] One of the theories is that musicians could get away from fees charged by the Chicago musicians' union by recording outside the city limits. Another theory is that the Sky Room had ideal acoustics since it was on the top floor of the second-tallest building in the state of Illinois at that time.[27] From 1937 through 1938, Sonny Boy had five recording sessions and made a total of forty-four cuts.

Sonny Boy's first session featured guitarist/vocalist Big Joe Williams and another guitarist/vocalist, Robert Lee McCoy. This was Big Joe's third session with Bluebird. As well as Sonny Boy, McCoy and Big Joe each had a session as a leader; everyone took a turn, as was typical of Lester Melrose's recording technique.

Robert Lee McCoy, aka Robert Nighthawk, was born Robert Lee McCollum on November 30, 1909, in Helena, Arkansas, and died there in 1967. McCoy was originally a harmonica player but switched to guitar in his early twenties after he learned it from his cousin Houston Stackhouse. Around 1935, McCoy moved to St. Louis for the same reason as Big Joe Williams. McCoy made his debut at the 1937 Aurora session.

Sonny Boy was the first artist to have a leader session, followed by McCoy and then Big Joe.[28] "Everything [*sic*] set up when you get there. Piano and everything. Two, three fifths of whiskey. Lester Melrose had that, 'cause Sonny Boy ain't gonna play, less [*sic*] he got him some whiskey," remembered Yank Rachell.[29]

Sonny Boy recorded six compositions: "Good Morning, School Girl," "Blue Bird Blues," "Jackson Blues," "Got the Bottle Up and Gone," "Sugar Mama," and "Skinny Woman." He did not move out of Jackson until 1942. Until then he cut six to ten sides per session. After he moved to Chicago, four sides per session became typical.

All the recordings sound like country blues in varied tempi, using a harmonica and two guitars. Sonny Boy employs three songwriting styles. First, he writes original lyrics while borrowing existing melodies, such as "How Long How Long Blues" by Leroy Carr or the familiar musical structure that was used in popular songs especially in the Memphis area, such as "You Gotta Have That Thing" by the Picanniny Jug Band. Second, he creates a variation of an existing song. In this case, he kept the musical foundation and the most recognizable lyrical part (usually the refrain), while rewriting other sections of the lyrics. Third, he writes original lyrics for a medium-slow blues pattern. Of the compositions from this session, "Good Morning, School Girl" and "Jackson Blues" belong to the "borrowing" type; "Got the Bottle Up and Gone," "Sugar Mama," and "Skinny Woman" belong to the "variation" type; and "Blue Bird Blues" belongs to the medium-slow blues formula type, while the accompaniment pattern for "Sugar Mama" follows the medium-slow blues pattern.

As shown in the appendix, in particular Sonny Boy Williamson's leader sessions from 1937 to 1940, these formulas—borrowing musical material, variation of preexisting songs, and following the medium-slow blues mold—were Sonny Boy's basic compositional methods almost throughout his entire career. Though he started to incorporate up-tempo swing music around 1939, he was still writing many songs based upon the medium-slow blues pattern, as if this was his signature style, until the end of his recording career in 1947.

As briefly discussed previously, many of Sonny Boy's lyrics are based on everyday events involving himself. As the songs are biographical and personal, Sonny Boy himself and his half brother T. W. often appear in the lyrics. According to T. W., many names of women in the songs were those with whom Sonny Boy had actual relationships. Names of places derive from where he lived or visited. In other words, he often personalized and localized lyrics.

While many songs are about relationships, one of the most frequent lyrical themes is alcohol and its bad effects. Occasionally, though, he composed songs around topical events, such as the effects of the Great Depression, the New Deal, and World War II. These are some of the subjects that are considered as social or political commentary. On the other hand, he was hardly ever inspired by folk themes, as other blues musicians were at the time, such as "Frankie" by Mississippi John Hurt in 1928 and "Razor Ball" by Blind Willie McTell in 1930.

Another outstanding characteristic of Sonny Boy's writing style is that he tended to compose long lines. He sometimes crams too many words into a very short space, which sounds comical especially when he sings with his distinctive lisp.

* * *

"Good Morning, School Girl"—loosely based on the vocal melody of Son Bonds's "Back and Side Blues" from 1934 with Sonny Boy's original lyrics—reveals Sonny Boy's most salient musical style: seamlessly inserting well-organized harmonica phrases with dexterous techniques between expressive vocal phrases. Sonny Boy's performing style—playing instrumental fills by harmonica between vocal phrases—was not practiced much then.

Will Shade of the Memphis Jug Band, for example, usually played a countermelody to the vocal line and added response fills between vocal phrases, as heard in their earliest recording, "Sun Brimmers Blues" in 1927. A similar pattern is heard in "Down South Blues" by Sleepy John Estes with Hammie Nixon in 1935. There were artists who alternated voice and harmonica, such as "Man Trouble Blues" by Jaybird Coleman in 1927 and "I Want You by My Side" by Jazz Gillum in 1936. However, the singing section is clearly separate from the harmonica part. In other words, when they sing, they do not play their instruments. Rather, they insert instrumental sections between stanzas.

On the other hand, as soon as Sonny Boy ends the introduction by playing the harmonica, he starts singing. While singing, Sonny Boy punctuates each vocal passage with his instrument. By doing so, he places the harmonica in the foreground of the music, and it acquires an equal musical importance to the vocal.

How did Sonny Boy learn such a performing style? The closest precedent of the same style is heard in "Mississippi Swamp Moan" and "Friday Moan Blues" by an obscure vocalist and harmonica player, presumably from Mississippi, by the name of Alfred Lewis, in 1930.[30] In his recordings, Lewis inserts harmonica fills between his falsetto vocal phrases. Occasionally he sings and plays the harmonica simultaneously, as heard around 0:17–0:19 and 0:55–0:57 on "Friday Moan Blues." However, there is no evidence that Lewis and Sonny Boy ever met.

Sonny Terry was another harmonica player with the same performing style. Sonny Boy may have been inspired by Terry, but it is not very likely. Terry's main territory was North Carolina, and he did not make his first solo recordings, "Mountain Blues" coupled with "The New John Henry," until December 1938.[31] In addition, the ways Sonny Boy and Sonny Terry create harmonica licks are different to a large extent. Compared with Sonny Terry, Sonny Boy tends not to rely on "chugging"—a repetition of a rhythmic breathing pattern—that Sonny Terry often incorporates to create his patterns. In short, while Sonny Terry creates more rhythmic phrases by quickly changing the direction of breaths, Sonny Boy prefers a more melodic approach.

It is very possible that Sonny Boy invented the technique of switching vocal and harmonica quickly by himself. When he was adopting a song from Son Bonds's "Back and Side Blues," he might have tried to sing Bonds's vocal part and play Hammie Nixon's harmonica at the same time.

More important, however, after Sonny Boy learned to alternate vocals and the harmonica, he continued to develop and explore the ramifications in his own way. He did this by replicating the effect of Hammie's harmonica for Son Bonds or Sleepy John. At the same time, inferring from the contrasting stylistic approaches between Sonny Boy and Hammie as detailed below, it is also possible that Sonny Boy adopted Yank Rachell's playing style to the harmonica. As discussed in chapter 1, Yank tends to structuralize music by inserting short, recurring mandolin riffs between vocal phrases, as heard in his collaboration with Sleepy John Estes on "Divin' Duck Blues." Sonny Boy possibly on occasion had to sing and play fills that Yank was supposed to play, experimenting with this performing style under stressful circumstances or, perhaps, just doing it for fun. Sonny Boy may not have been the first artist to come up with the style of quickly changing vocal and harmonica, but he was the first to popularize it.

"Good Morning, School Girl" is a showcase of harmonica techniques as if it is an étude for every harmonica learner (see figure 2.1). Sonny Boy plays an F-harmonica in the key of C. The introduction is clearly borrowed from the vocal line. Since this phrase keeps recurring throughout, it can be called a theme. This car horn–like motive gives the composition a recognizable character. Here (measures 1–2) he starts from a combination of two techniques—playing two holes simultaneously (holes 2 and 3) and pitch bending (hole 3: E is bent to E-flat). This passage rests on B-flat (measures 2 and 4: hole 2) with another pitch-bending technique. The same phrase in a different code (measures 7–8) is connected to a transitional phrase (measures 9–11), which is, as explained in chapter 1, probably a derivative of the melodies he learned from Hammie Nixon. The second half of the theme starts with a phrase that leans on the melodic potential of the instrument—an impressive wah-wah effect over a whole and a half step bent from E down to D-flat on hole 3, multiplied by a hand vibrato (measures 13–14). This section is followed by a cadential figure and a link—turnaround—to the first measure (measures 15–19).

[Wah-wah effect]

He-llo lit-tle school girl.   He-ll-o little

Figure 2.1. "Good Morning, School Girl," entire introduction.

Interestingly, while Sonny Boy learned bluesy licks most likely from Hammie Nixon, their approaches to connect sections are very different. Compared to Hammie's free-flowing accompaniment behind Sleepy John Estes or Son Bonds, Sonny Boy organically unites sections. He recycles the introductory phrase for an interlude—solo—after the fourth stanza. In addition, it is noticeable that Sonny Boy refers to what he learned from Hammie Nixon (see figure 2.2, an excerpt from "Jack and Jill Blues" by Sleepy John Estes with Hammie Nixon), but Sonny Boy adds thickness to Hammie's phrase when he plays it to punctuate vocal melodies.

[Harmonica doubles the vocal line.]

Now the sun gon-na shine in my ba-ck door some-day,

[Harmonica responses to the vocal phrase.]

Figure 2.2. "Jack and Jill Blues."

As opposed to Hammie, who has more of a single note–dominated style (puckering), Sonny Boy freely alternates a rich chordally dominated figure (chording) and single notes—the style that is heard at the very beginning of this recording. As Lawrence Hoffman describes, "Redoing this rural mix into a concept which he was to pioneer in Chicago in just a few years—a concept that was to shape the blues harp style into what it is a half century later."[32]

"Sonny Boy was the master at getting the most sound out of the harmonica," says Joe Filisko. "This is important because of how small the harmonica is and how good it can be at sounding loud regardless of its size."[33]

Sonny Boy's playing style is known for its volume—he is loud! He created such a rich-sounding style for two possible reasons. First, he often had to compete with other instruments of the ensemble, especially when he worked with a pianist and guitarist. Second, because he did not have a regular band, he had to fill up all the space by himself. Guitarist/vocalist John Brim said, "All them [sic] guys had this, watchacallit [sic]—down home style. Wasn't no style then really, until Sonny Boy Williamson around '36, blowing the style he had, you know. Back in like the [old-] timey music—then later years he'd blow. He'd just blow and wanted to blow some. Didn't have a band, you know."[34] With his debut recording "Good Morning, School Girl," Sonny Boy Williamson gave the harmonica a new role as a lead instrument.

"Good Morning, School Girl" also demonstrates Sonny Boy's characteristic vocal style. As Big Bill Broonzy once said, "I never heard a man couldn't speak well, but he could sing."[35] Sonny Boy has a lisping and stuttering way of singing, which was likely caused by a speech impediment. For example, as heard when he sings the phrase "Now, you can tell yo' mother an' yo' father, um, / that Sonny Boy's a little school boy, too"—especially when he stretches "mother and father"—he phrases slightly both behind and ahead of the beat. He does not sing powerfully like Muddy Waters and Howlin' Wolf but sounds warm and intimate.[36] He also sounds like a country boy. Blues historian David Evans noted Sonny Boy's singing style was widely imitated.[37]

As discussed in chapter 1, Sonny Boy composed "Good Morning, School Girl" when he was about thirteen years old, thinking of a schoolmate he fell in love with. Reflecting his age at the time, the lyrics appear childish. The third verse is an innocent marriage proposal.

> ["Good Morning, School Girl" Verse 3]
> Now, you be my baby, come on and be my baby,
> I'll buy you a diamond, I'll buy you a diamond ring,
> Well, if you don't be my little woman,
>   and I won't buy you a doggone thing.

The last verse can even be called naive. Although he doesn't know what to do, he will always be kind to her regardless of what happens in the future:

> ["Good Morning, School Girl" Verse 5]
> I don't know hardly, I don't know hardly,
> Baby, what in this world to, baby, what in this world to do,
> Well then I don't want to never hurt your feelings,
>   or either get mad with you.

"Good Morning, School Girl" was an influential record. Jimmy Reed listed it as one of the platters that helped him acquire a taste for the blues. "I used to listen to Sonny Boy Williams [*sic*] . . . and this thing he put out about 'School Girl,' and oh, it was quite a few of 'em I used to listen to," he said.[38] One of Memphis Minnie's best-known songs, "Me and My Chauffeur Blues" in 1941, is clearly based on "Good Morning, School Girl" in its melodic and verse structures.

* * *

The second cut from the May 5, 1937, session was "Blue Bird Blues." This song is in a medium-slow tempo with a rigid boogie-woogie bass pattern played by two guitars—one plays the bass line, and the other plays chords. Sonny Boy plays a C harmonica in the key of G. Similar to "Good Morning, School Girl," he plays instrumental fills between vocal phrases. In this way, he creates a call and response between his voice and the instrument. Because "Blue Bird Blues" has a slower tempo, he has more room to add fills than in "Good Morning, School Girl."

Sonny Boy tends to combine chordally dominated phrases with percussive effects, which can supply both thickness and a driving feel to the ensemble. The fills are clearly derived from his vocal lines. A two-pitched motive—D and F in this particular recording—occurs after the tremolo (measures 3 and 4), followed by the motive consisting of a series of triplets on the IV chord (measure 5), the I chord (measures 7 and 8), and a cadential figure (measures 11 and 12). These are formulaic passages he often utilizes for medium- and slow-tempo, twelve-bar blues compositions. This song is also an example of cramming many words into a small musical space—in this case "Please take this letter down south for me" in measures 3–4 and its repetition in measure 7 (see figure 2.3). After the third verse, Sonny Boy plays solo. The basic idea is juxtaposition: stillness and movement, and thick and thin (see figure 2.4).

Similar to "Good Morning, School Girl," "Blue Bird Blues" is a virtual library of harmonica techniques—a wah-wah effect in the introduction, a series of tongue slaps immediately after the fourth verse, and a hand-cup vibrato combined with chording for the solo, as well as switching between playing chords and melodies. He includes whatever he can produce from the instrument into his music making. The most outstanding feature here is a fat sound coming out of a small instrument and the impeccable timing with which he punctuates vocal lines—though, of course, it would be easier to rhythmically correspond to his own vocal.[39]

Joe Filisko calls this performance a good example of showing the stylistic continuity and difference between Sonny Boy and Hammie Nixon:

> Sonny Boy probably got his basic playing foundation and blueprint from Hammie Nixon. Hammie was quite accomplished at getting a seamless sound by working the inhaling notes and their corresponding bends. The result was a very potent and smooth blues sound not broken up by too many changes of breathing direction, which can result in the blues having a more folk-like sound to it. Sonny Boy seems to have picked this up from Hammie along with his song repertoire. But you don't hear a lot of percussive sounds in Hammie's playing. Hammie played cleaner. He didn't use much of split chord sounds. It's sort of like Sonny Boy took Hammie's style and made it more driving and got more sound of harmonica. He kind of put it on Steroids.[40]

Figure 2.3. "Blue Bird Blues."

"Blue Bird" is the name of Sonny Boy's record label (though, strictly speaking, it is spelled "Bluebird"); however, this song is not about the record company he was recording with but about a man who is asking a bird to carry a letter from St. Louis to his girlfriend in Jackson, Tennessee.

["Blue Bird Blues" Verse 2]
Now blue bird when you get to Jackson,
  I want you to fly down on Shannon Street,
Now blue bird when you get to Jackson,
  I want you to fly down on Shannon Street,
Well, then [?] I don't want you to stop flyin',
  until you find Miss Lacy Belle for me.

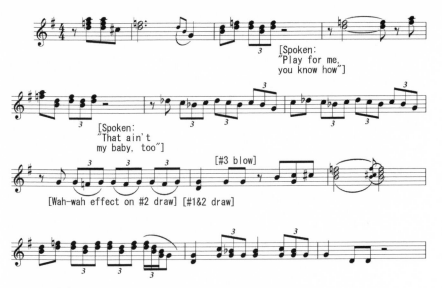

Figure 2.4. "Blue Bird Blues," solo.

As discussed in chapter 1, "Blue Bird" is an example of a personalized—
that is, biographical—composition; it is the compositional technique that
Sonny Boy learned from Sleepy John Estes. Lacy Belle Davidson was
Sonny Boy's fiancée at that time. She was from Houston, Mississippi. T.
W. remembered how Sonny Boy got to know her: "Her dad was working
for a railroad up here in Jackson. He got transferred up here on railroad.
And her mother was there. And her grandmother raised [her]. . . . She'd
come up here and stayed in the summertime when school's out. That's
how he met her."[41] And this song also shows an example of localized
lyrics with the inclusion of "Shannon Street." In the 1930s, Shannon
Street was the main African American business and entertainment street,
similar to Beale Street in Memphis. Along with "Good Morning, School
Girl," "Blue Bird Blues" personifies Sonny Boy's entire recording career
in the display of his performing and compositional styles.

"Got the Bottle Up and Gone," the third cut from the May 5, 1937,
session, is suited for social gatherings. Although the lyrics are sometimes
unintelligible, the protagonist sings that he doesn't run a filling station.
Nor does he sell gas but

> ["Got the Bottle Up and Gone" Verse 1]
> Well I don't run no filling station, I don't sell no gas,
> [Unintelligible], my burner heats too fast [?]
> You go the bottle up and go,

> You go the bottle up and go,
> You know the high-powered mama,
>   that papa got your water on [?].

The accompaniment pattern is in the style of the Hokum Boys (Tampa Red and Georgia Tom), and a lighthearted backup vocal in the refrain by Robert Lee McCoy arouses joyous, party-like feelings.

This recording is proof of Sonny Boy Williamson's strong connection to the musical tradition in Memphis. The same melody pattern is common in the repertoires of many other artists of the area. For example, the earliest recording of the same melodic pattern is found in "Your Friends Gonna Use It, Too—Part 1" and "Part 2" by Walter Vincent with Chatman's Mississippi Hot Footers, recorded in the Peabody Hotel in Memphis in September 1929. It also appears in "You Ought to Move Out of Town" and "Save Me Some" by Jed Davenport and His Beale Street Jug Band in 1930, followed by "You Got to Have That Thing" by the Picaninny Jug Band in 1932. With the same musical structure—the fast couplet/refrain pattern (but with a different lyrical pattern)—Will Shade's Memphis Jug Band recorded "Bottle Up and Go" in 1934, the direct precursor of Sonny Boy's version. Outside Memphis, those who recorded this song and variations included Tommy McClennan, Blind Boy Fuller, Leadbelly, Sonny Terry with Brownie McGhee, Blind Willie McTell (as Blind Willie), and country and western artists the Maddox Brothers and Rose.

In the chorus section, Sonny Boy punctuates the vocal line with a syncopated, car horn–like, three-note motive by the harmonica: "You got the bottle up and go—'A'–'A'–'A' / You got the bottle up and go—'A'–'A'–'A.'" The way Sonny Boy adds fills sounds highly similar to that in "You Ought to Move Out of Town" by Davenport.[42]

Another cut from the same session, "Sugar Mama," which contains a classic sexual metaphor of a woman as "sugar," is a variation of "Sugar Mama Blues" and was recorded by Tampa Red in March 1934. Sonny Boy's version is taken almost directly from Tampa Red's recording, but it is not Tampa's original. It can be at least traced back to "Sugar Farm Blues," Yank Rachell's February 1934 recording with Dan Smith, and another recording by Yank, "Sweet Mama," with Sleepy John Estes and Jab Jones in May 1930.[43]

Musically Sonny Boy's "Sugar Mama" is a variation of "Blue Bird Blues." The harmonica phrases in both recordings are very similar though they are in different keys. As we will observe in this chapter, Sonny Boy kept returning to this medium-slow blues pattern that he used in "Blue Bird Blues" and "Sugar Mama" for many other compositions.

One of the criticisms against the Lester Melrose productions is that some songs he produced sound very similar to one another. His priority—the business formula he relied on—often suppressed creativity. A Chicago blues composer from the next generation, Willie Dixon, who also worked in his early career as a session bassist for Melrose, was critical of Melrose's practice: "Melrose wanted all those things to sound alike and we would have quite a few arguments about it."[44] To be fair to Melrose, who had varying degrees of business acumen, these records with the pattern of medium-slow country blues sold well, especially in the Deep South.[45] While the single record was the main medium, the similarity to previous hits was one of the common factors that helped increase sales—the same tendency can be observed in numerous hit records.[46]

It seems that Melrose had wanted to cut six sides in total for this occasion, while Sonny Boy prepared only four compositions. He made up "Jackson Blues" and "Skinny Woman" on the spot, but they lack the artistic quality that the other four compositions have. "Jackson Blues" is an example of Sonny Boy's original lyrics set to the well-known melody—in this case, the popular eight-bar blues "Trouble in Mind," by Richard M. Jones from 1924. Sonny Boy sings what look like some unrelated verses: for example, the first verse is about leaving Jackson, while the second verse refers to different preferences of cars. While she likes Chevrolets, he prefers V-8 Fords. "Skinny Woman" is a variation of "Gravel Road Woman" by Yank Rachell, as mentioned in chapter 1. The first verse of Sonny Boy's version is almost identical to Yank's original—and his preference for a large female. From the second to the fifth verse, he again seems to be singing verses unrelated to the first verse, and other verses have nothing to do with any other verses—a man having too many choices in women to decide which one he likes in the second verse; having the blues because of a woman's mistreatment toward him in the third verse; a man's regret about his bad behavior in the past in the fourth verse; and a woman leaving a man in the fifth verse.[47]

The lack of quality control in "Jackson Blues" and "Skinny Woman" implies that the musicians and staff tried to record something within a limited time and budget. Since this was the era of disc cutting, it was not unusual for engineers to hesitate to waste another disc for a different take.

In addition, the general atmosphere of recording was often their priority rather than the small mistakes or subtle sound deficiencies that often occur—almost no one had high-quality professional audio equipment that could make performing flaws noticeable.

Though there were defects, Sonny Boy's first recording session successfully produced widely popular records, including "Good Morning, School Girl," "Blue Bird Blues," and "Sugar Mama." These recordings also show his mastery of compositional techniques that contain biographical and localized lyrics. More important, artistically he showed not only the past but also revealed the future of harmonica performance. Sonny Boy gave the harmonica a role as a starring instrument. He built the foundation of the Chicago blues sound that the next generations furthered—especially Muddy Waters and Little Walter.

* * *

Sonny Boy accompanied Robert Lee McCoy and Big Joe Williams in the same session. McCoy recorded "Tough Luck," "Prowling Night-Hawk," and "Sweet Pepper Mama," and Big Joe recorded "I Know You Gonna Miss Me," "Rootin' Ground Hog," "Brother James," and "I Won't Be in Hard Luck No More."

The quality of these recordings is uneven. Sonny Boy's harmonica on "Tough Luck" sounds aggressive. He is competing with McCoy's vocal by getting full sounds out of the instrument rather than creating subordinate phrases. For the next cut, "Prowling Night-Hawk," which is a variation of "Tough Luck" but with different words, Sonny Boy was probably told to keep it down. Here when McCoy is singing his part, Sonny Boy mostly offers soft harmonic support with an occasional tremolo, refraining from full sounds and busy rhythmic movements. On the other hand, Sonny Boy's performance in "Sweet Pepper Mama"—another variation of "Tough Luck"—is similar to the original. Musically, he is not in sync with the vocalist. The recording sounds like the only way to balance the vocal and instruments is to position Sonny Boy farther away from the microphone.

Big Joe Williams's four cuts for the May 5, 1937, session also are based on a theme and variations of blues in a medium-slow tempo. Accordingly, Sonny Boy's accompaniments fall into a routine. All of the recordings start with the formulaic two-pitch motive that we have observed in "Blue Bird Blues" (see figure 2.3), and as expected he plays the triplet figure in the IV chord section. At this early stage, he was still learning to be a creative accompanist.

* * *

Sonny Boy had a follow-up session on November 11, 1937, about a half a year after his first session. The location was again the Sky Room, on the top floor of the Leland Hotel in Aurora. This time he worked with guitarists Robert Lee McCoy and Henry Townsend and pianist Walter Davis.

Henry Townsend was born in Shelby, Mississippi, in 1909, and died in Mequon, Wisconsin, in 2006. With his father, he kept moving from one place to another, a small town called Lula between Shelby and Memphis; Memphis, Tennessee; Caruthersville, Missouri; Cairo, Illinois; and Miller City, Illinois. When he was around ten years old, they ended up in St. Louis. His first instrument was the harmonica, but he was inspired to pick up a guitar after hearing it played by a friend of his father. In 1929, Townsend recorded four sides for Columbia. Henry's "Worry Blues" captures his signature playing style—tremolo-like upper string figures and melodic rhythm, which is also heard in recordings by Henry Spaulding, his contemporary in St. Louis. Townsend recorded for Bluebird from 1933.

In his memoir, Townsend admitted he had high regard for Sonny Boy as a harmonica player. Sonny Boy, he said, could get a performing job anywhere he wanted. All he had to do was to walk into the place where he wanted to play:

> He [Sonny Boy] played up in houses, anywhere he could, but I don't know of any regular engagements that Sonny Boy ever got here [St. Louis]—he would muscle his way in on everything. If he wanted to play across town, he'd wait until evening and go in one of them places and take him a job, and he was accepted—that's the way he would do it. He was also one of the only guys that I know that could go to the job with a harmonica by himself. He walk in on his own [*sic*] and take him a job [*sic*] and they would accept him.[48]

Townsend also said that his A-Model Ford was the car "Walter Davis, Big Joe [Williams], Sonny Boy, and I were in when we all went up to Aurora to record,"[49] even though Big Joe was not part of the recording personnel at that time.

Sonny Boy recorded eight compositions. They are all slow or medium-slow blues songs. This time he prepared. "Up the Country" and "Collector Man Blues" are highly influenced by Walter Davis. These songs feature Davis's gloomy piano and Sonny Boy's wailing harmonica. In both recordings, which feature two other guitars, the idiosyncratic, limping ensemble and Sonny Boy's tired voice well express the down-and-out feelings of a man who, in "Up the Country," is desperately looking for his woman anywhere and everywhere he can think of: "highway 61," "up the country," "all the stations," and even in "England." In "Collector Man Blues," the protagonist is running away from a persistent debt collector man. With one line, "Why don't you tell him [collector man] any man ain't got no money, can't find a place to stay," Sonny Boy makes a strong social commentary that describes the life situation of his core audience—black farmers and factory workers.

A medium-slow tempo song, "Worried Me Blues," the second cut of the day after "Up the Country," establishes a musical mold for other compositions in this session. It starts with an introduction built upon a two-note motive by guitar and a wah-wah effect by harmonica. As with "Blue Bird Blues," Sonny Boy punctuates vocal lines with formulaic fills—sustained notes followed by the two-pitch motive, IV chord and I chord figures with triplets, and a cadential figure.

"Worried Me Blues" is about a mistreated man's feelings toward a girl who spent all his money and left. "Frigidaire Blues" is an analogy between a brand-new refrigerator (a novel, high-in-demand appliance of the times) and women; nothing works in a sufficient manner for him: "Now I just bought me a brand new Frigidaire, and I bought me a kitchen set, too . . . Well, I been I been [sic] lookin' around all over this town, I swear I want none of these women, too." "Black Gal," a eulogy for a dark-skinned woman, is a variation of Charlie Pickett's "Crazy 'Bout My Black Gal" recorded on August 2, 1937. Not much is known about Pickett, except that he was one of the Brownsville-Jackson-based artists.[50] More likely Sonny Boy got to know him and his songs through this circle. Sonny Boy plays "Black Gal" with the same musical pattern of "Worried Me Blues" and "Frigidaire Blues." This could be another of his biographical songs. His little brother—T. W.—appears in the second verse:

> ["Black Gal" Verse 2]
> Well now looky here, Black Gal, Black Gal,
>   you oughta be ashamed,

> The way that my baby brother know you, Black Gal,
>> he's scared to call your name,
>
> [Refrain]
> My brother says he's wild about you, Black Gal,
>> he's just as crazy as he can be,
> My brother says wild about you, Black Gal,
>> you ought to be a fool about him.

In the third verse, Sonny Boy himself appears: "Well now here is my picture, black gal / I want you to keep it in your frame, / Now when Sonny Boy says he's goin', / You can look at that Sonny Boy just the same." T. W. said, "He sang about all women [laugh]. Yes, Sir! He had a lot of them!"[51]

"Suzanna," another song from this session, is derived from Johnnie Temple's big hit "Louis Louis Blues," recorded on November 12, 1936. Sonny Boy's version appears to be composed around a woman with whom he actually had a relationship. Suzanna has "two dimples on her jaw":

> ["Suzanna" Verse 2]
> Now then Suzanna is just my type of woman,
>> with two dimples on her jaw,
> Now then if she ever mistreats me, man,
>> I'll be forced to break the law,
> But Suzanna, Baby, why don't you change your way,
> Well, I don't want you to wait till you get old, Suzanna,
>> change your young way [?].

T. W. remembered Suzanna and her sister: "Suzanna! Oh, Suzanna! [To his cousin Fred Utley in the same interview:] You met her sister, Brownie. You couldn't get browner than her."[52] The lyrics of "Suzanna" display Sonny Boy's ability as a storyteller.

Another cut, "Early in the Morning," is a good example of Sonny Boy's ability to vary preexisting songs. It is based on a classic song passed on to many artists. One of the earliest recordings is "Soon This Morning" by pianist Charlie Spand in June 1929. This is medium-tempo blues featuring Spand's own boogie-woogie piano. A recurring phrase— "soon this morning, 'bout the break of day"—in the fifth measure on IV chord is a recognizable musical trademark that other composers have used. Other versions before Sonny Boy include "Early This Morning—

'Bout Break of Day" by Walter Roland (July 1933), "At the Break of Day" by Big Bill Broonzy (released under Big Bill in June 1934), "Soon in the Morning" by Jimmie Gordon (July 1935), and "'Bout the Break of the Day" by Bill Gaither (October 1936). After Sonny Boy, two of his Bluebird label mates recorded it—"Early in the Morning" by Speckled Red (December 1938) and "So Early in the Morning" by Washboard Sam (November 1939).

Sonny Boy recorded "Early in the Morning" three times in his career. The second verse includes the following:

> ["Early in the Morning" Verse 2]
> Well then I've got a little woman, her name is Miss Kate,
> She told me to come to her house this morning,
>   I got there about half past eight,
> She asked "I told you to come early in the morning, Baby,
>   'bout the break of day,"
> Now you oughta see me grab the pillow,
>   where my baby used to lay.

The depiction of the circumstance of an affair with Kate stirs up listeners' imaginations, as though this was a real story. Possibly "Kate" was a woman with whom Sonny Boy had a relationship. While this song usually features lively piano, which adds citified feelings, Sonny Boy's version with just his harmonica and two guitars retains a strong flavor of the country blues. Similar to "Suzanna," Sonny Boy plays a very artful solo for "Early in the Morning"—powered especially by a throat vibrato technique (see figure 2.5).

"If you really wanna understand the blues tradition of the harmonica, the power for blues sounds is coming from inhaling sounds," says Joe Filisko.[53] He explained the secret of Sonny Boy's power.

> He had a very clever way of phrasing that most people from my cultural background would not likely find to be intuitive. Inhaling on hole 2 will give you exactly the same note as exhaling on hole 3 on a diatonic harmonica. Sonny Boy figured out how to use the best one at any given time to keep the sound full and groove driving.
>   Very often in his playing if you listen to what he does on bars 7 and 8, especially on bar 8, you hear idling—he's got this momentum going between hole 2 and hole 3. It is kind of building a momentum before he goes into the dominant chord. . . . The lick here is switching between the 2 inhaling and the 3 exhaling, which allows him to get his

breath ready for something stronger. . . . Knowing where to exhale, that's one of the things that John Lee was clever about.[54] (see figure 2.5)

Figure 2.5. "Early in the Morning," solo.

The last cut from the November 11, 1937, session was another slow-tempo blues, "Project Highway." This song reflects the times, more specifically, the Works Progress Administration (WPA), the largest and most ambitious of the New Deal agencies, which was formed to provide jobs for three million people to create useful projects, such as building or improving hospitals, schools, airport landing fields, and highways. Sonny Boy sings about a V-8 Ford, the popular vehicle of the time,[55] and a newly built "Project Highway," where he wants to drive his V-8. While the song is topical, the last verse is, in fact, autobiographical:

["Project Highway" Verse 4]
Now when peoples gather around, now in front of my baby's door,
Eeh-eeh, crowd of people stand in front of my baby's door,
    wah, wah, then I'm going to tell them don't get excited,
Ooh, same Lacey Belle I was singing about before.[56]

John Lee "Sonny Boy" Williamson and his fiancée Lacey Belle Davidson registered their marriage at the office of Madison County, Tennessee, on November 13, 1937, two days after this recording session;[57] they lived on Wells Alley (near North Shannon Street in Jackson, which he sang about in "Blue Bird Blues" from the last session). Sonny Boy was twenty-three years old; Lacey Belle was reportedly just fifteen years old at the time.[58] Compared with other recordings on the same date, especially "Up the Country" and "Collector Man Blues" with Walter Davis, Sonny Boy's vocal in "Project Highway" is much more brisk and vigorous. Even with a piercing sustained note in his solo, he expresses his excitement about his new bride.

Once again Sonny Boy accompanied other musicians when they took turns for their leader sessions—first Robert Lee McCoy and then Henry Townsend. "My Friend Has Forsaken Me," the first side McCoy cut, captures how Sonny Boy adjusts his performing style. During the first verse, his harmonica is louder than McCoy, but from the second verse, Sonny Boy reduces the volume and relies more on sustained notes without busy rhythmic movements. He provides enough harmonic support for the vocal line instead of competing with it; we observed a similar change in the last session. Probably he was again told to reduce the volume.

For another cut, "Mean Black Cat," in a slow tempo, Sonny Boy alternates two styles: relying on either sustained notes or obbligato phrases that rhythmically go along with the vocal lines, as well as adding fills between vocal phrases as he does on his own recordings. For "Take It Easy Baby" with a fast shuffle pattern, he offers a spirited support behind McCoy's vocal by alternating single note–dominated phrases and chords. As well as "Take It Easy Baby," Sonny Boy's exciting and graceful collaboration for three Henry Townsend compositions, "I Have Spent My Bonus," "A Ramblin' Mind," and "Now I Stay Away," is comparable to the forerunner of the forthcoming postwar Chicago blues style by Muddy Waters and Little Walter. Sonny Boy provides speed and thickness, though he can appear at times to be too loud, emitting a full, solid sound of the instrument, which is why he was placed at a fair distance from the microphone.

In this session, Sonny Boy was experimenting in the third position of the harmonica; however, probably because he was not confident enough, he used it only for accompaniment with "Brickyard" and "Mamie Lee" by McCoy and "CNA" and "Lose Your Man" by Townsend.[59]

The experiment did not prove effective, however. These compositions were not the best material for him to explore the potential of the third position. The purpose of using the third position is to create the mood of a minor key, whereas these songs are in major keys. By playing the higher register at random, he merely crushes against vocal melodies and the other instruments. It is clear Sonny Boy had some homework to do, though the November 11, 1937, session was still fruitful for him.

* * *

Sonny Boy went back to the Leland Hotel on March 13, 1938, for his third Bluebird session. He was accompanied by guitarists Elijah Jones and Yank Rachell; Rachell had not recorded for about four years; his last session was February 1934.[60] Sonny Boy recorded as a leader first. Subsequently Jones cut six sides with Sonny Boy and Yank, and then Yank took the last turn to record four sides.

Eight out of ten songs Sonny Boy recorded in this session follow the medium-slow blues formula. "My Little Cornelius" is a variation of "Blue Bird Blues" from his first session in May 1937. He changed words here and there while the music is almost the same—Yank Rachell's mandolin adds more country flavor to the overall sound, though. The original character "Miss Lacey Belle on Shannon Street, Jackson" is changed to "Miss Cornelius," a girl who actually lived on the Cornelius farm between Jackson and Brownsville.[61] Sonny Boy also changed the messenger of his special letter to a girl from a "blue bird" to a "special delivery man."

"Decoration Day Blues" is about remembering a lost wife. Pianist Curtis Jones claimed he was the composer of this song: "I was up in Sonny Boy's flat one day. Just after I composed it ["Decoration Day Blues"], I left my musical satchel behind with rough copy."[62] Sonny Boy sings very simple words in a twelve-bar, a-a-b, blues form about a woman who died and left him:

> ["Decoration Day Blues" Verse 1]
> Lord, I had a woman, she was nice lovin' in every way,
> Lord, I had a woman, she was nice lovin' in every way,
> Lord, but she died and left me,
>   I have the blues on every Decoration Day.
>
> [Verse 2]
> Lord, I hate to see her leave me,

because these's the last words my baby had to say,
Lord, I hate to see her leave me,
    because these's the last words my baby had to say,
She told me to brang [sic] her some flowers
    on every Decoration Day.

[Verse 3]
Peoples, you're havin' a good time now,
    just like the flowers that comes in May,
Peoples, you're havin' a good time now,
    just like the flowers that comes in May,
Now but Sonny Boy thinks about his baby
    on every Decoration Day.

[Harmonica solo]

[Verse 4]
Fare you well, Baby, I ain't got no more to say,
Fare you well, Baby, I ain't got no more to say,
Lord, but I always remember,
    I'll never forget Decoration Day.

[Nonmelodic] "Play along."

[Ending solo]

In the introduction, Sonny Boy uses a tongue block technique to create a "crying" sound on the harmonica (see figure 2.6) while Yank's mandolin offers a clever tone painting to produce the sad feelings of a man remembering his loss.

Figure 2.6.   "Decoration Blues," introduction.

The plain-spoken words and effective accompaniment here help listeners identify with the song and even imagine how the woman in the song passed away and how the man overcame the loss. This type of song was Sonny Boy's forte and appealed to his core audience. He depicts the everyday life of common people and sings about their feelings with simple words. This highly impressive performance inspired many artists who came later, including John Lee Hooker and another Sonny Boy Williamson (Rice Miller).

"Moonshine" (a variation of Sleepy John Estes's "Need More Blues" recorded on August 2, 1937) is about the often devastating effects of alcohol. It will make you want to shoot dice and make you want to fight:

> ["Moonshine" Verse 2]
> Now moonshine will make you shoot dice, make you wanna fight,
> Now when you go home, and you can't treat your wife right,
> You been drinkin' moonshine, moonshine do harm to many men,
>   now that is the reason why I believe I'll make a change.

Alcoholism is a recurring theme in Sonny Boy's songs. Although it is not known how serious his problem was around the time he recorded this song, he might have truly meant, "I believe I'll make a change," considering that other songs are based on his actual experience.

"Until My Love Come Down" is a variation of "Lemon Squeezing Blues" by Bumble Bee Slim in July 1935 and "Let Me Squeeze Your Lemon" by Charlie Pickett in August 1937. The chorus with the graphic expression "Now if you let me be your lemon squeezer, Lord, until my love come down" stokes listeners' imaginations.

Other slow blues songs like "Miss Louisa Blues," "Sunny Land," "Down South," and "Beauty Parlor" are all based on Sonny Boy's own medium-slow blues pattern. "Miss Louisa" sings of lost love, and "Down South" refers to nostalgic feelings toward his hometown—"Now I am going back down South, man, where the weather suits my clothes / Now I done fool around in Chicago, yeah, I [got?] done almost broke." Here Sonny Boy speaks for his listeners. The introductory melody is loosely based on "Roll and Tumble Blues" by Hambone Willie Newburn. The choice of melodic source fits the song theme—nostalgia for the South.

"Sunny Land" has more honesty than the other two songs. After the introduction that sounds like a train whistle, Sonny Boy sings about the dreary feelings of a man whose "baby" took a train—ironically called Sunny Land—and left him behind. Sonny Boy combines the images of train whistling and loneliness.

> ["Sunny Land" Verse 2]
> Lord, every time I hear that lonesome Sunny Land blow,
> Every time I hear that lonesome Sunny Land blow,

    Now you know it make me feel lonesome, Lord,
      just because I want to go.

In the fourth verse, he tries to convince himself to believe that someday she will be back, even as he knows this is only wishful thinking:

["Sunny Land" Verse 4]
Now but that's alright I know, my baby ain't goin' to stay away,
But that's alright I know, my baby ain't goin' to stay away,
Now she will get to sittin' down and thikin', yeah,
    and come runnin' back home some day.

"Sunny Land" proves that Sonny Boy could lend a sense of drama to complex human feelings, which many audiences could relate to. And his harmonica solo after the fourth verse is very powerful. Imitating a train sound was a classic method to demonstrate performing ability on harmonica when it was still considered a novelty instrument, but here he inserts additional layers of emotion to the sound and makes it a part of a musical drama, thereby raising harmonica performance to another level.

"Beauty Parlor," another slow blues song from March 13, 1938, is about a hairdresser who gives "my baby" the currently most popular type of curling, Kro Ken Know curls.[63]

Besides eight slow or medium-slow blues songs, Sonny Boy recorded two songs in faster tempi. "You Can Lead Me" derives from "Good Morning, School Girl." The vocal melody is borrowed from the previous hit, but he rearranged the new version with mandolin and rewrote words with rather shallow expressions: "Now here's my hand, Baby . . . you lead me where you want me to go . . . now if I don't make you happy, you won't have to fool with me no more."

"I'm Tired Trucking My Blues Away" is a hokum pop song. The similar musical pattern is found in "Whitewash Station Blues" by the Memphis Jug Band (1928), "Hittin' the Bottle Stomp" by the Mississippi Jook Band (1936), and "They're Red Hot" by Robert Johnson (1936).[64] They all sound like party songs in the rural South. And yet Sonny Boy's solo is rich in both volume and speed, demonstrating his quick, sharp, and rhythmical performance in full volume.

Elijah Jones and Yank Rachell, each of the two sidemen for the March 1938 session, had leader sessions after Sonny Boy. There is no information about guitarist/vocalist Elijah Jones. Sonny Boy played harmonica for "Only Boy Child," "Lonesome Man," and "Mean Actin' Mama."

These are all medium-slow blues songs. Sonny Boy builds harmonica passages in his typical medium-slow blues manner (shown in the discussion of "Blue Bird Blues" in this chapter) while Yank Rachell's mandolin helps to create a rustic atmosphere.

It is evident from Yank Rachell's leader recordings with Sonny Boy that they had been spending a long time polishing their efforts as a team. A medium-slow blues song, "J. L. Dairy Blues"—inspired by Yank's occupation—shows their matured music making for the genre. Sonny Boy is fully engaged in embellishing Yank's vocal. "Rachel Blues," a loose variation of Sleepy John's "Someday Baby," is a medium-tempo dance tune. Here Sonny Boy appears in the lyrics: "Better go down, Sonny Boy, I ain't going be here long . . . Yeah, I got the blues for my baby, I want to go back home." Sonny Boy inserts delightful response phrases after every vocal phrase, as if commenting musically on what Yank says. Sonny Boy's performance for "Lake Michigan Blues," which borrowed the main melody of the Delta blues classic "Roll and Tumble Blues," is hardly inspiring. On the other hand, the country dance tune "I'm Wild and Crazy as Can Be," a variation of "Bottle Up and Go" by the Memphis Jug Band, shows that they are performing well in tune with each other.

* * *

For the June 17, 1938, session at the Leland Hotel, pianist Walter Davis returned to play with Sonny Boy and Yank Rachell. Also "Jackson" Joe Williams—not Big Joe Williams again—participated in the session, cutting four sides as a lead singer. Not much is known about Williams except that he was in the Jackson-Brownsville blues community circle.

Davis accompanied two slow blues compositions by Sonny Boy, "Honey Bee Blues"[65] and "My Baby I've Been Your Slave." These are strange recordings. Sonny Boy plays his usual medium-slow blues pattern, while Davis maintains his idiosyncratic piano style. In addition, it sounds like "Jackson" Joe Williams's guitar is out of tune. With each player heading in a different musical direction, these recordings may sound too abstract for some ears; others may simply conclude that the music is falling apart.

One of the fast-tempo cuts from this session was "Whiskey Headed Blues," which later inspired "Whiskey Head Woman" by Tommy McClennan, Sonny Boy's Bluebird label mate. McClennan recorded this song more than a year after Sonny Boy—November 22, 1939. While McClennan's variation is built upon a Delta-blues style like a steady boogie-woogie bass pattern in a medium-slow tempo, Sonny Boy's original is in a fast-driving beat, similar to "Good Morning, School Girl." Although this song is about an alcoholic woman, it appears that Sonny Boy is depicting himself when he is intoxicated:

> ["Whiskey Headed Blues" Verse 3]
> Well now and I took you out of the street, Baby,
>   when you didn't have no place to stay,
> You ain't acting nothing but a fool, doggin' me round this way,
>
> [Refrain]
> 'Cause you's a whiskey headed woman,
>   now you stay drunk all the time,
> Now if you don't stop drinkin',
>   I believe you're going to lose your mind.

Sonny Boy's solo based on the vocal melody sounds very strong. He freely alternates a single note–dominated style (puckering) and a chordally dominated style (chording), but here he tends to use chords more in order to match up with the volume produced by the combination of guitar and mandolin. Especially when playing chords, he creates an acute, piercing sound.

"Shannon Street Blues" is a medium-slow blues similar to "Blue Bird Blues," "Decoration Blues," and others. As the title indicates, this is a composition with both localized lyrics and autobiographical lines. Shannon Street is near where Sonny Boy lived with Lacey Belle—she appears in the third verse—and supposedly this is also where he could buy liquor.

> ["Shannon Street Blues" Verse 1]
> I went down on Shannon Street, now to buy some alcohol,
> I went down on Shannon Street, now to buy some alcohol,
> I told him to put it half full of water,
>   but they didn't put in any drop at all.
>
> [Verse 2]
> So, I drank my straight whiskey,
>   now I staggered on the street,
> So, I drank my straight whiskey,
>   now I staggered on the street,
> Now but my head got so heavy,

my eyes couldn't even give a peep.

[Verse 3]
Lacey tells me, 'Papa, Papa, well, you ain't no good at all,'
Lacey tells me, 'Papa, Papa, well, you ain't no good at all,'
Now she say, 'You don't make me happy,
    so long as you fool with this alcohol.'

[Verse 4]
Sometimes I tell her, 'Oh, Lacey, this alcohol is killin' me,'
Sometimes I tell her, 'Oh, Lacey, this alcohol is killin' me,'
Well, now they told me if I ain't quit drinkin',
    in some lonesome cemetery I would be.

[Harmonica solo]

[Verse 5]
I say, 'Lacey, Baby, won't you go ridin',
    can I take you ridin' with me in my car?'
I say, 'Lacey, Baby, won't you go ridin',
    can I take you ridin' with me in my car?'
She say 'Sonny Boy, I'm scared you'll get a drink of whiskey,
    and I'm scared we won't ride very far.

"Shannon Street" is clearly personal. As alcohol was becoming a serious problem with Sonny Boy, the record sounds painful, as if he is describing his own battle against the habit he could not break. In 1947, Sonny Boy wrote a variation of "Shannon Street Blues" with a new title: "Alcohol Blues." I will discuss this song in the next chapter.

Nearly every artist who remembered Sonny Boy talked about his good-natured character, but they always stressed his reckless drinking habits as well. Yank Rachell was no exception: "He was a friendly fellow. Kept on him all the time, but he loved that whiskey."[66] As mentioned previously, Lester Melrose served whiskey even at the recording sessions. Yank mentioned that Sonny Boy and Walter Davis got drunk, had an argument, and nearly had an accident involving a gun:

One time I was in a car with Sonny Boy and Walter Davis. Big Joe Williams was drivin' and Sonny Boy and Walter started fightin'. Well, neither one was scared of the other and both of 'em want to fight. They were good friends, but Walter get mad 'cause Sonny Boy drinks. Sonny Boy drink [sic] his whiskey, and they got to arguing about it and drinkin' until they want to stop the car and get out. There's a pistol in dashboard. It wadn't [*sic*] Joe Williams' pistol. It [*sic*] my pistol, so I got it and put it in my pocket so nobody got hurt, 'cause I know they would hurt one another.[67]

Yank felt compelled to monitor Sonny Boy's behavior during the recording sessions because his mindless behavior could often be life threatening. "Sonny Boy [was] always gettin' into trouble over women. There's one time I carried him out of a club we were playin'. He tried to court a man's wife, and the man wanted to kill him. He young [*sic*], you know. . . . Yeah, he'd hug 'em and kiss 'em anyway. Keep playin', and would fight 'cause he wasn't scared of nobody."[68]

Four compositions from this session are related to well-circulated songs, including Sonny Boy's own recording. The vocal melodies of "Lord, Oh Lord Blues" and "You Give an Account" are borrowed from two blues classics—"Roll and Tumble Blues" by Hambone Willie Newbern and "Sitting on Top of the World" by the Mississippi Sheiks in 1930, respectively. "You Give an Account" has a taste of hillbilly music rather than blues because of the way Yank plays the mandolin. Here Sonny Boy sings "I told I'd buy her a Chevrolet, because she wanted a V-8 Ford."[69] "You've Been Foolin' Round Town" is a variation of "Got the Bottle Up and Gone."

"Deep Down in the Ground" has a similar verse pattern and musical structure—especially the opening melody—to "Good Morning, School Girl," but the rest is somewhat different. This recording captures one of the best moments of the Sonny Boy–Yank ensemble. In the tempo of prestissiomo (bpm/beats per minute = 208), Yank plays virtuosic guitar in which he switches from chording to single note–dominated phrases and a tremolo technique that he developed from playing the mandolin. Complementing Yank's tricky accompaniment, Sonny Boy provides a driving harmonica performance for the introduction (see figure 2.7).

Figure 2.7. "Deep Down in the Ground."

The music, with highly syncopated—almost jerking—phrases, effectively describes an upset feeling of a man toward his woman:

> ["Deep Down in the Ground" Verse 1]
> You hear that rumblin', you hear that rumblin'
>   deep down in the ground,
> Oh Lord, you hear that rumblin' deep down in the ground,
> Now it must be the devil, you know, turnin' my woman around.

* * *

Sonny Boy again accompanied Yank Rachell on four sides at the June 17, 1938, session. The recording sounds like a social country gathering when they would often jam together. A medium-slow blues song, "When You Feel Down and Out," is similar to "J. L. Dairy Blues" from Yank's last Aurora session with Sonny Boy on March 13, 1938. It also sounds similar to Sonny Boy's slow blues compositions such as "Shannon Street Blues." "Texas Tommy" is a country dance tune, which Yank once said he learned as "Texas Tony" from Brownsville local musicians Walter Franklin, Hambone Willie Newbern, and Stoke Franklin.[70] The vocal melody of "It's All Over" is taken from "Sittin' on Top of the World," which Sonny Boy also used in the same session with "You Give an Account." It is possible that Yank developed his variation by hearing Sonny Boy's version. The vocal melody of "My Mind Got Bad" is adapted from "How Long, How Long Blues," one of the most popular blues records in the late 1920s by pianist/vocalist Leroy Carr with guitarist Scrapper Blackwell. Yank probably learned this song from "My Love Is Cold," the Memphis Jug Band's recording from November 1934. In fact, Yank sings the same refrain "My love is cold" throughout, while changing lyrics here and there. To avoid a possible conflict over copyrights, he used a different title.

After Yank Rachell, "Jackson" Joe Williams recorded four compositions as a leader, while Sonny Boy accompanied him on only two songs, "Peach Orchard Mama" and "Haven't Seen No Whiskey." The recordings indicate that "Jackson" Joe was influenced by Sleepy John Estes's crying vocal style. For "Peach Orchard Mama," Sonny Boy plays his familiar slow blues style similar to "Blue Bird Blues." The up-tempo dance song "Haven't Seen No Whiskey," another song on which Sonny Boy played an accompaniment, is an obvious derivative of "Milk Cow Blues" by Sleepy John.

Sonny Boy sounds more restrained in his session work this time compared to his early sideman recordings such as those for Robert Lee McCoy and Henry Townsend. At no time does his harmonica dominate the vocalists. By now, he had learned how to back up the singers effectively.

* * *

On December 17, 1938, Sonny Boy was again in the Sky Room of the Leland Hotel with pianist/vocalist Speckled Red, mandolin player Willie Hatcher, and guitarist Robert Lee McCoy. This was Sonny Boy's last recording session in Aurora.

Before Sonny Boy, Speckled Red had a leader session. Born Rufus Perryman in 1892 in Monroe, Louisiana, Speckled Red learned church organ after his family moved to Hampton, Georgia.[71] With his brother Willie, later known as Piano Red, Speckled Red learned piano throughout his childhood and adolescence. By the time he became a teenager, he was proficient enough to financially support himself by playing the piano. With his 1929 hit "The Dirty Dozens," he made his reputation in the blues community of Memphis and St. Louis. For the December 17, 1938, Aurora session, Speckled Red cut ten sides, while Sonny Boy played only the last of the set, "You Got to Fix It," a derivative of "You Got to Have That Thing" by the Picaninny Jug Band in 1932. Speckled Red's version features his gorgeous boogie-woogie piano, accompanied by Sonny Boy's aggressive harmonica, as if in competition with him.

Sonny Boy himself cut ten sides. Except for two adaptations—"Susie-Q," a song about popular lindy hop steps and based on the fast couplet/refrain pattern of "Got the Bottle Up and Gone" and "Good Bye Red" (a variation of "Oh Red" by the Harlem Hamfats in 1936)—all the recordings for this session follow his medium-slow blues pattern like "Blue Bird Blues," with slight changes in tempo and in keys—C, F, and G. As mentioned earlier, the similarity to a previous hit was one factor to make another hit around this time, though eventually, the pattern would run its course and musicians would get tired returning to the same formula again and again, which eventually happened to Sonny Boy.

"Number Five Blues" is about a man who wishes for a woman to return to him on the train known as "Train Number 5." "Christmas Morning Blues" is, as the title suggests, about asking Santa Claus to bring toys for his girlfriend. In "Blue Bird Blues—Part 2," "blue bird" is a personification of a girl who has left her man, while in the original, "blue bird" functions as a proxy for him to send his love from St. Louis to Jackson. "Little Girl Blues" and "Low Down Ways" are about a woman failing to treat her man with respect.

"Low Down Ways," a little faster in tempo than other cuts from the session, is an interesting recording for Sonny Boy's stylistic development. This is the first indication of the integration of his harmonica with swing jazz. While he is in the framework of a basic four-beat pattern at this point, he gradually grew out of the country blues style and brought his music into fast swing and jump blues.

This composition is in a sixteen-bar quatrain refrain blues form with fairly long lyrics. Sonny Boy again returns to the theme of alcohol. This time, her "low down, dirty ways" are amplified by whiskey.

> ["Low Down Ways" Verse 1]
> Now listen here, Baby, do you think I'm gon' be your fool?
> You want to think, Baby, you want Sonny Boy to be your mule,
> Every time I meet you, Baby, walkin' up and down the street,
> You walk by me, smilin', act like you don't wanna speak,
>
> [Refrain]
> But, ah, little girl, I've got tired of low down, dirty ways,
> Well, now drinkin' whiskey and runnin' around,
>   little girl, that's all you crave.

As Sonny Boy was growing as a musician, he was also growing up as a person, as seen in the autobiographical "The Right Kind of Life," a variation of "Mistake in Life" by Roosevelt Sykes, recorded on March 31, 1938.

> ["The Right Kind of Life" Verse 1]
> Now I'm only twenty-four, I just declare
>> I been married twice, yes, I been married twice,
> Oh now I'm only twenty-four, I just declare
>> I been married twice, yes I been married twice,
> Well now you people know but then,
>> oh that I ain't been livin' the right kind of life,
>> no, not the right kind of life.

Sonny Boy was actually twenty-four years old when he recorded this song. He reflects on his life thus far, for which he had not necessarily made the right decisions: as mentioned earlier, his first marriage to a maid named Sallie Lee Hunt did not last long. In the second verse, he sings of his mother's worry: "Well, then she said, 'I'm scared that women and whiskey is gon' be the ruin of my only child.'" In the third verse, he blames young people's reckless behavior that makes their mothers cry, and in the fourth verse, he blames himself for chasing women and getting drunk all the time.

In "Insurance Man Blues," Sonny Boy sings about a poor living condition in which he cannot afford an insurance payment. This song is similar to "Collector Man Blues," which he recorded with Walter Davis in November 1937.

"Rainy Day Blues," the last cut from the session on December 1938, is complex. He sings about a man who is returning to take care of "[his] wife and baby" on a "rainy day"—when he realizes, "Now you know that the woman that I'm lovin', you know, she don't mean me no good." This is a long song compared to his other compositions—it takes six verses to tell the whole story, so that he had no time for soloing.

The musicians and producer called it a day after Sonny Boy's last cut. They returned to the Leland next day (December 18, 1938) to have Robert Lee McCoy's leader session. He recorded four compositions, all of which were released under "Rambling Bob." Sonny Boy and Speckled Red participated in all the cuts. For a light dance tune, "Next Door Neighbor," Sonny Boy sings a second vocal part, "You shouldn't do that, you shouldn't do that," a response phrase to McCoy's lead vocal. For the other three songs—"Big Apple Blues," "Freight Train Blues," and "Good Gamblin'," all of which feature McCoy's typical, melancholy blues in a medium-slow tempo—Sonny Boy offers reserved support. They all sound like his usual slow- or medium-tempo blues licks.

* * *

We have examined the early stage of Sonny Boy Williamson's recording career. Even at this point, Sonny Boy achieved artistry as a songwriter, with compositions including such blues classics as "Good Morning, School Girl" and "Decoration Blues"; as a vocalist, with his infectious, lisping vocal style; and, more important, as a harmonica player, with harmonica-playing techniques that have come to be studied by many other artists: quick alternation between vocal and the instrument; thick sounds with percussive, driving effects to compete with other instruments; and successive use of hole 2 and 3.

Sonny Boy tended to use the same melodic patterns more often than not, especially his medium-slow blues formula. As stated previously, that was in part a commercial strategy at the time, though it could be too excessive and run its course. Sonny Boy's artistic achievements, nevertheless, make up for his shortcomings.

Many of his song lyrics derive from his own experience and reflect the times he was living—"Project Highway," "V-8 Ford," "Frigidaire," "Collector Man," and "Flowers for the Decoration Day." With simple expressions, his songs deal with the life and times of his audience—working-class African Americans. His voice and lyrics echo their views, dreams, and struggles. While he sings of women with whom he actually had relationships in songs such as "Suzanna," "Early in the Morning," and "My Little Cornelius," he professes regret for the bad choices he has made in only one song—"The Right Kind of Life." Either way, he represents the common people and their often self-contradictory nature. Moreover, Sonny Boy, who was getting caught up in the mire of alcoholism, depicts whiskey as an ugly social disease, as seen in "Moonshine" and "Shannon Street Blues." Interestingly, he never sings about the joy of drinking.

In the following chapter, we will study Sonny Boy's recordings in Chicago. Here he incorporates his harmonica into swing jazz and increases the tempo of his music. Here, too, he departs from the country blues tradition altogether to the urban blues and, in the process, creates the sound of Bronzeville.

3

WINDY CITY BLUES

Chicago: 1939–1941

From 1939, all the studio work of Sonny Boy Williamson took place in Chicago. One of the most important characteristics of recordings during this period is that he started to incorporate swing jazz and jump blues into his sound. As a result, his performance acquired a fast tempo with quick techniques, even though he still composed many songs on the medium-slow blues pattern.

By this time, the Windy City had become a thriving blues capital. Bluebird Records was one of the most important forces in the blues recording market with such Chicago-based artists as Lonnie Johnson, Tampa Red, Big Bill Broonzy, Memphis Minnie, Memphis Slim, Big Maceo, and Little Brother Montgomery, as well as Sonny Boy on its roster.

At this point, however, Sonny Boy still lived in Jackson, Tennessee. His name is listed in the 1939–1940 edition of the *Jackson and Bemis, Tennessee City Directory*.[1] When he had recording sessions, he traveled all the way to Chicago by way of St. Louis, where he stopped to meet his uncle Fred. Fred remembered Sonny Boy had to go back and forth between Jackson and Chicago to cash a check as payment for the recording session: "He'd make his records and get a check. . . . Now it's too big to cash here [in Jackson]. Come back here and cash it, but nobody cash it. So he had to go back to Chicago for him to get check cashed."[2]

Until 1942, Sonny Boy stayed in Tampa Red's house when he was in Chicago, as many other blues musicians did. Tampa Red's house on 35th and State was known as the headquarters of the Chicago blues community. This is where many musicians congregated and Lester Melrose found new talent and new recording material. Willie Dixon remembered, "He [Tampa Red] had a place up over a pawnshop. And a lotta [sic] the musicians used to go up there and write songs, lay around in there, and sleep. Melrose always came there when he was in town."[3]

* * *

Pianist Walter Davis and guitarist Big Bill Broonzy were sidemen at Sonny Boy's first Chicago session on July 21, 1939. The recordings from this session sound like Broonzy is leading an ensemble by providing a steady rhythmic support with his amplified guitar, while Davis plays his free-floating piano. They cut eighteen sides, enough to secure materials for almost a year. In fact, Sonny Boy did not return to the studio until May 1940.

Eleven out of the eighteen sides are variations of the medium-slow tempo blues pattern. Generally they are not very impressive. Blues historian Neil Slaven writes about this session for the liner notes on Sonny Boy's complete recordings: "The session continued with a series of songs at a medium tempo that merge together in the listener's mind."[4] Though there might have been commercial demands, the formula for medium-slow blues songs was running its course. It is noticeable in many sections in the recordings that Sonny Boy himself is feeling bored with playing cliché-like phrases over and over. In some songs, he does not even play a solo.

One of the medium-slow blues songs, "Bad Luck Blues," is autobiographical. A barber named Dennis Morrison, a cousin of Sonny Boy and T. W., was shot to death near his shop on Biddle Street, St. Louis:[5]

> ["Bad Luck Blues" Verse 1]
> People did you hear about the bad luck,
>   the bad luck that happened just about six month ago,
> Now did you hear about the bad luck,
>   the bad luck that happened just about six month ago,
> Now my cousin Morrison got shot down,
>   just as he was walking out of the door.

Other slow blues songs, "Doggin' My Love Around," "Little Low Woman Blues," "Good for Nothing Blues," "Sugar Mama Blues No. 2," "Something Going on Wrong," and "Miss Ida Lee" have the almost identical opening with the cupped hand vibrato technique, which Sonny Boy previously used for many recordings, such as "Sugar Mama Blues" (1937), "Moonshine" (1938), and "Shannon Street Blues" (1938), though keys are varied—he uses three harmonicas for this session: G, D, and B-flat.

Sonny Boy plays the first position harmonica (straight harp) for "Little Low Woman Blues"—a B-flat instrument in the key of B-flat. This is an awkward recording. The ensemble is falling apart—obviously three players are not working together. His use of the straight harp is also heard in "My Little Baby," a different version of "Good Morning, School Girl." This is another unpolished side since his instrument—a C harmonica in the key of C—is not in tune with the piano. "Good for Nothing" is another song about alcohol:

> ["Good for Nothing" Verse 1]
> My baby says I ain't good for nothing,
>> Lord, now, I just keep on runnin' around,
> My baby says I ain't good for nothing,
>> Lord, now, I just keep on runnin' around,
> Now she says when you get a drink of whiskey, Lord,
>> you don't do nothin' but act like a clown.

"Miss Ida Lee" is about yearning after an Eastern woman, who "look[s] something more like a Japanese." Sonny Boy recorded this song before the attack on Pearl Harbor in December 1941.

Another medium-slow blues from this session, "T. B. Blues," is based on the well-circulated subject of the times, tuberculosis. Famous recordings before Sonny Boy include "T. B. Blues" (1927) and "Dirty T. B. Blues" (1929) by Victoria Spivey, "T. B. Blues" by Jimmie Rodgers (1931), and "T. B. Is Killing Me" by Buddy Moss (1936). Except Jimmie Rodgers's, all the versions including Sonny Boy's have a punch line— "T. B. is killing me." The vocal melody of Sonny Boy's version and the lyrics are based on that of Spivey's "T. B. Blues." He even mentions where he wants to be buried when he dies:

> ["T. B. Blues" Verse 1]
> Now when I was upon my feet,
>> now I couldn't even walk down the street,

> With the women lookin' at me from my head to my feet,[6]
> But, oh, T.B. is killing me, now that I want my body buried,
>   way down in Jackson, Tennessee.

"T. B. Blues" is one of the cuts from this session on which Sonny Boy does not play a solo.

"Good Gal Blues" sounds like something Sonny Boy composed on the spot. The less creative words are sung in a vocal melody similar to that of "T. B. Blues," while the tempo for "Good Gal Blues" is faster. "Joe Louis and John Henry Blues" is about the historical heavyweight championship match on January 25, 1939, in New York City—Louis knocked out John Henry Lewis in the first round. Similar to "T. B. Blues," "Joe Louis" had been an inspirational folk hero for African American singers.[7] Recordings before Sonny Boy included "Joe Louis Is the Man" by Joe Pullum in 1935, "Joe Louis Blues" by Carl Martin in 1935, and "He's in the Ring (Doin' the Same Old Thing)" and "Joe Louis Strut" by Memphis Minnie, both in 1935. According to the lyrics, Sonny Boy bet fifty cents on Joe Louis as he was "woophin' with them men and women in Jackson." "Joe Louis and John Henry Blues" gave an idea for the introductory phrase for another medium-slow blues, titled "I'm Not Pleasing You." "Thinking My Blues Away" has a somewhat impressive vocal melody with an ascending figure, though he still relies on much of his blues-lick cliché.

Again similar to "T. B. Blues," Sonny Boy composed a song around another well-circulated theme—"New Jail House Blues."[8] He actually spent some time in jail in a newly built courthouse on East Main Street, Jackson.

> ["New Jail House Blues" Verse 1]
> Now were you ever in the new jail in Jackson,
>   Man, you didn't know what to do,
> Now were you ever in the new jail in Jackson,
>   Man, you didn't know what to do,
> Now then you wanted to go out walkin',
>   but they wouldn't let you out on the avenue.

Sonny Boy's half brother T.W. told the story behind the song. Sonny Boy made friends with the police officer who arrested him:

> A policeman named Harold Newman used to be a speed cop here in Jackson back in the first of the '30s. He arrested Sonny Boy once and carried Sonny Boy to jail. Sonny Boy whooped on down that hall goin'

"Please don't arrest me, I've done nothing wrong, drank a little beer and that's all." He just made a song of it. And that guy [Harold Newman] liked him [Sonny Boy] and brought him on home to Mama. And every time they ever picked Sonny Boy up, they'd carry him to the police headquarters in Jackson and . . . lock him until Harold Newman came in. And Harold Newman would take him on his motorcycle and take him home and say, "Nancy, take this boy and make him go to bed."[9]

"Lifetime Blues" appears to be another autobiographical song. Sonny Boy borrowed lyrics and melodies from "Viola Lee Blues" by Cannon's Jug Stompers in 1928. The title sounds like another jailhouse song, but this song is actually about drinking: "Now I've been drinking White Lightnin' / It's done gone to my head." In the last verse, he reworks the lines from "Viola Lee Blues" to describe his and Walter Davis's alcoholism as if it were a prison sentence:

> ["Lifetime Blues" Verse 3]
> Some got six months, some got one solid (mmm),
> Some got one solid (mmm), indeed Lord,
>   some got six months, some got one solid year,
> Now but me and Walter Davis, we both got lifetime here.

Three other songs from the July 21, 1939, session are adaptations from previous hits. Sonny Boy recorded "Honey Bee Blues" for the June 17, 1938, session, but he rerecorded it this time. The new version is clearly based on the very popular records "Bumble Bee" by Memphis Minnie and Kansas Joe in 1930 and "Honey Bee Blues" by Bumble Bee Slim in 1931. Sonny Boy's phrasing and the idea of the honeybee, or bumblebee, personifying sexual prowess are identical in all three versions, although there are subtle differences. He combines his lyrics with the introductory phrase for "Decoration Blues"—a variation of the medium blues pattern.

> ["Honey Bee Blues" Verse 1]
> Now honey bee, honey bee,
>   I want you to please make some honey for me,
> Ah now honey bee, honey bee,
>   I want you to please make some honey for me,
> Now that you can make the sweetest honey
>   of any honey bee I ever did see.

In order to understand Sonny Boy's future musical direction, two other adaptations from this session are important—the lively romping "Good Gravy," based on the musical pattern that Sonny Boy had previously used for "I'm Tired Trucking My Blues Away" on March 13, 1938, and "Tell Me Baby," a variation of the well-known "(Hey) Lawdy Mama," premiered as "Oh Lordy Mama" by Buddy Moss in 1934.[10] These songs indicate that Sonny Boy's musical style was moving toward fast-tempo swing jazz.

Joe Filisko pointed out how Sonny Boy amalgamated his thick sound playing with speed: "With melodic style in a fast tempo, Sonny Boy would also know how to exhale with 'Tell Me Baby.' It's like using 3 blows and 2 draws sometimes with chords. It's the same kind of chord sound, but he is mixing it all up between 3 exhales, 2 inhales, and a chord. Very very clever stuff"[11] (see figure 3.1).

Figure 3.1.   "Tell Me Baby."

From the following session in 1940, Sonny Boy almost always prepared songs with a faster tempo in which he could display his musical strength without being trapped in the medium-slow blues licks that he tended to overuse.

"Good Gravy" and "Tell Me Baby" also capture the fabulous teamwork of Sonny Boy and Big Bill Broonzy. With very solid chord stroking, Broonzy supports Sonny Boy who contributes a warm vocal performance.[12]

* * *

Sonny Boy returned to the studio on May 17, 1940. This was a pivotal session. He started to increase his recording band. This time he introduced a drummer, but he later added a bassist as well. Drummer Fred Williams and a new pianist, Joshua Altheimer, were Big Bill Broonzy's sidemen. Williams, by providing a clear rhythmic support, tightened up Sonny Boy's ensemble. Compared with the previous pianist, Walter Davis, Altheimer gave much more versatile harmonic background, especially for the up-tempo compositions. Influenced by a series of Big Bill's recordings, Sonny Boy departed from the country blues style to the citified swing style—the tendency observed in "Good Gravy" and "Tell Me Baby" in the last session.

"I Been Dealing with the Devil" is a variation of Sonny Boy's medium-slow tempo blues, but it sounds more energetic than his previous recordings with the same formula. Altheimer's delightful piano opening is followed by Williams's simple but clear-cut drum work, primarily with bass and snare drums. Right at the beginning, it is obvious that these musicians give stability to the ensemble. Sonny Boy's voice sounds very enthusiastic, as if his new backups are energizing him. When he is singing the chorus part "I been dealing with the devil," the way he stretches the vowel—"e" for "devil"—sounds very catchy.

Sonny Boy plays two rounds of solo—after the third verse and the fourth (last) verse for an ending. The second solo is breathtaking. He juxtaposes a long sustained note and very tricky licks: a smooth descending of "D–C–B–G," a quick descending of the same pitches, trill, and then a series of triplets (see measures 5–7 of figure 3.2).

Figure 3.2. "I Been Dealing with the Devil."

For other songs he recorded in this session—"Decoration Day Blues No. 2," "New Early in the Morning," and "Welfare Store Blues"—he plays a solo part in a similar way, with a contrast between a motionless (sustained) section followed by a speedy passage. This is an ideal solo that every harmonica player should learn to build a musical drama.

Later, "I Been Dealing with the Devil" contributed to a controversy over Sonny Boy's untimely death. As discussed in chapter 5, the following line led to the rumor of the cause of his death, that he was stabbed by a woman with an ice pick:

["I Been Dealing with the Devil" Verse 2]
Well now I've got the meanest woman,
   the meanest woman you most ever seen,
She sleeps with an ice pick in her hand, Man, she fights all in her dream,
I'll soon be sleeping with the devil, I'll soon be sleeping with the devil,
I'll soon be sleeping with the devil, my woman don't love me no more.

He concludes that his woman "don't love me no more."

"War Time Blues," "Train Fare Blues," "Decoration Day Blues No. 2," "Welfare Store Blues," and "My Little Machine" are all derivatives of his medium-slow blues pattern, while these songs are a little slower in tempo than "I Been Dealing with the Devil." In all of the medium-slow compositions, Williams's thumping bass drum gives a steady, rhythmic support to the performance, and Altheimer's cascade-like piano adds a tasteful harmonic background. Sonny Boy's harmonica sounds soaring on top.

"War Time Blues" is a product of the times. On May 10, 1940, a week before the recording session, Germany invaded France, Belgium, and the Netherlands. The song was intended to lift fighting spirits for the war.

["War Time Blues" Verse 2]
Now it ain't no use of you worryin', Buddy, that ain't gon' to help you none,
Now it ain't no use of you worryin', Buddy, that ain't gon' to help you none,
Now if you can't fly no airplane, maybe you'll be able to carry a gun.

He later recorded a more patriotic song when the United States joined the allied forces after Japan's Pearl Harbor attack in December 1941.

"Train Fare Blues" is about asking his mother to send money for a train fare to come home. This seems to be another song that was inspired by a personal story. According to T. W.'s daughter Linda Utley King, Sonny Boy was quite a dresser: "His mother said Sonny Boy bought suits and bought clothes. And he liked to dress and stuff . . . the choice of best suits and he loved hats, too."[13] But sometimes he spent too much money on clothes so that he could not afford to travel back home. T. W. remembered when Sonny Boy was traveling with an artist named Ella Green:

> Mama wrote a letter for him to call her. He called her. . . . And she talked to Ella about Sonny Boy. "Ella, what's my boy doin'?" "He's doin' alright." "He's got clothes?" She [Ella] said, "Yeah, plenty of clothes." "Send him home." She [Ella] said, "That's the trouble. He spent all the money on clothes." (*laughs*) So Mama wired him money to come home . . . he showed up with three suitcases of clothes . . . two suitcases of suits and a suitcase full of shirts. [14]

"Decoration Day Blues No. 2" is a new version of his earlier hit "Decoration Blues," recorded on March 13, 1938. Similar to the original, "No. 2" is a remembrance of a deceased wife. The May 20, 1944, issue of *Billboard* gave "Decoration Day Blues No. 2" coupled with "Love Me Baby" a positive review: "The holiday for Sonny Boy is also the anniversary of his sweetheart's death and the side should show its biggest strength in the particular race sectors at this time of the year. . . . 'Love Me Baby,' also an original, takes on a brighter lyrical aspect, with the full implication contained in the title of the tune. This side will unquestionably enjoy wide circulation among the race fans at the phono locations." [15] To our modern ears these recordings may seem dated, but this review suggests that his medium blues pattern combined with melancholy lyrics and sexual innuendo had broad appeal back then. This was the first time that *Billboard* reviewed a Sonny Boy record.

While "War Time Blues," "Train Fare Blues," and "Decoration Day Blues No. 2" start with Altheimer's piano, "Welfare Store Blues" and "My Little Machine" open with Sonny Boy's harmonica. For these two songs, he explores an octave embouchure technique, which will be discussed later in the chapter. "Welfare Store Blues," a song that is associated with the Depression, is based on "Red Cross Blues" by Walter Roland, in 1933. As blues lyric researcher Guido van Rijn points out, Sonny Boy sings "how difficult it was for many blacks under sharecropping to receive welfare goods." [16] It is imperative to get a sign from "some really white man" to get welfare goods—army surplus such as "keen-toed shoes" and "pea black soldier coats":

> ["Welfare Store Blues" Verse 2]
> Now you need to go get you some really white man,
>   you know, to sign you a little note,
> They give you a pair of them keen-toed shoes,
>   and one of them pea black soldier coats,
> But I told her no, baby, I sure don't wanna go,

I say I do anything in the world for you,
but I don't wanna go down to that welfare store.

"My Little Machine" is about low-quality gasoline damaging the car. Willie Dixon, a house songwriter at Chess Records, referred to this song when he composed "Oh Yeah," which he offered to Muddy Waters in 1954.

Sonny Boy recorded two swing compositions for this session: "New Early in the Morning [Early in the Morning No. 2]" and "Jivin' the Blues." In "New Early in the Morning," supported by Altheimer's marvelous boogie-woogie piano and Williams's steady backbeat, Sonny Boy is playing much faster—vivace (160 bpm = beats per minute)—than the original slow allegretto (96 bpm). For the introductory phrase and solo after the third verse, he creates a phrase with a succession of octaves by tongue blocking and then shifts to a chordal phrase. He produces very powerful, layered sounds as though performed by multiple players (see figure 3.3). While Sonny Boy has very articulate rhythms in the instrumental sections, he never sings words on the beat. This is part of his charm.

Figure 3.3.   "New Early in the Morning."

"Jivin' the Blues," based on his previous recording "Susie-Q" on December 17, 1938, is even faster than "New Early in the Morning"—presto (184 bpm). Sonny Boy effortlessly plays a fast lick. He has great control in volume and rhythms. His harmonica performance is clearly now at a new level. As the title indicates, this song is "jiving" musically and literally, a fast dance instrumental featuring his nonsense talks between solos. In fact, the "jiving" vocalization sounds like a forerunner of rap or hip-hop.

["Jivin' the Blues"]

[Harmonica solo]

[Nonmelodic talk]

I don't care nothin' about your engagement ring,
    oh come on here, at least you can talk with me, you know,
Just let me, shhh, tell you something, you know,
    oh, I don't wanna marry no way,
Now watch!

[Harmonica solo]

* * *

The year 1941 was a productive time for John Lee "Sonny Boy" Williamson. He had three recording sessions during this year and cut twenty sides in Chicago.

Sonny Boy still lived in Jackson, Tennessee. It appears, however, that he temporarily lived in Beloit City, Wisconsin. The population schedule for the census taken on May 30, 1940, lists "Williamson, John L" and "Lacey Belle" as lodgers who resided at 956 Third Street.[17] As his occupation is listed as "laborer,"[18] he might have held a temporary job there. Sonny Boy finally moved out of Jackson to Chicago in 1942, as will be discussed in chapter 4.

When Sonny Boy was in Jackson, he performed with local musicians. Dave Clark, a *DownBeat* magazine contributor based in Jackson, reported in the November 15, 1941, issue that Jackson local band leader Alar [*sic*] Green produced a show for state fairs throughout the South with musicians including Sonny Boy. "The show will use Ziggy Forte, former Green front man, and four other musicians in the cast, Ike Price, bass, Rush Gates, guitar, Christine Chatman, piano, and Sonny Boy Williamson, harmonica."[19] This was the first time Sonny Boy's name appeared in printed media, besides the *Billboard* review mentioned earlier in this chapter.

The first 1941 recording session was scheduled in early spring. On April 3, a day before Sonny Boy's leader session, Yank Rachell was in the studio. He had not made records for nearly three years—the last session was on June 17, 1938. Sidemen were Sonny Boy on harmonica, William Mitchell on imitation (oil-can or washtub) bass, and Washboard Sam on washboard. The compositions Yank recorded for this session were two types: variations of a country blues in a medium-slow tempo that Sonny Boy often used—"Hobo Blues," "Army Man Blues," "38 Pistol Blues," "Worried Blues," and "Up North Blues (There's a Reason)"—and two songs based on the fast couplet/refrain pattern of a popu-

lar song in the Memphis area known as "Bottle Up and Go"—"It Seems
Like a Dream" and "Biscuit Baking Woman," respectively. [20]

"It Seems Like a Dream" is a great example demonstrating Sonny
Boy's sideman work. By offering a thick harmonic and rigid rhythmic
support, he not only collaborates with Yank but also competes with him
musically. Joe Filisko assured me he learned a great deal about blues
guitar–harmonica duo performance by observing Sonny Boy's performing style:

> When I started playing music more in a duo, I started to really see that
> thinner toned style just don't make it. If you play the harmonica like
> John Lee "Sonny Boy" Williamson, when you play with a guitar
> player, you should get a really full, powerful sound—with that guitar
> and the harmonica blend together. Otherwise, the guitar is doing the
> work, and the harmonica is doing a little fill over the top, which any
> instrument can do that. But Sonny Boy's playing is connected to the
> rhythm of the guitar, and the two drive together. . . . He figured out
> how to play the coolest licks plain to basically the blues scale but he
> also figured out how to do it with a very big full sound.
>
> Here's something about Sonny Boy Williamson's playing that is
> not in my opinion, it is not intuitive to many other modern, contempo-
> rary players. You have to really think differently to figure out what he
> is doing . . . really think consciously what he is doing. [21]

Sonny Boy returned to the studio on the following day—April 4, 1940—
with Big Bill Broonzy on guitar, Blind John Davis on piano, and William
Mitchell on imitation bass; Yank Rachell and Washboard Sam were not
included. Blind John Davis was a member of Tampa Red's Chicago
Five. [22] Although Davis said in an interview "I could play with any-
body," [23] the way he adjusts to different performers is somewhat limited—he just plays block chords in his left hand part no matter whom he
plays with and what types of compositions he is required to play. More
important, this was the first session of Sonny Boy as a leader supported
by a bassist. The heavy sound coming out of his extended ensemble is a
precursor of the postwar Chicago blues sound later exemplified by Muddy Waters and Howlin' Wolf.

While Sonny Boy's band produced a loud sound, his music in this
session sounds like his old, circa 1939, pattern. Six out of eight compositions are based on the medium blues formula—"Western Union Man,"

"Big Apple Blues," "My Baby Made a Change," "Coal and Iceman Blues," "Drink on Little Girl," and "Mattie Mae Blues." Musically there is not much variety here. Sonny Boy plays a C harmonica in the key of G—the second position harp (cross harp)—on all the songs. It is possible that he had only one harmonica with him for this session.[24] His harmonica performances here generally follow the patterns that we have observed in earlier discussions—inserting response phrases between vocal lines, full volume sounds, alternations of thick and thin tones, tongue block techniques to create a succession of octaves, alternating no. 2 hole inhale and no. 3 exhale, and so forth.

"Western Union Man" is based on "Mailman Blues" that Sleepy John Estes recorded just about a year before—June 4, 1940—about a man who is anxiously expecting a telegram from his sweetheart. Sonny Boy changes some parts of Estes's lyrics to fit his own story, as he includes his wife's name: "I'm expecting a call from Miss Lacey."

"Big Apple Blues"[25] is about a crop from "Mr. Rudolph's Farm." It is not difficult to read sexual allusions in this song:

> ["Big Apple Blues" Verse 4]
> Lord, I can see your little apple,
>   hangin' way up in your little apple tree,
> Lord, I can see your little apple,
>   hangin' way up in your little apple tree,
> Now you made like you love me so much,
>   Baby, please drop one down for me.

It sounds comical when he sings a very long line for the beginning of the third verse like a tongue twister: "Now my grandmother say she wanna buy a bushel of your apples, she want to make her some apple sauce."

"My Baby Made a Change" is a derivative of Casey Bill Weldon's "Somebody Done Changed the Lock on My Door" of 1935. Similar to "Western Union Man," Sonny Boy changed original lyrics while he recycles Weldon's famous line "Because the key I've got, oh well well, won't fit in my (that) little lock no mo'" almost as is. In his own original lines, Sonny Boy sings that he was warned by his mother and grandmother: "Ah now my mother, she said one thing, my grandmother jumped up and said the same, 'I say if you keep on foolin' around, Sonny Boy, say I'll swear women gon' change your name." Sonny Boy was a playboy according to his half brother T.W. The names of women that appeared in his songs are the ones with whom he actually had relationships. In one of his latest recordings, "Lacey Belle" in 1947, he expresses regret over many episodes of "foolin' around."

"Coal and Iceman Blues" is another song full of sexual innuendo. It includes a very creative stanza, which implies a secret relationship that the two can only achieve through a backdoor:

> ["Coal and Iceman Blues" Verse 4]
> Now tell me what's the matter with your basement,
> > I don't believe you use Sonny Boy's coal no mo',
> Oh tell me what's the matter with your basement,
> > I don't believe you use Sonny Boy's coal no mo',
> Well I always been nice to you,
> > I would bring it in through your back door.

"Drink on Little Girl" is a song about lost love. A man is losing his girlfriend but he still asks her to have a drink with him. Musically it is a little different from other songs in a similar style. In the second and third verses, Blind John Davis plays the stop time—playing only the first beat of a measure—instead of filling all the space. "Mattie Mae Blues" recalls a girl with two dimples on her jaw—remember "Suzanna" also has two dimples on her jaw[26]—and the songs are probably based on a real relationship. Sonny Boy recorded one more slow song, "Springtime Blues." Lyrically, it derives from "Sail On, Little Girl, Sail On" by Amos Easton (Bumble Bee Slim) in 1934, while musically it sounds somewhat similar to "How Long How Long Blues" by Leroy Carr—one of the most popular blues songs in the 1930s.[27]

Sonny Boy recorded only one up-tempo swing composition for this session, "Shotgun Blues." This song contains a line that later became cited in other blues songs—"Now when my baby left me, you know, she left me a mule to ride."[28] In four rounds of solo, he demonstrates his mastery of building a mini musical drama. Especially in the second round, he juxtaposes a very simple phrase consisting of pitches of the G-major triad for four measures and a cascade-like figure that he alternates *forte* and *piano* (see figure 3.4).

Figure 3.4. "Shotgun Blues."

* * *

When Sonny Boy returned to the studio on July 2, 1941, with pianist Blind John Davis and bassist Ransom Knowling, he recorded more up-tempo compositions than usual—four out of six cuts, in fact. The melody pattern of "I'm Gonna Catch You Soon" is a recycle of his previous records "I'm Tired Trucking My Blues Away" in 1938 and "Good Gravy" in 1939. The main feature of the new version is Sonny Boy's lisping vocal. "Sloppy Drunk Blues," another song about alcoholism, is almost an exact recreation of Leroy Carr's recording with the same title in 1930.[29] The music is built on a medium-fast, eight-beat pattern like early rock 'n' roll songs by Chuck Berry, such as "Maybellene" or "Thirty Days." A response phrase by his harmonica after each vocal line may sound formulaic but, actually, it proved to be quite instructive for budding harmonica beginners.

While most of Sonny Boy's songs are about love or lost-love relationships between a man and a woman (with occasional songs about alcohol), "She Was a Dreamer" is slightly different in that it touches on sociocultural issues, for example, the peculiar attitude toward gender in the society they lived in. Sleepy John recorded the same composition with a different title, "Little Laura Blues" on September 24, 1941, about two months after Sonny Boy's. Because this song has a style similar to other Sleepy John songs like "Down South Blues," this is possibly Sleepy John's song although Sonny Boy recorded it before Sleepy John.

Sonny Boy's version has a fast swing feel compared to Sleepy John's country blues style. Regardless of the title, the song is about a girl that the man dreams of. The first verse describes a teenage girl dreaming of "that old Southern dream." But her mother finds her daughter's dream too unrealistic to even listen to: she was "the dreamest girl I most ever seen."[30] Sonny Boy's version has a fast swing feel compared to Sleepy John's country blues style. Regardless of the title, the song is about a girl that the man dreams of. The first verse describes a teenage girl dreaming of "that old Southern dream." But her mother finds her daughter's dream too unrealistic to even listen to:

> ["She Was a Dreamer" Verse 1]
> Now my baby was a girl, she was a sweet sixteen,
> Her mother wouldn't listen to her dream,
> I know she was a dreamer, she dreamed that old Southern dream,
> She was the dreamest girl, the dreamest girl I most ever seen.

In the second verse, it is clear that this is a man's idea of a dreamy girl who loves and kisses him as he dreams.

> [Verse 2]
> Well she knowed about lovin' and kisses on down,
> She was the dreamest girl from miles around,
> I know she was a dreamer, she dreamed that old Southern dream,
> She was the dreamest girl, the dreamest girl I most ever seen.

The third verse is still about his dream that she was expecting kisses and hugs from him. In this context, "that old Southern dream" is likely her expectation to be treated nice by him.

> [Verse 3]
> Well she dreamed that I was kissin' and huggin' her close to my breast,
> She told that much of the dream but she wouldn't tell the rest,
> I know she was a dreamer, she dreamed that old Southern dream,
> She was the dreamiest girl, the dreamiest girl I most ever seen.

The fourth verse is again his fantasy—she dreamed they were kissing by the mill.

> [Verse 4]
> Well she dreamed that we was kissin' down by the mill,

> She dreamed that she had taken me from the girl on the hill,
> I know she was a dreamer, she dreamed that old Southern dream,
> She was the dreamest girl, the dreamest girl I most ever seen.

It is not clear what is meant by "She had taken me from the girl on the hill." Possibly it refers to her removing him from his old girlfriend whom he was having an unwilling relationship with—because now he was in love with the "dreamest girl." In the recording, the second verse, with a slight change, is repeated before the end.

"She Was a Dreamer" captures the times. In many cases, women, who were often socially weak, relied on men. While a woman may use a man to attain her goal, he often took advantage of her. This song describes a typical young girl's dream and a man's wistful feeling toward her.

The introductory harmonica phrase in "She Was a Dreamer" is taken from "Shotgun Blues" from the previous session on April 4, 1941. In addition, there are similarities between them. He freely alternates between stillness and motion, between thin and thick sounds. With another swing number from this session, "You Got to Step Back," Sonny Boy was expanding the realm of expressions by adding speed.

Two medium-slow blues cuts, "Million Years Blues" and "Shady Grove Blues," follow the formulaic pattern. The title "Million Years Blues" is taken from the punch line in the first verse—"You only been gone 24 hours, but it seem like million years now"—but this impressive line is used only once in the whole song. The second verse is full of feelings that many of his listeners could relate to.

> ["Million Years Blues" Verse 2]
> I notice [?] if I ever mistreat you, God knows,
>   I don't mean no harm,
> I notice [?] if I ever mistreat you, God knows,
>   I don't mean no harm,
> Because I ain't nothin' but a little country boy,
>   and I'm right down off the cotton farm.

Sonny Boy's expression is simple, but it is a true voice of the people with similar social and cultural backgrounds.

Another medium-slow blues, "Shady Grove Blues" (a reference to a common name for cemeteries), is similar to "Decoration Blues." This song is about a man who carried the body of his deceased wife to the cemetery in "Shady Grove." Interestingly, Sonny Boy sings of his own death and some form of bad luck, though we never know how seriously he was thinking, for example, "I said if these good lookin' women kill me, Mama, you just leave your poor Sonny Boy dyin'" in the third verse and "she says Sonny Boy, you's a bad luck child, and you just catch the devil everywhere you go" in the fifth verse.

On December 11, 1941, he returned to the studio again. This was his third recording session that year. Sidemen were Blind John Davis on piano and Charlie McCoy on guitar. In addition, imitation bassist Alfred Elkins and washboard player Washboard Sam played for three tracks, respectively. Two types of compositions are in this session: variations of the medium-slow blues formula and a medium-fast, eight-beat pattern influenced by Leroy Carr. Sonny Boy recorded three songs of each type. Two of the eight-beat songs are based on existing compositions.

"Ground Hog Blues" is about a man in a dark frame of mind, comparing himself with a ground hog. All the variations of the medium-slow blues pattern have a clearly faster tempo and steady boogie-woogie feel than those he had recorded previously. This is another influence from swing music. Sonny Boy mentions he wants to hear Fats Waller in the third verse:

> ["Ground Hog Blues" Verse 3]
> Now I wanna hear some swingin' music,
> I wanna hear a Fats Waller sound,
> Now if I start Jitterbuggin',
>   I will get [?] my hole down in the ground.

While the man is compared to a ground hog, a woman is compared to a black panther in "Black Panther Blues," which describes a ruling and cunning girlfriend. Musically this song is almost identical with "Ground Hog Blues." Another medium-slow blues variation, "My Black Name Blues," given the confusing lyrics, sounds like it might have been composed in the studio on the spot. The first verse originated from a levee camp holler, while the second verse —"Well I had this blues before sunrise, with tears standing in my eyes . . ." —is almost a direct quote from "Blues before Sunrise" by Leroy Carr with Scrapper Blackwell in 1934. Blind John Davis's piano is louder than Sonny Boy's harmonica in this recording; this is a tendency of most of the cuts from the December 1941 session, but it is especially noticeable in this song. In addition, Sonny Boy is not playing his instrument as much as usual.

"Broken Heart Blues" is a variation of "Broken-Hearted, Ragged, and Dirty Too" by Sleepy John Estes recorded in 1929. The original, which sounds similar to Sleepy John's "Milk Cow Blues" and "Black Mattie Blues," is built upon a succession of eighth notes in four-four time. In Sonny Boy's version, pianist Blind John Davis is recreating the same rhythmic feel with the way he plays boogie-woogie bass line and chords, though he plays them a little faster than in Sleepy John's version.

"She Don't Love Me That Way" shares the same musical structure of "I'm Tired Trucking My Blues Away" in 1938.[31] Another song on the eight-beat pattern, "I Have Got to Go," is a call to young men to join the army —"Now you go to wear Uncle Sam's uniform, so you can be in style." The recording session was held four days after the attack on Pearl Harbor on December 7, 1941.

These cuts also have an uneven mix; as already indicated, the piano is louder than the harmonica, for example. Actually, Sonny Boy's harmonica sounds full in the studio but is placed farther away from a microphone. Possibly he (and the engineer) had difficulty controlling the balance between the instruments.

"She Don't Love Me That Way" has a flavor of "Jivin' the Blues" from the May 7, 1940, session, and possibly inspired Little Walter's debut record "Just Keep Loving Her," released under Little Walter and Othum Brown in 1947.

Born Marion Walter Jacobs in Marksville, Louisiana, in 1930, Little Walter grew up listening to Sonny Boy. Harmonica player Billy Boy Arnold, who knew both players, once said, "Little Walter was unique but still his style was derived from John Lee (Sonny Boy) Williamson. He once admitted to me that Sonny Boy would tell him he played too fast. He also said that 'Sonny Boy was the man,' and that 'we'll never beat him.'"[32] Walter's thick, chordally dominated solo is apparently inspired by Sonny Boy's performing style, while Walter later added more speed to his performances. Sonny Boy's influence on Little Walter and other players will be explored in the next chapter.

T. W. acknowledged that Sonny Boy had a direct contact with Little Walter in St. Louis. Their meeting occurred around the late 1930s or early 1940s.[33] According to what T. W. said to Jim O'Neal, on one occasion Sonny Boy borrowed a harmonica from Walter: "Can I play your harp, Little Walter?"[34] When he returned the instrument to him, Walter played Sonny Boy's tune to him in response. "That's what I wrote," said Sonny Boy to Walter.[35] They jammed together sometimes in nightclubs and at other times on the street.

After cutting six sides on December 11, 1941, Sonny Boy, along with Alfred Elkins and Washboard Sam, stayed in the studio to accompany Yank Rachell. The eight sides he recorded are categorized into four types. "Yellow Yam Blues" and "Rainy Day Blues" are based on the medium-slow tempo blues pattern like "Army Man Blues" and "38 Pistol Blues" from his last session on April 3, 1941. "She Loves Who She Please," "Bye Bye Blues," "Loudella Blues," and "Katy Lee Blues" follow the same medium-slow blues formula, but the tempo is faster than his earlier recordings in the same pattern.[36] "Tappin' That Thing" originates from Charlie Burse's recording with Will Shade in 1932. The structure of the song is similar to that of "It Seems Like a Dream" and "Biscuit Baking Woman." A country dance, "Peach Tree Blues," is a variation of "Rachel Blues."

The highlights are compositions on the medium-slow pattern in a faster tempo. "Katy Lee Blues," especially, captures the best moment of the nonpareil country blues ensemble, consisting of Yank's vocal and guitar, Elkins's imitation bass, Washboard Sam's washboard, and Sonny Boy's harmonica. Sonny Boy sounds very lively and vibrant, more so than the performance for his own leader recordings on the same day.

This was Yank Rachell's last recording session on the Bluebird label, though he produced several good sellers from the above cuts. "Bye Bye Blues" coupled with "Katy Lee Blues," which was reissued in July 1944, received a positive review from *Billboard*: "Using his own home-spun lyrics, set in the race blues pattern, Yank Rachell hits the mark for those finding favor in the blues shouting."[37] Though he never talked about it, possibly the label dropped him, while his old recordings were style recycled. Otherwise, he might have been just happy with playing around the Brownsville-Jackson community and Memphis. He did not resume his recording career with Hammie Nixon and Sleepy John Estes until 1963 —the period known for linking the blues with the folk music revival.

The following day—December 12, 1941—Sonny Boy with bassist Alfred Elkins returned to the studio for Big Joe Williams's leader session. Big Joe recorded six compositions. "Throw a Boogie Woogie" sounds like a spontaneous work based on the fast couplet/refrain pattern that has been observed in "Got the Bottle Up and Gone."[38] Sonny Boy's harmonica is a little too reserved overall. He plays solos after the second and third verse, but he sounds like he is not sure if he is even allowed to take a solo.

After the third verse, however, Big Joe gives a cue for Sonny Boy, "Here Sonny Boy!" In response, he plays a very swingy solo.

"North Wind Blues" is a variation of the medium blues pattern. Similar to "Katy Lee Blues," Yank Rachell's composition for this session, this recording captures a superb performance of a country blues ensemble. "Please Don't Go" and "Highway 49" are new versions of Big Joe's own hits in 1935, respectively. These recordings are good examples of Sonny Boy's role as a collaborative player. The way he plays response phrases and obbligato add good spice to Big Joe's vocal. The collaboration of Big Joe Williams and Sonny Boy Williamson anticipates the Muddy Waters–Little Walter ensemble. "Someday Baby" is based on Sleepy John Estes's recording in 1935. While all of the above Big Joe Williams recordings are in the key of A, for which Sonny Boy uses a D harmonica (second position), "Break 'Em on Down" is in the key of B, and Sonny Boy plays the D harmonica in the key of B—in fourth position. Sonny Boy stays in the higher range, but there is a moment when he mistakenly plays the first position of D harmonica.

* * *

As we observed, Sonny Boy Williamson was expanding his artistic realm. He was departing from the laid-back, down-home country blues style to the frantic city blues. His music became faster in tempo, as heard in "Tell Me Baby," "New Early in the Morning," "Jivin' the Blues," and "Shotgun Blues." His music was getting louder, too, since he was now performing in noisy venues. In addition to piano and guitar, he incorporated his harmonica with rhythm instruments—drums, washboard, and "imitation" (using an oilcan or washtub) bass. The larger sound of this up-tempo music—the Bluebird Beat—was a precursor of what would become the "postwar Chicago blues," which was developed by Muddy Waters, Little Walter, Howlin' Wolf, and many others. In this sense, one of Sonny Boy's musical contributions was building the foundation for the next generation.

On the other hand, Sonny Boy did not completely discard his down-home style. His sideman work with Yank Rachell and Big Joe Williams displays the state-of-the-art country blues ensemble—the exquisite musical collaboration and competition among acoustic instruments and vocal performances.

As his music matured, his fame spread. In 1944, Sonny Boy's name appeared again in *Billboard*. As he became more nationally famous and his music became more urbanized, he found that he could no longer remain in the rural South of Jackson, Tennessee.

Sonny Boy Williamson, circa 1947. Courtesy of T. W. Utley, Jackson-Madison County Library.

Sonny Boy Williamson playing an amplified harmonica, circa 1947. Courtesy of T. W. Utley, Jackson-Madison County Library.

Billy Altman of RCA Records and Sonny Boy's half brother T. W. Utley at the opening ceremony of the marker, June 1, 1990. Courtesy of Jackson-Madison County Library.

Librarians of Jackson-Madison County Library (from left Michael Baker, Judy Pennel, and Jack Wood) and Sonny Boy's half brother T. W. Utley at the opening ceremony of the marker, June 1, 1990. Courtesy of Michael Baker.

The original metal marker at the place where Sonny Boy was buried in 1948.
Courtesy of Michael Baker.

A newly purchased headstone near Blai's Chapel in 1990.

Club Georgia advertisement that appeared in the *Chicago Defender*, August 16, 1947, with Sonny Boy's name misspelled "Williams." Courtesy of *Chicago Defender*.

Club Georgia advertisement that appeared in the *Chicago Defender*, September 13, 1947, with Sonny Boy sharing the bill with Lonnie Johnson, the blues guitar virtuoso. Courtesy of *Chicago Defender*.

Permanent

CORONER'S CERTIFICATE OF DEATH

ORIGINAL
State File No.

STATE OF ILLINOIS
DEPARTMENT OF PUBLIC HEALTH
Division of Vital Statistics and Records

NO CORONER'S FEE COLLECTED

1. PLACE OF DEATH:
County of _Cook_ Illinois
Registration Dist. No. 3104
City, Township, Village, Road Dist _Chicago_
Primary Dist. No. 3104
Street and Number _Michael Reese_ Hospital
Registered No. 16599

LENGTH OF STAY: In Hospital or Institution _Yrs._ / _Mos._ / _Days:_ In Community where death occured 2 Yrs. 1 Mos. 2 Days.

2. PLACE OF RESIDENCE: State _Illinois_, County _Cook._, Township, Road Dist. City or Village _Chicago_, Street and No. _3226 Giles Ave._
19. Int. List Number

3.(a) FULL NAME _John Lee Williamson_ 16 3A

Coroner's Certificate of Death

3.b). If Veteran name war _No_
3(c). Social Security No. _Unknown_

20. DATE OF DEATH _June_ Month _1_ Day _1948_ Year

4. Sex _Male_
5. Color or race _Negro_
6(a). SINGLE, MARRIED, WIDOWED, DIVORCED

21. I HEREBY CERTIFY, that I took charge of the remains of the deceased herein described, held an INQUEST INVESTIGATION thereon, and from the evidence obtained find that said deceased came to HIS HER death on the date stated above and that death was due to ACCIDENT SUICIDE HOMICIDE more fully described below.

6(b). Name of husband or wife _Lay B._
DATE OF INJURY OR ONSET _6-1-48_ DISEASE

6(c). Age of husband or wife (if alive) _27_ years

MANNER OF INJURY AND DEATH FROM UNDUE MEANS or MEDICAL CAUSE OF DEATH:

7. BIRTHDATE OF DECEASED _March_ Month _30_ Day _1914_ Year

8. AGE OF DECEASED _34_ Years _2_ Months _1_ Days If less than one day (Hrs.) (Min.)

Skull fracture with
cerebral laceration
Intra-cranial hemorrhage.
Assault on Street

9. BIRTHPLACE OF DECEASED _Jackson_ City or County _Tennessee_ State or foreign country

Murder

10. USUAL OCCUPATION (Kind of job _Musician_
11. INDUSTRY OR BUSINESS: _Nite Club_

Father 12. Name _John Ray Williamson_
13. Birthplace _Jackson Tennessee._
Mother 14. Maiden Name _Nancy Utley_
15. Birthplace _Jackson Tenn._

Use reverse side for additional space, if needed.

22. Was injury or cause related to occupation of deceased? _No_

16. INFORMANT _Lacy B. Williamson_ (Pen and ink signature)
P. O. Address _3226 Giles Ave._
If so, how? _None_

23. Place of Injury _Chicago_ Village, Township, City, Road Dist.

17. PLACE OF BURIAL, Cremation or Removal
(a) Cemetery _Local_
Location _Jackson_
County _Tenn_ State

Accident or injury occured AT HOME, AT WORK, IN PUBLIC PLACE
(Signed) _Robert L. Brodie_ Coroner

(b) DATE: _6-3-19_

By _Deputy Coroner_
Address _#54 County Bldg._
Date _1-15-19 48_ Telephone _Da 13 un_

18. FUNERAL DIRECTOR:
Signature _Theo Harvey_
Address _4445 South Parkway_
License Number _128_
Firm Name _Metropolitan_

FILED
(Signed) _Harman R. Sunderson_ Registrar
P. O. Address _Jul 11 1948_ Illinois

Sonny Boy's death certificate.

A. L. BRODIE, Coroner of Cook County

PATHOLOGICAL REPORT

The undersigned has this date June 1, 1948 (examined) (performed an autopsy on)

the dead body of John Lee Williamson at Metropolitan Funeral Parlors.

identified to me by the Undertaker.

DESCRIPTION: Age: 26 yrs. Race: Colored. Sex: Male Color of eyes: Black.

Hair: Black. Weight: 165 Lbs. Length: 5 ft. 9 in. Date of death: June 1, 1948.

1. Linear fractures of the occipital bone.
2. Hemorrhage into the posterior cranial fossae and diffuse leptomeningeal hemorrhage.
3. Hematoma of scalp.
4. Laceration of lower lip.
5. Contusion in the region of the left eye brow, lateral half.

In my opinion cause of death was due to Fractures of the skull and intracranial hemorrhage.

A. C. Stehl, M. D.
601 E. 36 St.
Atlantic 2222.

118 Form 19A 10M 10-47 (682)

Sonny Boy's pathology report included in the coroner's inquest, detailing the cause of his death.

Billy Boy Arnold.

Joe Filisko. Courtesy of Joe and Michelle Filisko.

Marker placed at Tennessee 18 and Caldwell Road.

The record label of "Western Union Man."

The record label of "Shotgun Blues."

BLUES CLASSICS BY

SONNY BOY
WILLIAMSON

GROUNDHOG BLUES	BLACK PANTER BLUES
COLLECTOR MAN	BAD LUCK BLUES
UNTIL MY LOVE COME DOWN	MY BLACK NAME
YOU GIVE AN ACCOUNT	JIVIN' THE BLUES
WESTERN UNION MAN	MY LITTLE MACHINE
SHOTGUN BLUES	JOE LOUIS AND JOHN HENRY
WELFARE STORE	SLOPPY DRUNK BLUES
SHE DON'T LOVE ME THAT WAY	CHECK UP ON MY BABY

Blues Classics 3

The album cover of *Blues Classics by Sonny Boy Williamson*, released by Chris Strachwitz's independent label Blues Classics in 1964.

4

THE SOUND OF BRONZEVILLE

1942–1948

T. W. said, "When Sonny Boy left here [Jackson], he went to Chicago."[1] In response to Jim O'Neal's question, "When did Sonny Boy leave Jackson?" T.W. answered, "Oh, I remember '42 . . . something on," while it is written in some sources that he moved to Chicago in 1934.[2] It makes sense that he was in Chicago from 1942. Sonny Boy recorded only four sides per session—except one session when a recording ban was anticipated. Previously he usually recorded six to ten sides to gather enough materials: in one session on July 21, 1939, he cut eighteen more sides. The number of cuts he made at each session corresponds to when Sonny Boy had a home in Chicago.

Though the peak of the Great Migration from the South occurred between 1910 and 1920, the African American population in Chicago was still increasing during the war years because many blacks arrived there to look for jobs in war-related industries—"some sixty thousand more new arrivals between 1942 and 1944, swelling the black population to 337, 000, one tenth of the city's total and double what it had been before World War II."[3] Bronzeville, also known as the "Black Metropolis" in the early twentieth century, is the area that stretched from Twenty-Second to Sixty-Third streets between Wentworth and Cottage Grove. It was a "city within a city" as well as the "second largest Negro city in the world" in the 1940s, next to Harlem as the center of African American culture. Famous residents included Andrew "Rube" Foster, founder of the

Negro National Baseball League; Ida B. Wells, a civil rights activist, journalist, and organizer of the National Association for the Advancement of Colored People (NAACP); Bessie Coleman, the first African American woman pilot; Joe Louis, acclaimed fighter; John H. Johnson, *Ebony* magazine publisher; Elijah Muhammad, the leader of the Nation of Islam; and musicians Mahalia Jackson and Louis Armstrong.[4] Pilgrim Baptist Church, where Thomas A. Dorsey worked as a director, had been in the heart of Bronzeville until it was destroyed by a fire in January 2006.

Sonny Boy and Lacey Belle lived in a house on Giles Avenue, between Thirty-Second and Thirty-Ninth streets in Bronzeville. This area had the largest African American population on the South Side. Many were newcomers and settled there only temporarily. This was also the location of the famous red-light district with its cabarets, nightclubs, taverns, gambling houses, and whorehouses.[5] It was a joyous place, but it could also be deadly. T. W. remembered what Sonny Boy's mother Nancy said to him when he moved out of Jackson, "If you stay Sonny Boy, you can make it. You live in Chicago. Don't let Chicago live in you."[6]

* * *

In 1942, Sonny Boy had only one session, on July 30—about half a year after the previous December 1941 session. Many record companies were forced to reduce production because shellac, the important material to make phonograph records, was now primarily used for the military industry. In addition, on August 1, 1942, the American Federation of Musicians, at the instigation of union president James Petrillo in Chicago, initiated a strike against the major recording companies because of disagreements over royalty payments. Although Sonny Boy was not a union member at this point—because the harmonica was not considered a legitimate instrument then—no union musicians, including most of his sidemen, could record for any companies, beginning at midnight of July 31.

With Blind John Davis on piano, Big Bill Broonzy on guitar, and Alfred Elkins on bass, Sonny Boy recorded four compositions: "Love Me, Baby," "What's Gettin' Wrong with You," "Blues That Made Me Drunk," and "Come on Baby and Take a Walk." Except for "Love Me, Baby," they ended up unissued at that time—they were included in compilation albums later. No spirit is felt in any of these cuts. Sonny Boy might not have had enough time to prepare compositions for the unplanned session. In addition, he literally sounds drunk, slurring words more than usual, inserting empty shouts, and constructing incoherent verses. In "Blues That Made Me Drunk," he might be ironically singing about himself: "You know that this slow consumption killin' you by degrees."[7] Since the songs appeared to be musically organized, at least someone was sober enough to lead the session.

The strike ended on November 11, 1944. Subsequently Sonny Boy went back to the studio, where he recorded two compositions about women, "Miss Stella Brown Blues" and "Desperado Woman," and two compositions that were inspired by the ongoing war, "Win the War" and "Check Up on My Baby"—with Blind John Davis on piano, Ted Summit on electric guitar, and Jump Jackson on drums. The sidemen, especially Davis's chording with a successive use of triplets and Jackson's thumping drum work, provide a thick and stable musical background for the front man who responds to them with the fat sound of the harmonica. This is the typical urban blues sound, though it would have been a perfect Bluebird Beat with an addition of bass. Because of the presence of the drummer, the recordings from this date sound similar to some cuts from the May 17, 1940, session—also with drummer Fred Williams, including "I Been Dealing with the Devil" and "War Time Blues." Musically, all the cuts are based on Sonny Boy's medium-slow blues formula in a medium boogie-woogie tempo, while "Desperado Woman" is a little faster than the others. "Win the War" is a propaganda song to urge young men to go to war—"He [Uncle Sam] want to drop a bomb on the Japanese, I really got to make my baby proud." As will be discussed later in the chapter, Sonny Boy probably tried to enlist in the army himself.

The third verse of "Desperado Woman" contains lines describing an unfair trial. Possibly such an occurrence was very common in the community in which Sonny Boy lived.

> ["Desperado Woman" Verse 3]
> Now for killin' her daddy, my baby didn't even get no time,
> She winked her eye at the judge,
>   the judge didn't even charge her a single dime.

Sonny Boy's voice sounds confident and energetic since he was in the studio for the first time in more than two years. He must have been highly excited when he recorded another cut, "Check Up on My Baby." In the beginning of the second verse with a stop time, he demonstrates his

trademark vocal technique—cramming a long stream of words into a
four-measure phrase without any flaws.[8]

> ["Check Up on My Baby" Verse 2]
> Now don't you know what Hitler told President Roosevelt,
>   said "We raised the fastest airplane of the world."
> [Ah] President Roosevelt said "I think you're telling a lie,
>   Brother, we got our plane that builds up like a squirrel."[9]

About a year later, on July 2, 1945, Sonny Boy was again in the studio.
The sidemen for this session included Big Sid Cox on guitar, Ransom
Knowling on bass, and Eddie Boyd on piano. "G. M. & O. Blues" is
about a woman leaving him on the Gulf, Mobile, and Ohio Railroad,
which operated from Jackson to New Orleans and extended to St.
Louis.[10] As discussed earlier, Sonny Boy learned to compose songs with
localized lyrics from Sleepy John Estes. The melody is taken from "How
Long How Long Blues" by Leroy Carr with Scrapper Blackwell in 1928,
one of the most popular blues songs in the late 1920s and the 1930s.

The recording shows that the musicians, including Sonny Boy and the
usually versatile Eddie Boyd, did not understand the musical structure (a
harmonic progression including the fourth chord with a flatted third) of
the original. Curiously, when Sonny Boy borrowed a melody from "How
Long How Long Blues" for "Springtime Blues" in 1941, he used the first
position harmonica (straight harp). This time again he plays the first
position—a C harp in the key of C.

As the title indicates, "We Got to Win" is a patriotic song. This was
Sonny Boy's fourth song supporting the war effort; the others included
"War Time Blues" (1940), "Win the War" (1944), and "Check Up on My
Baby" (1944).[11] Supporting the war was the general attitude of his audience living in an industrial city—Chicago. In the second verse, he sings,
"I didn't pass the army, but I'm really doing everything I can." He might
have tried to enlist in the army, though it is not difficult to imagine that
recruiters noticed his alcoholism. Perhaps it was his breath or his demean-
or.

"Sonny Boy's Jump" is an adaptation of "Shotgun Blues," a swing
number that he recorded in 1941. For the new version, he increased the
tempo from fast vivace (160 bpm = beats per minute) to presto (170
bpm). While the original is a good example to show off his ability to
build drama of soloing from a static to animated movement, the new
version demonstrates his mastery of the figures and the speed of alternat-

ing vocal and harmonica back and forth (see figure 4.1). Even when he plays a succession of fast licks, he sounds very stable. In addition, he inserts fills between vocal phrases with amazing timing—at the same time he finishes singing or sometimes even before he finishes the last phrase, he starts playing a response phrase.

Figure 4.1. "Sonny Boy's Jump."

"Elevator Woman," a song full of sexual allusions, is based on the medium-slow blues pattern. Even in such a moderate tempo, it is highly noticeable that he switches between vocal and harmonica very quickly and accurately. Willie Dixon, one of the house bassists of Lester Melrose at that time, claimed in his autobiography that he played bass on this song. It is possible that Ransom Knowling played the first three songs and Sonny Boy switched Ransom with Willie for "Elevator Woman."[12]

Sonny Boy made friends with Eddie Boyd, the pianist for the July 1945 session, sometime in 1941.[13] Born Edward Riley Boyd in 1914, he grew up in Stovall, Mississippi—Muddy Waters was his neighbor. Soon after Boyd settled in Chicago, he started his career as a club piano player and then became Sonny Boy's musical partner. Boyd said, "after Johnny Shines and me worked together a little while, I started working with Sonny Boy number 1,"[14] "and after I recorded with him, then we started playing together. . . . 'Cause we worked in Gary [Indiana] a long time, about a year and a half with just the two of us: piano and harmonica."[15]

"Sonny was a heck of a drinker,"[16] remembered Boyd. "He was a good cat, man, but that whiskey, it'd turn him into a [*sic*] ape real quick."[17] But they were good friends. Many times Boyd mediated arguments between tavern customers and Sonny Boy when he got drunk. When he overtipped waiters and overpaid for his drinks, Boyd secretly held on to Sonny Boy's money and returned it to him when they got home—they lived in the same area of Bronzeville. Boyd even saved Sonny Boy's life once. Getting drunk again at his regular venue, Club Georgia, Sonny Boy accidently stepped on a customer's foot. The angry patron then pulled out a switchblade, intending to stab Sonny Boy in the chest. Boyd stepped in: "I was trying to explain to him that Sonny Boy is harmless, he's drunk, and he's sorry he stepped on your foot, man."[18] The following day Boyd explained the incident to Sonny Boy: "'Hoo-ooo,' you know, tears went over him."[19]

With a recommendation to Lester Melrose, Sonny Boy opened the door for Eddie Boyd to be a recording artist. Although he enjoyed only limited commercial success with RCA Victor, his "Five Long Years" for the J.O.B. label became a number-one hit on the *Billboard* R&B charts in 1952.

As well as Eddie Boyd, guitarist Henry Townsend from St. Louis was also in the blues community of Bronzeville. Similar to Sonny Boy, Henry Townsend was "in and out of Chicago periodically from 1945 almost up into the 1950s."[20] When he was in Chicago, he stayed at Thirty-First and Giles, which was not even a mile from where Sonny Boy lived. Townsend remembered, "At first I didn't know exactly where Sonny Boy was, but he heard about me being in town. He was living on South Parkway then, and he found me, and we started bumming around together."[21]

Around this time, guitarist/vocalist Lonnie Johnson also had his regular venue on Thirty-First and Indiana, "right around the corner at Thirty-first and Giles," where Henry Townsend stayed.[22] As will be discussed later in the chapter, in 1947 Johnson shared the bill with Sonny Boy at a party given by Club Georgia on State Street, Sonny Boy's regular venue.

* * *

On October 19, 1945, Sonny Boy had a great session with pianist Big Maceo, guitarist Tampa Red, and the Melrose session drummer Charles Sanders. The first cut was Sonny Boy's third recording of "Early in the Morning." Each version has a different feel. The first one with two guitarists (Robert Lee McCoy, Henry Townsend, or Joe Williams) on November 11, 1937, sounds like a reserved country blues song. The second version with Joshua Altheimer on piano and Fred Williams on drums on May 17, 1940, released as "New Early in the Morning," is a swing number in fast tempo. For the newest version, Sonny Boy updated the lyrics of the earliest version. While the girl in the song was originally twelve years old, now she is eighteen. The combination of Big Maceo's heavy, percussive piano touch and Sonny Boy's loud response to Maceo produces a much plumper sound than its original. And Sonny Boy's vocal sounds more mature.

"The Big Boat" and "Stop Breaking Down,"[23] both of which are based on Sonny Boy's medium-slow blues formula, have the same characteristics as "New Early in the Morning"—heavy sound and mature voice. The last cut for the session, "You're an Old Lady," is a sound depiction of the Bluebird Beat—a mixture of older black blues with the newer swing rhythm featuring electric guitar, harmonica, and piano accentuated by the addition of drums—as defined in chapter 2. The first half of the music employs the stop time rhythm on the first chord, and the second half is on a swing rhythm. This is an exciting track with Sonny Boy's flowing harmonica powered by the buzzing sound of electric guitar, driving piano, and drums capably responding to voice and harmonica. This is the sweaty sound of the city—the sound of Bronzeville.

"You're an Old Lady" coupled with "Early in the Morning" received a positive review from *Billboard*: "Williamson gives the lilting blues, 'You're an Old Lady,' plenty of power . . . 'Early in the Morning,' a slower tempoed [*sic*] blues with lots of good singing from Williamson."[24]

* * *

Around this time, another important meeting in the history of blues took place—Sonny Boy Williamson and Muddy Waters. Born McKinley Morganfield in Jug's Corner near Rolling Fork, Mississippi, in 1913, Muddy grew up on Stovall's Plantation outside Clarksdale. He arrived in Chicago in 1943. In 1945, he was still establishing himself as a professional musician while working day jobs. One of the musicians he met on the networks was Eddie Boyd. They went to the same school on Stovall's Plantation.[25]

Sonny Boy was one of the first well-known blues artists in Chicago with whom Muddy became acquainted.[26] Probably through Boyd, who was then Sonny Boy's accompanist, Muddy became Sonny Boy's other sideman. They played regularly at a place on the South Side in South Chicago. Muddy remembered his early days in Chicago with Sonny Boy: "He was nice . . . but he was Sonny Boy, and I wasn't Muddy Waters . . . and in fact Eddie Boyd and myself and Sonny Boy was [sic] together. . . . But, see, they wanted to keep me in the background, and they sung."[27] And the real reason that Sonny Boy hired Muddy was because Muddy had a car—"They wasn't carrying me for guitar playing. Just carried me 'cause it was for transportation."[28]

Yet, Muddy occasionally had a chance to get the spotlight. When Sonny Boy got too drunk to perform, Eddie Boyd took the vocal microphone, but he also became tired of singing from time to time. Then he said to Muddy, "'Why don't you sing one?' I [Muddy] said, 'Ok, I'll sing,' and I sung one and brought the house down, boy, and Sonny Boy woke up, and he ran back up there, and got his harp, [and sang] 'My baby left me, left me a mule to ride.' . . . [Sonny Boy said to Muddy] 'Check it out first with me, man.' And the people say, 'Let him sing! Let him sing!'"[29] It seems that there were many occasions when Sonny Boy could not control his appetite for alcohol. Eventually they all got fired from this venue.

* * *

Muddy Waters admitted that Sonny Boy was one of the first artists he heard that played amplified harmonica: "I'd see Sonny Boy used to be with Big Joe [Williams] back there, put the mike [sic] up against it and make it come out, you see, because he was blowin' through an amp, you know."[30] Muddy also said, in a different interview, "And when I first got to Chicago, the first Sonny Boy would blow over the house mike [*sic*] sometimes. So the electric thing had started a little bit."[31] One of the existing photos of Sonny Boy shows him playing an amplified harp—he is holding a bullet-type microphone with his harmonica (see the photospread).

In the history of Chicago blues, the idea of amplification was practiced as far back as the 1930s. In fact, electric guitar was commercially available as early as 1932. George Barnes, who was sixteen years old at the time, played the electric guitar on Big Bill Broonzy's "Sweetheart Land" and "It's a Low Down Dirty Shame" on March 1, 1938.[32] Tampa Red also used an electric guitar for "Forgive Me Please" at the December 16, 1938, session at the Leland Hotel.[33] Robert Lockwood Jr., though he had a base in Helena, Arkansas, said, "I bought the De Armand pickup when it first came out in 1939. So did Charlie Christian."[34] By the early 1940s, electrification of instruments in Chicago blues was a common practice, as heard in Arthur "Big Boy" Crudup's recordings from the April 15, 1942, session, including "Standing at My Window" and "Gonna Follow My Baby Blues." Muddy Waters—who arrived in Chicago in 1943—said, "[Big Bill Broonzy] was the first one I saw playing electric with my own eyes."[35] And Muddy himself acquired his first electric guitar in 1944.[36]

By 1945, several years after the rise of electric guitars, some harmonica players started to use an amplification system. Snooky Pryor, a harmonica player based in Chicago, mentioned he got an idea of amplification when he played a bugle through a PA system when he was in the army. Pryor said:

> When I got discharged out of army, November the 16th, 19 and 45, from Camp Grant, Illinois. . . . I went down on State Street, 504. . . . That's where I bought me a PA system with two speakers, and a mike [*sic*] look like a snuff box . . . then I come back to Maxwell Street: just me, the harmonica, and a microphone. And hooked up. And it was loud.[37]

Maxwell Street or "Jew Town," as it was then known, was filled with blues musicians performing for vendors and customers of an open-air flea market. This was the place for them to develop their musical skills. Sonny Boy was no exception. Henry Townsend remembered: "Jew Town was Sonny Boy's hangout, over on the West Side. We used to have musical duels, Otha Brown and Little Walter, Eddie El, Sonny Boy, and myself.

We used to all get together and do what they called battle royals."[38] It is not difficult to imagine how noisy the crowded streets were. Using an amp was a reasonable solution for any harmonica players to catch the attention of passersby. Townsend said:

> At first he [Sonny Boy] was just playing acoustic harmonica, and somehow that acoustic harmonica was good enough—a reasonable size crowd could hear it. The places that he worked at could hear it, and that was good enough. Later on he got an amp; I think he picked him up an amp about the same time Joe Williams got one. Joe had one of them old-time square tin boxes. [39]

While Sonny Boy was one of the pioneers of amplified harp, he did not make any recordings with it—in other words, he used it exclusively for live performances outside the studio. Willie Dixon once said, "[Lester] Melrose and them had electric instruments but were keeping 'em turned down to sound acoustic style. I couldn't even get them to put the harp electric."[40]

In fact, Melrose did produce recordings with an amplified guitar, as discussed earlier in the chapter. Sonny Boy's "You're an Old Lady" with Tampa Red's "buzzing" electric guitar was one of them; more notably, "That's Alright Mama" by Arthur "Big Boy" Crudup, in 1946, was another. Apparently, Melrose was not impressed by the sound of the amp, mainly due to the low quality of the equipment that musicians brought in. Bob Koester, who had a business relationship with Lester Melrose, shared what he heard about Melrose's impression of amps:

> Lester Melrose didn't like it [an amplified sound]. According to Ransom Knowling—the house bassist of Melrose production—[he felt] "you are not gonna get good guitar sound if you use an amplified guitar." I remember I felt the same way when I first recorded Big Joe Williams' *Piney Woods Blues* [in 1958] and *Blues on Highway 49* [in 1961]. He had an electric guitar and an amp. You know what it was? It was a very old portable radio from the 1930s. He converted it to an amplifier with a speaker—god knows where he got it. They were trashy things. . . . I suspect some of those amps didn't sound very good. They had a lot of hum. You would not want that on record. That's what Melrose insisted. [41]

As a matter of fact, Sonny Boy had a decent amplifier, for which he paid $200 cash, according to Billy Boy Arnold. Regardless of the quality of the amp, Sonny Boy himself was probably not fond of amplification either. He established his own performing style with the use of chordally dominated phrases (chording) combined with percussive rhythms. In other words, his loud playing style was designed for acoustic performance with two or three other instruments but not for an amplified harp. Playing Sonny Boy's style with an amp can be overkill. Joe Filisko shared his insights:

> Playing Sonny Boy's style through an amp is almost too much. If you are playing with the band—you have got a piano player, a guitar player or two, a drummer, and a bass player—it is almost like harmonica is too much if you play in that style with an amp. To me, Sonny Boy's style really shows itself when you play acoustically in a smaller situation with a duo or a trio.
>
> I do think that after amplification became commonplace, players were able to rely more on the amp than the aggressive driving full sounds associated with his style. The general excitement of the big sounding harp was still there as they remembered the lessons of copying him. The players who remained very true to his [Sonny Boy's] sound were mostly acoustic players. [42]

T. W. also acknowledged that for a while Sonny Boy was having difficulty being accepted with amplification:

> Well, different group(s) [*sic*] from Chicago, they had their own amplifiers. So every time he [Sonny Boy] would play with them, he had to bring his amp and they didn't like that. . . . He messed around about two years in Chicago before he was accepted . . . up to their playing. . . . First they gotta test the harp. They didn't wanna deal with it. . . . When he first went, they liked his singing but they wouldn't start wanting his harp. But in two years time, they liked the harp and him, too. [43]

How Sonny Boy adjusted his playing style with new equipment will be described later in the chapter. Of equal importance, in addition to his performing style, the amplification at least partly affected his status as a professional musician. Around the same period when his new playing style with an amp was accepted, he joined the musicians' union—the Chicago Local 10-208 of the American Federation of Musicians.[44]

When Sonny Boy started his professional career in the late 1930s, he was not required to join the union, because, inconceivably, the union did not consider harmonica a musical instrument—hence, harmonica players were technically not musicians.[45] But there were at least three factors for the harmonica to be accepted as a legitimate instrument. First, of course, Sonny Boy was a highly commercially successful artist by this time. Second, several other harmonica soloists and ensembles—such as John Sebastian (Sr.), father of John Sebastian of Lovin' Spoonful and Jerry Murad's Harmonicats—recorded with recognizable success during the union strike. The union could no longer ignore harmonica players since their memberships could bring substantial revenues into its coffers. Third, with a microphone and an amplifier, the harmonica no longer looked like a novelty toy but rather more like professional gear.

Willingly or unwillingly Sonny Boy Williamson became a member of the musicians' union, but it seems that there were more disadvantages than benefits. Now he had to pay union dues. In addition, his payments as a sideman and for his club performances were regulated by union rules. Pianist Sunnyland Slim talked about the days that he and Sonny Boy were free from union rules:

> What really turned me on after I got here [Chicago], after I left my pad in Cairo, was Sonny Boy calling me. "Do you know we made twenty Dollars?" The union scale was $8.50 for sidemen. Me and Sonny Boy played for these parties, we'd leave there with $10 or $12 apiece and go on to another place, and sometimes I'd be so drunk I couldn't get up the stairs, but we played all of 'em, shit. I had more money, me and Sonny Boy was playing them parties. . . . Then they put my ass in the union. I stayed up here two or three years before I done anything else but just run up and down the road with Sonny Boy.[46]

In 1946, Sonny Boy's popularity was reaching its peak. For the first time the mail-order service advertisement of the *Chicago Defender* listed his record—"Desperado Woman."[47] In the issue of March 6, his performance at the Purple Cat Lounge at 2119 West Madison Street was announced, though his name was misspelled "Williams." He had a band called the Purple Cat Trio and played there every Friday, Saturday, and Sunday night.[48]

On August 6, he was in the studio with Blind John Davis on piano, Willie Lacey on electric guitar, and Ransom Knowling on bass. "Sonny Boy's Cold Chills," "Mean Old Highway," and "Hoodoo Hoodoo" are based on his medium-slow blues pattern. "Hoodoo Hoodoo" is the origin of "Hoodoo Man Blues," one of the best-known Chicago blues songs by harmonica player/singer Junior Wells, recorded on the States Records label in 1953 and for Delmark Records in 1965.

These cuts reveal that the musicians, including Sonny Boy, did not have a clear sense as to who would take a solo. For example, at the end of the second verse in "Sonny Boy's Cold Chills," Sonny Boy gives a cue for John Davis, "All right, John," but Sonny Boy himself is playing his part just as loud as Davis. The same flaw is also found in "Mean Old Highway"[49] and "Hoodoo Hoodoo." Regardless of the somewhat low quality of the performance, "Hoodoo Hoodoo" coupled with "Sonny Boy's Cold Chills" received a positive review from *Billboard*: "Shouting the race blues with fine feeling for the blues idiom, and just as earthy when giving groovy lips to his harmonica blowing, Sonny Boy Williamson rings the bell for both of these slow blues."[50] His medium-slow blues pattern with the typical Bluebird sound secured strong popularity.

The last cut, "Shake the Boogie," is based on the fast couplet/refrain pattern that has been seen in "Got the Bottle Up and Gone." This song is again about a man who is lamenting his relationship with his partner. Except for Ransom Knowling on bass, all the members—John Davis, Willie Lacey, and Sonny Boy—take a solo. By this point, they recognized the flaw. While other members are soloing, Sonny Boy, while still playing accompaniment, is stepping back from the microphone. When he takes his turn, he explodes, building a climax by powerfully emphasizing one pitch, "D," and rolling his tongue while exhaling. This is an exciting side.

This was the first time Sonny Boy's record was reviewed in the *Chicago Defender*. In its issue of January 11, 1947, it read:

> Sonny Boy Williamson is in fine voice as he tells his favorite gal [*sic*] friend to "Shake That Boogie" for RCA Victor, with strong fervor in his vocalizing. The rhythm is rugged and Sonny Boy accents the groove beat with his husky vocalizing while his harmonica's amazing breadth of expression provides additional color to the trio accompaniment of guitar, string bass and piano.[51]

Reflecting the *Defender*'s confident review, "Shake the Boogie" reached number four on *Billboard*'s chart on February 1, 1947.[52] This was Sonny Boy's first national hit and his most commercially successful record.

* * *

Sometime in 1946 Sonny Boy, Big Bill Broonzy, and pianist Memphis Slim were involved in an oral history interview along with a jam session organized by folklorist Alan Lomax. Previously, in 1942, as the researcher of the Library of Congress, Lomax approached Broonzy for his study on race, blues, and American life. As a director of a series of concerts, under the name "Midnight Special," at the Town Hall in New York City, Lomax called Broonzy again. Broonzy appeared with two of his friends, Sonny Boy and Memphis Slim. Lomax reflected on the concert in his *The Land Where the Blues Began*; "the trio tore down the house at Town Hall, discovering that their Delta music was appreciated by an audience they had never known about."[53] After the concert, Lomax brought them to the Decca Records' studio to record their performance and interview. Lomax described the three participants. Broonzy, who was the oldest, took a Socratic role, drawing his friends into deeper levels of drama. Memphis Slim offered humorous counterpoint to Broonzy's graver observations. And Sonny Boy, whom his friends would gently kid, would take the comic role in the play.[54]

The existing recording starts with a slow blues song, "Life Is Like That," featuring Memphis Slim's melancholic piano and vocal. Sonny Boy's harmonica behind Slim is barely heard. He is placed too far from the microphone. Then Broonzy talks about the life situations that give rise to the blues. He throws a question, "What do you think about . . . when someone would say the reason why you have the blues?"[55] Sonny Boy introduces a story behind "Good Morning, School Girl," as explained in chapter 1.

After Sonny Boy sings "My Black Name Blues," their topic shifts to hard times and racial experiences in the South. They discuss the inhumane labor conditions in levee camps and penitentiaries. Memphis Slim explains how blues works in such a situation. "Yeah, blues is kind of a revenge. You know you wanna say something, you wanna signifying like—that's the blues. We all have had a hard time in life, and things we couldn't say or do, so we sing it."[56]

During the interview, Broonzy and Slim mostly talked, while Sonny Boy—possibly because of his speech impediment—says very little. Besides two musical performances, a short segment of a field holler and "My Black Name Blues," Sonny Boy speaks for just about two minutes out of forty-five minutes of total recording time—this is his only existing interview to this day. As they talk about racism and violence, Sonny Boy shares his experiences, introducing his mother's trouble with a white man from whom she bought a mule:

> My mother, she bought a mule from the . . . they called him Captain Mack. You know, he is the boss of the county road in Jackson, Tennessee. . . . They take you out on trucks and you build bridges and dig ditches and things like that. Of course they didn't use no chain. He sold my mother a mule. So by me bein' young and everything, my mother gave me the mule, and naturally, young boys [*sic*], I'd run the mule. . . . Well, finally, the mule, he got mired up in the bottom . . . and the mule died, [like] a quicksand. . . . So this Captain Mack, he told mother, say "I'm crazy to get that damn boy out there on the county road. I'm gon' do to him just like he did that mule." And so my mother had to scuffle to keep me off there. . . . And after all, he'd done sold the mule, and she paid him . . . I was around fourteen years old.[57]

Many blacks in the South had similar stories to share. Broonzy breaks in: "That word . . . we'll go back to the word, what they say 'kill a nigger, we'll hire another'n. Kill a mule, we'll buy another'n.' See . . . all these things come into the same word. The fact of the business, back in those days, a negro didn't mean no more to a white man than a mule."[58]

"The session was a triumph," Lomax reflected. "Here at last, black working-class men had talked frankly, sagaciously, and with open resentment about the inequities of the Southern system of racial segregation and exploitation. An exposé of that system was on record."[59] But the three participants did not feel comfortable publicizing the interview under their own names. For the safety of themselves and their families, they made sure Lomax issued the recording only under pseudonyms. When it was released under the title *Blues in the Mississippi Night: The Real Story of the Blues* by United Artists Records in 1959, it was noted as "sung and told by three Mississippi Delta blues men—'Leroy,' piano and vocals; 'Natchez,' guitar and vocals; 'Sib,' harmonica and vocals; recorded and edited by Alan Lomax,"[60] though none of the performers were actually from Mississippi. The title of the album might have been another way to hide their identities.

* * *

The last year John Lee "Sonny Boy" Williamson made recordings was 1947. That year he had three sessions: March 28, September 19, and November 12. At midnight, January 1, 1948, the second American Federation of Musicians recording ban went into effect and lasted for eleven months. Probably anticipating that union members would not be able to record for a while, Sonny Boy cut eight sides for the November 12 session to secure enough material for the releases in the coming year. And there is another reason that 1947 became Sonny Boy's last recording year. He was murdered on June 1, 1948. His death and its aftermath will be detailed in chapter 5.

On March 28, Sonny Boy was in the studio with some of the finest recording personnel of the Bluebird sessions: Blind John Davis on piano, Big Bill Broonzy on electric guitar, Willie Dixon on bass, and Charles Sanders on drums. Dixon was then a member of the Big Three Trio on Columbia Records, and Sanders was a drummer for the Big Three Trio's recordings. For this session, Sonny Boy cut three swing numbers, following a big success with "Shake the Boogie." The first cut, "Mellow Chick Swing," indicates Sonny Boy was moving toward a new musical direction—blues harmonica in swing jazz or jump blues. Blind John Davis comps during the intro, and Sanders adds irregular snare attacks. Sonny Boy's harmonica is very light. He only plays simple single note–dominated (puckering) phrases while staying away from thick chording sounds. *Billboard*'s review for "Mellow Chick Swing" assured Sonny Boy's musical direction: "It's the solid rock and rugged rhythm as Sonny Boy Williamson shouts it out for his blues-styled 'Mellow Chick Swing' . . . with top race blues talent on tap, makes for a choice jazz collector's cutting, with Williamson's singular efforts on the flip also fitting in such folios."[61]

In the following observation, Joe Filisko finds evidence of Sonny Boy adjusting his playing style to the amplifier:

> I think the later recordings start to show that he was beginning to rely on amplification . . . "Mellow Chick Swing" is a good example to indicate how he was changing playing style. The tune starts off by going the hole 1 inhaling and 2 exhaling [see figure 4.2]. But you would often hear players play that phrase fuller [see figure 4.3]. I think maybe because he was trying to appeal much more to urban audiences that felt his style sounded a little bit too countrified. . . . I suspect he

probably didn't need to play full when he had an amplifier. Remember, to me, his style grew out of what would sound appropriate to his ears. So I think he was a listening man, always saying "what is gonna sound most appropriate." So if you put him in a band with an amp, he is going to adjust his playing.[62]

Figure 4.2. Actual introduction to "Mellow Chick Swing."

Figure 4.3. Imaginative introduction to "Mellow Chick Swing."

Similar to "Shake the Boogie," each musician takes a solo in the order of piano, guitar, and then harmonica. Sonny Boy's solo is simple (see figure

4.4). As Filisko points out, Sonny Boy does not rely on chords much until he plays an ending phrase. This may, too, be a fragment that indicates his new playing style, stripped down sounds for the use of an amp.

Figure 4.4. "Mellow Chick Swing," solo.

In addition, the way Sonny Boy composes a song is more citified, as seen in choices of such words as "wine" instead of "moonshine" or "whiskey" and "slick" and "hip" instead of "good lookin'." There is also well-polished rhyming here. In addition, he avoids one of his major compositional characteristics—cramming too many words in a small musical space:

> ["Mellow Chick Swing" Verse 1]
> She's kind of fine, she changed my mind,
> I want some wine, and take her time,
> I know you is kinda slick, but I'm hip to that mellow chick.

Other swing compositions, "Polly Put Your Kettle On" and "Apple Tree Swing" are more delightful than "Mellow Chick Swing." "Polly Put Your Kettle On" is based on an old English nursery rhyme. "Apple Tree Swing" is in an A-A-B-A, twenty-four-bar pop song form. In the "B" section, the music goes to the relative minor mode. This was a new musical device for him. Interestingly, the lyrics do not use many suggestive phrases even though the apple here is a metaphor of a plump girl. Compared with "Big Apple Blues" on April 4, 1941, Sonny Boy consciously avoids an overtone of eroticism in "Apple Tree Swing." In many ways, he departs from the countrified blues style to urbanized swing music. Using more universal and friendly song subjects, he tries to appeal to wider audiences, including minors.

"Apple Tree Swing" was coupled with "Alcohol Blues" and released in May of 1948. The anonymous reviewer for *Billboard* wrote that "Apple Tree Swing" was "a novelty jump, Sonny Boy is better at the blues."[63]

On the other hand, Sonny Boy also retains his old countrified style. "Lacey Belle," named after his own wife, is based on the medium-slow blues formula. It sounds like a confession about his infidelity:

> ["Lacey Bell" Verse 1]
> Oh, Lacey Belle, don't allow me to do nothin',
>   nothin' but just lay up in the bed and dream,
> Oh, Lacey Belle, don't allow me to do nothin',
>   nothin' but just lay up in the bed and dream,
> She said, 'Sonny Boy, what's the use of worryin'
>   about some other women, just as long as you got me.

Then he tells Lacey Belle about the woman with whom he had an affair, who dumped him and left him with nothing but his suitcase. Given that Sonny Boy was a playboy, this song seems to be biographical. What's more, compared with the swing compositions, he plays thicker phrases with tongue split techniques, consciously using different playing styles according to compositional types.

Again in these three cuts, in contrast to "Mellow Chick Swing," clearly the musicians did not organize their solos. For example, in "Polly Put Your Kettle On," the first solo is supposed to be by Blind John Davis—since Sonny Boy gives him a cue—but it sounds like the two are in conflict, while the second and the third solos are exclusively by Sonny Boy. In "Apple Tree Swing," Sonny Boy might have intended to offer subordinate licks for anyone who takes a solo, but the microphone picks up his harmonica more than the soloists.

On July 22, 1947, Sonny Boy went to the Columbia studio to accompany Big Joe Williams. Other musicians were bassist Ransom Knowling and drummer Judge Riley. Big Joe cut fives sides, including a rerecording of "Baby Please Don't Go" and its alternate take.[64] "Baby Please Don't Go" is in B-minor and stays on the tonic chord throughout. Playing the third position harmonica—an A harmonica in the key of B—Sonny Boy creates a chirping birds sound effect with a bluesy flavor in a higher range. The alternate take uses a bit faster tempo. Sonny Boy uses the third position technique also for "Stack of Dollars." His experiment with the third position in Robert Lee McCoy's session on November 11, 1937, fell flat, but this time—almost ten years later—it works, somewhat. While he controls his breath to hit the high notes, he does not come down to the lower range of the instrument, where he could have made more bluesy licks.

For the other two cuts, "Mellow Apples" and "Wild Cow Moan," Sonny Boy goes back to the standard second position harp—a C harp in the key of G. "Mellow Apples" sounds similar to Yank Rachell's country blues dance "Rachel Blues" and its variation "Peach Tree Blues" for both of which Sonny Boy played accompaniment. "Wild Cow Moan" captures one of the best moments of Sonny Boy as a sideman. The countermelodies and response phrases that he offers to Big Joe's vocal line testify to their equal musical relationship. In addition, Sonny Boy plays a creative solo that combines both elements of stillness and motion and that a harmonica instructor could use as a soloing model. This is further proof that Sonny Boy laid the groundwork for the future innovation of subsequent generations of blues musicians such as Muddy Waters and Little Walter.

* * *

Sonny Boy Williamson became a national superstar by the late 1940s, as did his Bluebird label mates Tampa Red, Big Bill Broonzy, Big Maceo, and Dr. Clayton. From early 1946, Sonny Boy's records were always included in the mail-order service advertisements in the *Chicago Defender*. In the issue of January 25, 1947, University Studio in Washington, DC, lists "You're an Old Lady" with "Early in the Morning," and Carver-Hampton Company in New York lists "Mean Old Highway."[65] His national hit "Shake the Boogie" appeared in ads in non-Chicago newspapers such as the Radio and Records Bar in the *Anniston (AL) Star*.[66] Harmonica player Billy Boy Arnold, who was born in Chicago and was an enthusiastic follower of Sonny Boy then, remembered Sonny Boy as a hero of the community: "His records were popular and dynamic, and the black audiences bought everything he recorded. . . . So it just made him a folk hero among black people. Sonny Boy was the man."[67] Billy Boy also remembered Sonny Boy as a popular figure on the streets of Chicago: "Sonny Boy Williamson was extremely confident and warm as a person. People would stop him on the street and ask him to play, and right there and then he would play his harp."[68]

Sonny Boy's regular venue in 1947 was Club Georgia at 4547 South State Street, which was within walking distance from his house on Giles Avenue. His performance dates at Club Georgia were advertised in the entertainment section of the August 9 issue of the *Chicago Defender* with his portrait, though his name was again misspelled. It reads, "'SONNY BOY' WILLIAMS [*sic*] NOW AT 'BIG WHITE'S'—'Big' White presents 'Sonny Boy' Williams and his nationally known recording trio, every Friday, Saturday and Sunday for your entertainment. 'Sonny Boy' is the man with the Blues, and he plays and sings his latest recordings, the 'Sonny Boy Jump' [*sic*], 'Mean Old Highway,' and many more."[69]

The September 13, 1947, issue announced Club Georgia's first anniversary party, which was held for four nights from September 15 to 18— "Sonny Boy Williamson vs. Lonnie Johnson in the Battle of the Blues featuring Jimmie [*sic*] Boyd's Trio."[70]

On September 19, Sonny Boy was back in the studio with Eddie Boyd on piano, Willie Lacey on electric guitar, Ransom Knowling on bass, and Judge Riley on drums. "Wonderful Time" is a happy song. Sonny Boy returned to the melody pattern that he had used for "I'm Tired Trucking My Blues Away" (1938), "Good Gravy" (1939), and "I'm Gonna Catch You Soon" (1941). The newest version has a very citified sound. It is a busy shuffle, starting with a drum solo followed by Sonny Boy's two rounds of solo based on the vocal melody. After the second verse, the proficient session guitarist Willie Lacey takes a solo for two rounds. One of the most exciting moments of the recording is in the last verse where Sonny Boy crams many words in a short, four-bar phrase—"I got a big fat mama and a skinny mama too, I don't tell my big fat mama what my skinny mama can do."[71] He must have been full of spirit after "The Battle of the Blues" at Club Georgia.

"Sugar Gal" is a variation of one of his earliest recordings on May 5, 1937, "Sugar Mama." "Sugar Gal" is now arranged like Louis Jordan's jump blues tune. In fact, for the second round of solo, Sonny Boy adds the rhythmic break copied from Jordan's "Caldonia" in 1945. Sonny Boy flawlessly plays a very fast presto tempo (about 190 bpm). At the same time, the full sound for the opening with a tongue split technique evokes more like the introduction to Chuck Berry's rock 'n' roll song "Johnny B. Goode."

In this session, it seems that the musicians, including Sonny Boy, clearly planned how to organize the music. Fast-tempo swing compositions, such as "Wonderful Time" and "Sugar Gal," are showcases for both vocal and harmonica—a long introduction by harmonica for "Wonderful Time" and an intro plus two rounds of solo for "Sugar Gal."[72] In the two other cuts, "Willow Tree Blues" and "Alcohol Blues," which are based on Sonny Boy's medium-slow blues pattern, he focuses on singing with a small portion of harmonica inserts. He does not even take a solo—Blind John Davis plays a piano solo for "Willow Tree Blues" as does Big Bill Broonzy on guitar for "Alcohol Blues." Since Sonny Boy was modifying his musical style to appeal to different audiences, this session might have been another strategy to make his music more urbane.

Joe Filisko talked about Sonny Boy's vocal performance and his shift to reduce the harmonica part:

> It sounds to me like maybe he is thinking of the story and telling the story with using his voice with the same exact passion and attitude that he switches and plays harmonica fills to. It's like two of them are really connected. It's not like he is a powerful singer with this amazing voice and he plays a little harmonica just to kill time. You can tell he is really in love with playing the harmonica. I can't help but wonder how he would feel later on if they told him, "Don't play so much. Sing more. Stop playing." But at that point he was already an established star. So almost anything he recorded was going to sell.[73]

"Willow Tree Blues" is about lost love with a woman who could "just shake like a willow tree"—a classic blues expression to describe an attractive female. "Alcohol Blues" is an adaptation of "Shannon Street Blues." But instead of "Shannon Street," he goes "down on 31st Street, just to buy me a drink of alcohol." Like the original, he sings about the awful effects of alcohol—he still wants to go for a ride with his girlfriend despite being in an inebriated state.

A Chicago-based guitarist/vocalist, Little Hudson, who claimed that he had jammed with Sonny Boy many times in different clubs, witnessed the compositional process of "Alcohol Blues."

> He was a mastermind. He could go down the street and see something and then make a song out of it. We was walking down the street together, and Thirty-first Street one day, and he saw a guy walking down there staggering, you know, drunk. Three weeks later he come out with the record "I was walking down on thirty-first street . . ." and I said, "I knew you was going to make the record." He say he drank so

much his eyes couldn't even give a peep. But that was a real funny record and we laughed about that a while. [74]

* * *

John Lee "Sonny Boy" Williamson had his last leader session on November 12, 1947. His sidemen were Blind John Davis on piano, Big Bill Broonzy on guitar, Ransom Knowling on bass, and Judge Riley on drums. Lester Melrose (and probably Sonny Boy, too) anticipated the forthcoming recording ban. Sonny Boy recorded eight songs, twice as many as usual. Four cuts are based on his medium-slow blues formula, and the other four are in faster tempi with different musical styles.

In this session, Sonny Boy follows the strategy that he found at the last session: for the songs with the medium-slow blues pattern, he focuses on singing but giving up a solo—the solo part is played either by piano or guitar; in contrast, the fast-tempo songs allowed him more room to play solo. In "Little Girl"—a different song from "Little Girl Blues" of December 17, 1938—his voice sounds very convincing, especially when he sings the line "You're the little girl that I've been thinkin' of" with his voice full of life. On the other hand, he limits his harmonica sections only to the formulaic introduction and response phrases. Here Blind John Davis takes a solo. The same strategy is observed in "Blues about My Baby" and "I Love You for Myself." The portion he plays on the harmonica is smaller than that for "Little Girl" because of the lyrical structure. "Blues about My Baby" and "I Love You for Myself" are both in a quatrain refrain form. Since each line is very long, as soon as he ends one line, he starts a pickup for the following line. By doing so, he reduces sections to insert harmonica passages. In these compositions, Big Bill takes a solo, and Sonny Boy supplies harmonic support.

"Blues about My Baby" with "Wonderful Time" was released in February 1949—almost nine months after his tragic death. A reviewer of the disc for *Billboard* wrote a short comment for "Blues about My Baby": "Well performed slow blues." For "Wonderful Time," the reviewer offered more: "Sonny Boy delivers a catchy, chuckle-voiced fast blues, smartly backed by a small harmonica and rhythm combo. A likely offering for southern buyers." [75] Though Sonny Boy himself could not know it, the marketplace had shifted from the medium-slow blues to fast swing type songs.

"No Friend Blues" is taken from the classic melody of "Four O'clock Blues," which a majority of his audience would have been familiar with.[76] Since Johnny Dunn's Original Jazz Hounds in 1922, many artists recorded this tune. While some of them such as the Original Memphis Five (1923) and Skip James (1931) kept the original title, others used different titles and lyrics—"Georgia Bound" by Blind Blake (1929), "Midnight Hour Blues" by Leroy Carr (1932), and "From Four until Late" by Robert Johnson (1937). It is not known which version Sonny Boy referred to, but it seems that the nostalgic lyrics for his hometown are original.

> ["No Friend Blues" Verse 1]
> Now but I'm goin' back South and start my life brand new,
> Now I'm goin' back South and start my life brand new,
> Now it seems like my baby don't know what she wanna do.

Sonny Boy's vocal performance is passionate, as if he is talking to his audience. In this song, Blind John Davis plays a solo.

One of the fast-tempo tunes, "Bring Another Half a Pint," is a rerecording of "Sloppy Drunk Blues" on July 2, 1941—a variation of Leroy Carr's recording in 1930.[77] The new version is a bit slower than the original, but it features a bass drum that hits every eight-beat pulse. Along with the drumbeat, the bass and piano with the same rhythms provide thickness to the ensemble and lend the song a frantic feeling. Big Bill Broonzy's jazzy electric guitar helps make the overall sound more urbane. Sonny Boy's harmonica sounds very crisp. He takes a solo twice—after the second and fourth (last) verses. In the second (ending) solo, especially, he displays virtuosic techniques—hand vibrato and slap, tongue rolling, and fully sounded phrases with tricky, percussive rhythms. What's more, his vocal sounds very confident.

The overall characteristics of "Southern Dream"—a rerecording of "She Was a Dreamer" on July 2, 1941—are similar to those of "Bring another Half a Pint." Here again Sonny Boy's harmonica sounds penetrating.

Similar to "Polly Put Your Kettle On" from the March 28, 1947, session, "Rub a Dub" is based on an old English nursery rhyme usually known as "Rub-A-Dub Dub (Three Men in a Tub)." It is an innocent song that he tried in order to appeal to a different type of audience, but lines such as "You know I met a little girl, she was all trimmed out in blue. She saw me rubbin', she started rubbin' too" can be interpreted as vulgar.

Like today's rap artists, Sonny Boy crams these words in a short, four-measure musical phrase. Reflecting its origins, the music sounds like a hokum song rather than a straight blues. The circle of I–I–IV–V accompaniment pattern in four-four time is similar to that of "Signifying Monkey"—a song based on a popular African American toast—by Willie Dixon's Big Three Trio, which was also recorded under Lester Melrose's wing. "Rub a Dub" coupled with "Stop Breaking Down" from the October 19, 1945, session was released in July 1948, after Sonny Boy's death.[78] Both sides received a positive review: "The deep, dark and dirty blues, with authentically elemental appeal" for "Stop Breaking Down,"[79] and "Lively chanting in deep South accent of a double entendre lyric based on a traditional race theme. Should get juke play in race spots" for "Rub a Dub."[80]

Sonny Boy's final recording as a leader, "Better Cut That Out," a cover of Big Bill Broonzy's 1940 recording, is a lively shuffle composition, which must have been an ideal crowd pleaser. Three rounds of solo demonstrate that Sonny Boy is a sheer swinger with a great sense of rhythm. And he is loud. He could produce a volume full of sound without using an amp. Sonny Boy's harmonica, piano, guitar, bass, and drums all roll as one to create a propulsive sound, with speed. This was a new stage for the Bluebird sound. Coupled with "The Big Boat" on October 19, 1945, "Better Cut That Out" was released in December of 1948. *Billboard* gave the disc a moderately positive review: "Earthy down-home blues warbling with hard-hitting rhythm" for "The Big Boat" and "Full-flavored shouting of a bouncy blues with torchy harmonica and rhythm" for "Better Cut That Out."[81] Sonny Boy's swing-influenced records were consistently well received.

"Better Cut That Out" is a message for everyone who gets deeply wrapped up in something that can cause harm; Sonny Boy might have been thinking of his own destructive drinking habits.

> ["Better Cut That Out" Verse 1]
> Ah now now when you say a drunk man makes you mad,
> When you get drunk you look-a just as bad,
> You better cut that out, yeah, you better cut that out,
> You better cut that out, boy, before it'll be too late.

This song clearly delivers some advice like some of the songs written by Willie Dixon such as "Don't Go No Further" and "Spoonful." There is no point of speculating how Sonny Boy would have developed his music if he had lived, but along with the dynamic sounds of his recording, message songs could have been his new musical direction.

* * *

On December 18, 1947, a week before Christmas, Sonny Boy returned to the Columbia studio to play harmonica for Big Joe Williams to cut eights sides,[82] with bassist Ransom Knowling and pianist Judge Riley. This was Sonny Boy's very last recording session—remember Sonny Boy's first session as a sideman was for Big Joe Williams and Robert Lee McCoy on May 5, 1937.

The overall tone of these cuts is rustic, especially evident in Big Joe's rough and rugged vocal style and throbbing bass drum coming from a distance, another example of the Bluebird Beat. By creating obbligato lines and response phrases, Sonny Boy competes with Big Joe's vocal—the style of which seems to be a direct model for the earliest recorded collaboration of Muddy Waters and Little Walter with drummer Baby Face Leroy—"Rollin' and Tumblin' (Part 1)" and "(Part 2)" on Parkway Records in 1950. Joe Filisko shared his thoughts about Sonny Boy's accompaniment for Big Joe Williams:

> I have personally always felt that much of his best stuff was playing behind Big Joe Williams. He played very strong with lots of confidence, though it sounds like the same basic stuff that he does in his own songs. . . . One of the last recordings he did, "Don't You Leave Me Here," the playing is so solid. He is playing with such confidence, such driving. It's so powerful. When I listened to that, I think "Man, no wonder he inspired so many people to play."[83]

"King Biscuit Stomp," one of the sides from Big Joe's session with Sonny Boy on December 18, 1947, was a theme song for the radio show *King Biscuit Time*, hosted by Rice Miller, the other Sonny Boy Williamson, on KFFA in Helena, Arkansas.

The real name of the other Sonny Boy Williamson is usually indicated as Rice Miller, but its variants are Alec, Alek, or Alex Miller, and his last name could very well be Ford. Bob Koester, who was assisting Chicago blues artists at the American Folk Blues Festival in Europe during the 1960s, saw the name "Willie Williamson" on his passport. For many years, his birthplace and birth date were mysterious, but it has been verified recently by census data that he was born in Glendora, Mississippi, in

1911, even though his tombstone says, "Born March 11, 1905 and Died June 23, 1965."

Rice Miller started playing the harmonica in the early 1920s. By the mid-1930s, he became a traveling musician. His musical partners included Robert Johnson, Robert Lee McCoy (Robert Nighthawk), Robert Lockwood Jr., Elmore James, and Chester Burnett (Howlin' Wolf). According to Snooky Pryor, Miller originally called himself "Little Boy Blue."[84] In 1941, Miller started hosting a radio show, *King Biscuit Time*, on KFFA in Helena. As the legend goes, Max Moore of Interstate Grocery, the owner of the sponsoring company of the show, renamed him "Sonny Boy Williamson," after the acclaimed harmonica player on Bluebird Records.

King Biscuit Time was a very popular thirty-minute-long live broadcast starting at 12:15 p.m. every weekday to match the lunch break of African American workers in the entire Delta area. It featured the music by Rice Miller (as Sonny Boy Williamson), Robert Lockwood Jr. on guitar, Pinetop Perkins on piano, and James Peck Curtis on drums. Miller left the program in 1947 but returned in 1965 for a short period just before his death.

When Big Joe Williams recorded "King Biscuit Stomp," Rice Miller's theme song, he let his audience know that his friend John Lee Williamson was the real "Sonny Boy Williamson": "Real Sonny Boy was on there with me. Well, sure, I stole it from Rice Miller because I wanted people to know that he wasn't the real Sonny Boy. That's why I knew to steal that song and make it. For sure. So Rice Miller didn't never get a chance to make it. Yeah, stole it. That was the way I did it, for the public."[85]

The arrangement is similar to one of the best-known Delta blues compositions, "Forty-Four Blues" by Roosevelt Sykes, recorded in 1929.[86] Over the musical background created by veteran rhythm section bassist Knowling and drummer Riley, Big Joe and Sonny Boy collaborate and compete with each other. Similar to other cuts on December 18, 1947, this is a powerful recording.

The relationship between John Lee "Sonny Boy" Williamson and Rice Miller "Sonny Boy" is thoroughly discussed in chapter 5.

* * *

Sonny Boy kept building his musical vocabulary by incorporating swing jazz and jump blues, as seen in "Sonny Boy's Jump" and "You're an Old Lady." His approach to the up-tempo music fully matured with his biggest commercial success, "Shake the Boogie." The vocal and instrumental performances in his last recordings, especially "Sugar Gal" and "Better Cut That Out," reflected his strong artistic confidence.

In addition, many other changes were taking place. He started to use amplification, focused on his vocal performance in medium-tempo tunes, and wrote songs with more universal appeal such as "Polly Put Your Kettle On" and "Rub a Dub." Interestingly, while he was exploring new fields of artistry, he was conscious of retaining his roots—countrified medium-tempo blues—which is especially evident on his final recordings with Big Joe Williams.

Most of Sonny Boy's songs are based on the everyday life of working-class African Americans. With simple expressions and choice of words, he shares his own stories with his listeners, and by doing so he represents their voices. Blues historian Derrick Stewart-Baxter pointed out that Sonny Boy was not a social rebel. "He was content to sing about everyday events. The ups and downs of Negro life, of loving and hating, of booze and relief from worry that it brings and of the unfaithful women. That was his world and the world of his people."[87] Occasionally Sonny Boy addresses social issues, as seen in a few patriotic songs such as "Win the War," "War Time Blues," and "Check Up on My Baby," but these songs still came from the everyday life of his audience and reflected his times. Remember many of his listeners in Bronzeville were war-related industry workers, and Sonny Boy himself possibly tried to enlist in the army. Other cultural issues, such as the gender stance in the African American migration, which is embedded in "She Was a Dreamer," and a preference for a particular type of car like "V-8 Ford," are also an extension of the everyday matters of people he was familiar with.

Writing protest songs such as "I Wonder When I Will Get to Be Called a Man" by his contemporary Big Bill Broonzy was not Sonny Boy's cup of tea. And he did not act as a menacing, powerful persona like Muddy Waters' "Hoochie Coochie Man" or the swaggering "Back Door Man" of Howlin' Wolf. Sonny Boy emphasized his own strengths with the subjects of his choice. And for his people he sang his blues from the bottom of his heart. As Billy Boy Arnold described, "Sonny Boy used to stand up and play sometime and tears just run down his face—he was so emotional y'know. I think that's what had a lot to do with his success."[88] It should be noted that it is very ironic that his final side as a leader,

"Better Cut That Out," is about his resolution to quit drinking, after so many songs about chronic alcoholism.

Sonny Boy Williamson was very a popular artist—so much so that his fame produced many imposters. And he was highly influential. His career served as a model for future generations of Chicago bluesmen. Sonny Boy's tragic death, which will be described in the following chapter, occurred when he was exploring new artistic territories.

5

THE FINAL DAYS
1948

The year 1948 was the last year of Sonny Boy Williamson's life. In the early morning of June 1, Sonny Boy was mugged on his way home after a performance at the Plantation Club. He received a deadly blow to his head and was pronounced dead at Michael Reese Hospital in Chicago.

Before his tragic death, Sonny Boy had three important connections. One of the most curious aspects of Sonny Boy's life was his relationship with Rice Miller, also known as Sonny Boy Williamson #2. The other two meetings were with Emma Bruce Ross and Billy Boy Arnold. Ross was Sonny Boy's elementary schoolteacher in Jackson, Tennessee. She became a family member when Sonny Boy's mother, Nancy, remarried a member of Ross's family. Billy Boy Arnold, who lived near Sonny Boy in Bronzeville, idolized the bluesman. One day he visited Sonny Boy at his apartment and received a harmonica lesson from Sonny Boy himself. These meetings will be discussed in the oral history interviews with Sonny Boy's half brother T. W., Ross, and Billy Boy, respectively, as well as supporting comments by Sonny Boy's musician friends.

In addition, the coroner's inquest from the medical examiner of Cook County will reveal the medical details of Sonny Boy's death. Surprisingly, no mainstream newspapers in Chicago, including the leading African American paper, the *Chicago Defender*, reported his murder. The lack of official coverage contributed to many contradictory stories regarding the circumstances surrounding his death.

* * *

Rice Miller was one of many artists with the pseudonym "Sonny Boy" Williamson or its variations. Billy Boy Arnold reflected on the time when John Lee "Sonny Boy" Williamson was a household name: "Anytime a man was good with his fists, people would tend to call him Joe Louis. And the same way, if you could play anything on harp, then people called you Sonny Boy Williamson."[1] While calling someone with good harmonica proficiency "Sonny Boy Williamson" could have been an innocent gesture, it could have also been a means for cashing in on the reputation of another more famous musician—and one with a recognizable name. In fact, in the postwar era, many artists nicknamed themselves after other popular blues or jazz figures, and "Sonny Boy" was one of the most commonly used names.[2]

According to two blues discographies, *Blues and Gospel Records, 1890–1943* and *The Blues Discography, 1943–1970*, there were two other artists called "Sonny Boy Williamson" besides John Lee "Sonny Boy" Williamson on Bluebird Records. One of them was, of course, Rice Miller, but the other one was Jeff Williamson, who recorded in 1961, long after John Lee "Sonny Boy" died.[3] Reportedly, Rice Miller sometimes called himself Sonny Boy Williams in order to avoid legal conflicts with John Lee "Sonny Boy."[4] In addition to Miller, there were at least three others with the name Sonny Boy Williams.[5] One of them, Enoch Williams—his musical style is more jazz than blues—recorded for Decca Records in the early 1940s, while the other two recorded in 1959 and 1968, respectively.[6] Enoch Williams also performed as part of the Sunny Williams Trio (recorded in 1947). Then there was Sonny Boy Johnson (recorded in 1947 and 1948). There was a duo Sonny Boy and Lonnie (recorded in 1947). Probably this Sonny Boy made another duo with an artist named Sam—Sonny Boy and Sam (recorded in 1947). Some of them were not even harmonica players.[7] Their names are found in discographies or listed as *Billboard* recording artists, but there must have been many others who did not have the chance to make any records or who are not included in current discographies even though they, in fact, recorded. John Brim mentioned a jam session partner he met in Gary, Indiana, who was one of the Sonny Boys: "I was playing, messing around with a guy named Edward Hollis, blowing harmonica. He called hisself [*sic*] Sonny Boy."[8]

Among them, the most commercially and artistically successful was Rice Miller. He later became one of the most prominent blues artists on Chess Records. John Lee "Sonny Boy" Williamson and Rice Miller "Sonny Boy" were acquainted with each other. In fact, Rice Miller told Bob Koester they were friends.[9] Billy Boy Arnold told *Melody Maker* what he had heard from John Lee's wife Lacey Belle: "Lacey said they [John Lee and Lacey] knew him [Rice Miller] well, that he used to come to their home in Jackson, Tennessee, before Sonny Boy became famous. Then she laughed . . . [and said] 'Dozens of 'em used to say they were Sonny Boy, remember?'"[10] Sonny Boy's half brother T. W. provided more details: "Rice Miller used to come to Jackson. Sonny Boy practically taught him about playing harp. Sonny Boy was getting along with Miller."[11]

Some sources, including Snooky Pryor's interview, say John Lee even traveled to Helena, Arkansas, to stop Rice Miller from using the name.[12] However, Robert Lockwood Jr., who was then a musical partner of Miller, was not sure if there was any conflict between the two Sonny Boys or legal settlement over the use of the name: "Me and Big Sonny Boy—Rice Miller was very tall—was [*sic*] together when Little Sonny Boy came to Helena and didn't a damn thing happen. . . . He and Big Sonny Boy knew each other. I just don't know what he came there for. John Lee couldn't play no harp with Sonny Boy [Rice Miller] . . . Rice Miller could play Sonny Boy's stuff better than he could play it! John Lee had to get the fuck away from there, couldn't stay. I don't know whether John Lee told him to stop using his name or not, but when this thing came to a point— when there was two of 'em there—the man who owned Interstate Grocery changed and spelled those last names different."[13]

T. W. told his side of the story: "We had a cousin down there in Arkansas. Sonny Boy went out to stay with him. That's when he met Rice Miller." When T. W. found out about the radio show [*King Biscuit Time* on KFFA], he asked, "Sonny Boy, the dude down there in Arkansas is using your name." Sonny Boy replied—"'Well, T., if he's taking my name and living off, let him do. I'm doing alright. Let 'em go.'"[14] T. W. concluded, "He didn't try to stop him. He didn't bother."[15]

The fact that John Lee "Sonny Boy" Williamson accompanied Big Joe Williams's "King Biscuit Stomp" might be a plausible indication that John Lee "Sonny Boy" did not even bother. Most of the time, they were geographically distant from each other. Rice Miller's territory, including the radio show, was mainly in the South, while Sonny Boy's main venues were in St. Louis, Aurora, and Chicago. Bob Koester shared his view: "He [Rice Miller] was in the South when he was on the radio show on the station that could not be heard in Chicago. I don't see any reason why [John Lee] Sonny Boy was worried about the guy using his name down South."[16] More important, Rice Miller at this point was not a recording artist. Although he was an influential radio personality, he was just another man who was impersonating a famous artist.

Their relationship developed in a strange way after Sonny Boy's death. Some of his compositions are copyrighted as Rice Miller's. This issue will be described in chapter 6.

* * *

During World War II, Sonny Boy's mother, Nancy, lost her second husband, Willie Utley, in the military action.[17] She later married Mack Taylor Reed, who was a relative of Emma Bruce Ross, Sonny Boy's fourth-grade teacher at Blair's Chapel School in Madison County, Tennessee. Ross moved to Chicago in 1935. Although she lost touch with Sonny Boy and his family for a while, she ran into Nancy when visiting Jackson. Nancy gave Ross Sonny Boy's phone number in Chicago. Ross and her sister Myrtle made a surprise visit to the West Side club where Sonny Boy and Memphis Slim were performing. Ross wrote, "It was bedlam for he loved his hometown friends."[18] She also said: "He was well loved there, when he'd come in there and start to playing, all the girls, you know, they'd cluster around Sonny Boy."[19]

Though Ross, who did not drink much, rarely went back to the club to hear Sonny Boy perform, they continued to renew their friendship. After Sonny Boy closed his show, he went to other nightclubs to sit in with fellow musicians. Around daylight, when they finished a long jam session, they often visited Myrtle and enjoyed food she prepared in her backyard. Sonny Boy probably felt he could confide in Emma Ross and Myrtle, who was around Sonny Boy's age. They could talk about the old times and share memories of back home. "All he talked about was Jackson. He never left; his body left Jackson but his heart never left Jackson."[20] The last visit Sonny Boy and his musician friends made to Myrtle was about two weeks before his death.

Emma Ross's impression of Sonny Boy as her student—she described him as "friendly" and "generous"—did not change when they reunited after many years. "He was even minded, very easy to get along with, sometimes probably too easy because a lot of people used him that way . . . he would come in these places and spend his money on them, buy[ing] a lot of 'set up the house.'"[21]

Reports about his alcohol abuse upset her. She did not remember him as being a heavy drinker: "But he didn't do much drinking. He might take a drink now and then, but he was not a person that drank. That riled me up when I read [that] one of the people that was supposed to have known him from St. Louis said he was an alcoholic."[22] When she was interviewed in 1990, she said, "All I knew is that he was a wonderful friend, a likeable person and a great, innovative artist."[23]

* * *

As described in previous chapters, alcohol was a serious issue for Sonny Boy. Though Emma Bruce Ross was offended when she was told Sonny Boy was an alcoholic—she only remembered him as her fourth-grade student—many people could not avoid talking about his addiction as well as his friendly and credulous nature, as if those characteristics were inseparable. Henry Townsend in St. Louis described Sonny Boy's character:

> Sonny Boy was well, not quite an ordinary guy. He was kinda loud when he'd be drinking. I wouldn't call him an overbearing guy, but he would speak up for himself without any hesitation. He wasn't a belligerent type of guy, but he was pretty strong-minded. And he had very high self-esteem; he thought quite a bit of himself.[24]

Big Bill Broonzy remembered:

> He was a good-hearted boy, and free-handed as he could be. He would give you anything he had, he would give the shirt off his back to his friend, and he had a lot of them, too. Me and Sonny Boy and Memphis Slim played together for a long time and every time Sonny Boy would get drunk he would jump on me or Slim for a fight. Sometime we would fight him and some other time we would go off and leave him arguing. Then when he would finally find us he would start crying and say to me and Slim: "Why did you all leave me?" and we would talk nice to him.[25]

Broonzy's observations were confirmed by Billy Boy Arnold. He told *Blues Unlimited*, in 1977, a story that he had heard from harmonica player Bob Myers: "I heard a lot of stories about when Sonny Boy and Memphis Slim, Big Bill played there, y'know. And he [Myers]'d say that Sonny Boy would get . . . drunk and they'd put him out of the club 'cause he'd want to fight, y'know, and the guys they hated to see Sonny Boy coming 'cause he'd take the show. Y'know he could—the people liked him so well, he would take over."[26] But Billy Boy also remembered: "He [Sonny Boy] worked to help the people with something to eat and something to drink. When payday come, he didn't have anything—he had no pay day. . . . He was good to the crowd around him. That's all he did, was work for them."[27]

Pianist Sunnyland Slim's description of Sonny Boy is similar to Big Bill's story: "He was a good fellow, but his attitude when he's drinking, for a person that don't know him, they would think he was some vicious man. And he was harmless as a lamb. Sonny Boy played sharp, had plenty of women and was dangerous to fool with if you made him mad. But you loved him just the same."[28]

By 1946 or 1947, when he regularly played at the Triangle Inn, Sonny Boy appeared drunk onstage and even disappeared from the venue altogether. Guitarist Jimmy Rogers recalled:

> We'd hang with Memphis Slim, too. There was a place on the West Side off Maxwell Street there—the Triangle . . . John Lee "Sonny Boy" [Williamson] and we all used to hang around there. Sonny Boy was a guy that, see, he'd get drunk and then he'd clown. [*Laughs.*] Him and Memphis Slim wrecked that joint one night when we was over there.
>
> Sonny Boy would get drunk. He would play awhile. He'd get him a few bottles there, man. He'd go on off somewhere. He liable [*sic*] to leave the club and go on home and leave somebody else up there playin'. He didn't care. That's the way he was. He didn't have no band.[29]

* * *

Billy Boy Arnold is the only living artist who had direct contact with Sonny Boy. And Billy Boy is the only living harmonica player who directly received harmonica lessons from Sonny Boy.

Billy Boy Arnold was born William Arnold on September 16, 1935, in Chicago. In 1952, he made his debut recording, "Hello Stranger," for the independent Cool Records, which gave him the nickname "Billy Boy."

He joined Bo Diddley's group. In 1955, Bo Diddley released a single, "I'm a Man," which featured Billy Boy's harmonica on Chess Records' subsidiary Checker label. In the same year, Billy Boy issued "I Wish You Would" and "I Ain't Got You" as a solo artist for Vee Jay Records. These songs were later rerecorded by the Yardbirds with Eric Clapton in 1963. "I Wish You Would" was also included in David Bowie's 1973 album, *Pin Ups*. In 2008, Billy Boy released a tribute album to Sonny Boy— *Sings Sonny Boy* (Electro Fi). He remains a Chicago resident today.

* * *

In the late 1930s and the early 1940s, Billy Boy Arnold and his family lived in Altgeld Gardens, a new housing project on 132nd Street. Around the age of five, he started to explore the blues records that belonged to his mother's sister who lived with them—Billy Boy's father preferred African American pop music such as Louis Armstrong and Nat King Cole rather than blues and gospel music. In an interview, Billy Boy named some of the records that impressed him as a child: "Cherry Red Blues" by Eddie Cleanhead Vinson, "Ain't That Just Like a Woman" by Louis Jordan, and "Driftin' Blues" by Charles Brown. Many of his favorites were on Bluebird Records. Most of the blues artists on Bluebird were residents of Billy Boy's hometown, Chicago: "Key to the Highway" by Jazz Gillum, "Worried Life Blues" by Big Maceo, "Mean Old Frisco" and "I'm Gonna Follow My Baby" (also known as "Greyhound Bus Station") by Arthur "Big Boy" Crudup, and "Coal and Iceman Blues" coupled with "Mattie Mae Blues" by Sonny Boy Williamson.[30] "I didn't know Sonny Boy 'till I was eleven years old," said Billy Boy.[31] Nor did he know what instrument he was playing: "I didn't know nothing [*sic*] about harmonica. I didn't know he was playing a harmonica or anything. . . . I just liked the way he was singing the song. I liked his voice."[32]

Because Billy Boy's aunt moved out with her records and record player, he didn't have access to any recordings for a good four or five years. But after a while, he started listening to blues records again. His grandfather gave his mother a record player and sent him old records from a jukebox. Billy Boy was eleven years old then. By this time he was conscious of what was written on the record labels—the personnel involved in the recording as well as the titles of the tracks and the name of the label. He also mentioned a certain quality of the harmonica sound that particularly captured his interest:

I didn't get interested in harmonica till I was eleven. And I heard another record by Sonny Boy Williamson, "G. M. & O. Blues" and "Mellow Chick Swing." When I heard that record, on the record there was a name of the guy that was singing and playing. It says, "Sonny Boy Williamson, blues singer with a harmonica," Bill Broonzy guitar, John Davis piano. So then I knew he was playing a harmonica. . . . I was just fascinated by the way he made the sound.

The harmonica sounded something like muted trumpet. And Sonny Boy made that sound of "wow wow wow" on "Mellow Chick Swing." I just was curious how he got that sound on harmonica. I went to Sears and Roebuck to buy a plastic harmonica. It was 50 cents or a dollar. That was a lot of money for a kid then. I bought that and played it along with the record. I didn't think if it was a right key. And I couldn't choke the harmonica to make a bluesy sound. [33]

Soon Billy Boy learned that the harmonica player on his favorite records regularly performed at the club that a family member owned. "As I was playing the harmonica, my father told my mother that he [Sonny Boy] came into Club Georgia—the club that my father's cousin Big White owned. My father also said he'd see Sonny Boy on 31st Street from time to time." [34] Club Georgia was on State Street, within walking distance of Sonny Boy's apartment on Giles Avenue.

Sonny Boy regularly sat in with the jazz band that performed at Club Georgia, but he soon became a popular act himself. Big White got rid of the band and gave Sonny Boy the spot that originally had been assigned to the band. The trio—Sonny Boy on harmonica, either Johnny Jones or Eddie Boyd on piano, and a guitar player whom Billy Boy could not remember [35]—performed there on Fridays, Saturdays, and Sundays, while they had another regular venue at the Plantation Club on Wednesdays and Thursdays.

Billy Boy talked about his obsession with Sonny Boy. "I went to the record shop and found ten other titles. I bought some of them. I bought 'Lacey Belle,' 'Polly Put Your Kettle On,' 'Cold Chills [Sonny Boy's Cold Chills],' 'Early in the Morning,' 'Sonny Boy's Jump,' and 'Elevator Woman.' [36] How did he manage money? "I worked in my uncle's store on Saturdays, a butcher shop on 31st and Giles, two doors down from the Plantation—one of Sonny Boy's regular venues. I also sold *Chicago Defender*, newspaper." [37]

purposes, and the coroner's verdict. The last page of the inquest, the
verdict, briefly summarizes what happened to Sonny Boy:

> John Lee Williamson came to his death on the first day of June A.D.,
> 1948 in Michael Reese Hospital, Chicago, Illinois, from and as the
> result of fractures of the skull, and intracranial hemorrhage, due to
> external violence, caused when the deceased was brutally assaulted by
> a person or persons unknown to this jury, at a point unknown to this
> jury; —the deceased herein returning to his home, 3226 Giles Avenue,
> Chicago, Illinois, on June 1st., A.D., 1948 about 2:30 o'clock A.M. in
> said condition.
>
> From the testimony presented, we the jury find the occurrence to be
> MURDER, and recommend that the police institute a diligent and
> vigorous search for the said person or persons responsible for said
> vicious attack, and that when apprehended, he, she or they be held to
> the grand jury on a charge of MURDER, until released by due process
> of the law.
>
> MURDER[45]

The pathology reports describe the cause of death as follows:

1. Linear fractures of the occipital bone.
2. Hemorrhage into the posterior cranial loss and diffuse leptomeningeal hemorrhage.
3. Hematoma of scalp.
4. Laceration of lower lip.
5. Contusion in the region of the left eye brow [*sic*], lateral half.

In my opinion cause of death was due to fractures of the skull and
intracranial hemorrhage.

[signed by] A. E. Webb, M.D.[46]

The first inquest was held on June 2, 1948—a day after his death—at the
Metropolitan Funeral Home. Because no details were found at this point,
the session was very short. It was continued on June 11 and July 2 at the
Fourth District Police Station. Before the second session, Lacey Belle
took Sonny Boy's body to Jackson, Tennessee, for a funeral service held
on June 6. At the second session, Officer Louis Frank stated that the
investigation required a little more time since two witnesses, club customers Willie Spain and his wife Mary Lee Walker, were detained. They

were the last people who saw Sonny Boy leaving the Plantation Club. For the third session, two officers, Terry McGovern and Louis Frank; customers Spain and Walker; and Sonny Boy's wife Lacey Belle Williamson were brought in.

Sometime on May 31, 1948, a Monday, Sonny Boy with Lacey Belle appeared at the Black and Tan tavern, called the Plantation, which was only a few blocks from their home. According to Billy Boy Arnold, Sonny Boy did not regularly perform on Mondays—he performed at the Plantation on Wednesdays and Thursdays and at Club Georgia on weekend days. Possibly he just went to have a meal or a drink and ended up performing, or he stopped by to sit in with a performer—guitarist Little Hudson claimed he performed with Sonny Boy that very day. [47]

Either way, Lacey Belle went home earlier, while Sonny Boy performed. He left the Plantation around 2:00 a.m. on June 1. Two club customers—Spain and Walker—recognized Sonny Boy leaving the tavern. Spain stated, in his testimony to Officer McGovern, that he had a brief conversation with the singer. Then Sonny Boy started to cross the street, from the east side of Giles Avenue, and Spain and his wife Walker also started to cross the street to their home, also on the east side of Giles. Sonny Boy kept walking south at Giles Avenue. That was the last time they saw him. The polygraph test taken at the Bureau of Criminal Information and Science collaborated Spain's statement. Around 2:30 a.m., Sonny Boy arrived home.

Lacey Belle told Deputy Coroner Martin what happened after she left Sonny Boy at the Plantation:

A [Lacey Belle]: I did not see him any more until about two thirty that morning when he rang the bell. He was standing down there leaning against the wall like that, I asked him: "Son, are you hurt?" and he didn't answer me, and he stumbled down a foot or so from the first step, and I helped him up the stairs.

Q [Coroner Martin]: Was he bleeding or anything?

A: I didn't notice anything until he sat down on the bed. I see spots on the left eye was bleeding and some blood from his head.

Q: Yes?

A: And his—well, yes he was bleeding, that's when I noticed anything.

Q: Did he ever tell you he had any trouble with anyone at the Plantation?

A: I didn't hear of nothing.

Q: Did he ever tell you anyone attempted to hurt him, do him bodily harm, or he feared for that?

A: No, didn't say anything at all. All he just said, when I got to him: "Lord haver [sic] Mercy."

Q: I mean before this occurrence happened?

A: No, I don't remember him saying anything about that, argument of no kind, nothing like that.

Q: And that's all you know about this matter?

A: Yes.

Q: Any questions? (no response)

Q: You are excused. (witness excused)[48]

In addition to the wounds, Lacey Belle noticed Sonny Boy's clothes were dirty as if he had been rolling on the ground, and she noticed that his wristwatch, wallet, and three harmonicas that he usually carried with him were missing. Soon he went into a coma. She called the patrol wagon and requested a "sick removal." Sonny Boy was taken to Michael Reese Hospital, where he was pronounced dead. He was only thirty-four years old. At 5:30 p.m. [sic in the transcription, but most likely 5:30 a.m.], Officer McGovern was summoned to the hospital.

Willie Spain and Mary Lee Walker were released. As stated earlier in the chapter, the verdict by six jurors was "MURDER." According to the inquest, there were no other material witnesses other than Spain, Walker, and Lacey Belle. The club owner, waiters and waitresses, cooks and bartenders, other club customers, and musicians were not interrogated. The case remains unsolved to this day.

* * *

T. W. described how Lacey Belle notified him of Sonny Boy's death: "Early one morning Lacey called us here. [She said], 'T. W., a sad message. Mama, did she go out?' I said, 'She's in here.' And she said, 'Well, Sonny Boy left us.' 'What do you mean [he] left?' She said, 'Well . . . he got killed last night.'"[49] T. W. recalled that he once overheard his grandmother telling his mother, Nancy, a bad premonition about Sonny Boy: "That boy's in a hurry. He's not going to live all of his days."[50]

The funeral service was held at Blair's Chapel CME Church in Jackson, Tennessee—the church across the creek that Sonny Boy used to walk to with Nancy and T. W. Perhaps someone remembered the line he once sang, "Now and I want my body buried, way down in Jackson, Tennessee" in "T. B. Blues" in 1939. T. W. recalled, "[T]he church was full, they were all way up to the back door."[51] The service was one of the largest ever held at Blair's Chapel. Admirers sent countless telegrams and letters and bushels of flowers. The attendees included Big Bill Broonzy and Tampa Red, though many others were unable to make it all the way to Jackson.[52] Yank Rachell in Brownsville, for example, was unable to attend: "I had to go get the bus to go over there, and I had to wait. But the bus go there too late for me, they had the funeral and gone to the cemetery. I didn't get to see him."[53]

After the service in Jackson, T. W. accompanied Lacey Belle to her home on Giles Avenue. He recalled, "I stayed at their house for three days when I was there. And she told me to take everything, 'cause she didn't wanna stay there no more. I thought she was kidding. I wish I had a number to call. He had 900 records. . . . She gave everything to a young man cleaning their house up."[54] Around the same time, Billy Boy Arnold met Lacey Belle:

> I came back [to Sonny Boy's house] a couple of weeks later, and his wife was there. She was moving. They looked like they were packing. And when I walked in, she said, "Oh, this is a little boy who was taking a lesson from Sonny Boy." She said, "He looked for you to come by to get your harmonica." She said, "let me pay you." I said, "No, I won't accept that. He was my friend." Then she said in the

morning they took him out, all the children was just crying 'cause they knew him. They traded comic books with him.[55]

By the third inquest on July 2, Lacey Belle had moved out. At the testimony, she gave her new address as 5417 South Prairie Avenue.[56] Lacey Belle and Sonny Boy did not have any children. She lost touch with all the musicians after Sonny Boy died. "She was completely out of the picture," Billy Boy said.[57] Perhaps she did not want to have any relationships that reminded her of Sonny Boy.

Nancy's disappointment was beyond imagination. T. W. later told the *Jackson Sun* that she could not bear to see her son's photos or hear his records. The family put them all away and discarded them over the years, though they did keep some items.[58] It took her years to be able to listen to her son's records and tell stories about him and Lacey Belle to the family.

T. W. told the *Jackson Sun* that he could not afford a headstone for his brother's grave then. He worked two jobs and farmed, while he and his wife raised nine children. For years, there was only a temporary steel grave marker. Before long, Sonny Boy was forgotten in Jackson.

On December 2, 1948, Forest City Joe (born Joe Bennie Pugh in Arkansas, July 10, 1926; died, April 1960), recorded a tribute for Sonny Boy, "Memory of Sonny Boy" for Aristocrat Records—later called Chess Records. Joe's vocal and harmonica, both of which very much sound like his idol Sonny Boy, are accompanied by (possibly) J. C. Cole's acoustic guitar.

* * *

Despite the tribute to Sonny Boy on Aristocrat Records, the musical trend in Chicago was shifting. In 1948, RCA Victor and Columbia reduced the number of recordings by blues artists. Indeed, Sonny Boy's death on June 1 marked the clear decline of the Bluebird Beat. Big Bill Broonzy, Tampa Red, and Big Maceo did not make any records in 1948, partly because unionized musicians went on strike over the issue of royalties from performances from new media—namely, television. On the other hand, Muddy Waters's "I Can't Be Satisfied" coupled with "I Feel Like Going Home" recorded in April 1948 for Aristocrat, indicated a new musical direction: the heavily distorted, crunching sound of electric guitar played in the bottleneck style from the Mississippi Delta.

By the end of 1949, RCA Victor stopped making blues records altogether, and in the following year it dropped the Bluebird label. While

Tampa Red stayed with RCA, Columbia did not renew its contract with
Big Bill Broonzy—he moved on to Mercury. Memphis Minnie had her
last Columbia session in 1949. In April 1950, Columbia halted its 30000
blues series.

* * *

No newspapers in Chicago reported Sonny Boy's murder—neither the
Chicago Sun-Times nor the *Chicago Tribune*, and not even the *Chicago
Defender*, the leading black newspaper. In the June 12, 1948, issue of the
Defender, his death was briefly announced not in the regular obituaries—
Deaths of the Week—but in the section for funerals held the previous
week—"Metropolitan Funeral Parlors": "John L. Williamson, born in
Jackson, TN, resided at 3226 Giles Ave., died June 1, 1948. Body was
shipped to Jackson TN for funeral services [*sic*] and burial."[59] In the
section titled "Jackson News" of the *Defender*'s June 26, 1948, issue,
there was one sentence about his death: "John Lee Williamson died June
1 in Chicago."[60] In the June 6, 1948, issue of the *Jackson Sun*, Jackson's
local paper, there was a small announcement of his funeral service in a
classified section with a headline "Colored Dead." "Mr. John Lee
Williamson alis [*sic*: supposedly alias] Sonny Boy Williamson departed
this life June 1, 1948 at 6 o'clock a.m. in Chicago, Illinois. Loving husband of Mrs. Lacey Belle Williamson of Chicago Illinois. Son of Mrs.
Nancy Utley, brother of Mr. T. W. Utley both of Jackson, Tenn. Seven
aunts, five uncles and other relatives and friends."[61] There was no explanation for the cause of death.

The only black media that covered Sonny Boy's death as a murder
was the Associated Negro Press (ANP) based in Chicago. ANP was a
news agency founded by Tuskegee graduate Claude Barnett in 1919.
Similar to the Associated Press (AP) and United Press International
(UPI), ANP provided news materials for its member newspapers, but
because of increasing debts and Barnett's failing health, ANP ultimately
ceased operations in 1964.

As a news source agency primarily for African American papers, ANP
sent a twice-weekly packet of general and feature news relevant to the
lives of African Americans. In the music news section of "Windy City
Chatter" dated June 16, 1948, Dave Clark—possibly the same person
who contributed to *DownBeat* as the first African American writer[62] —
wrote: "We received the sad news about the death of Sonny Boy Williamson, the blues singer and RCA Victor recording artist. At this writing, we

don't have the details of how Sonny Boy was murdered. It seems like yesterday, although it was nine years ago, that we were begging Sonny Boy to leave a little town in Tennessee and come north to try to his luck on the records."[63]

Not many people knew what happened to him. In fact, as quoted earlier in the chapter, Billy Boy Arnold did not even know Sonny Boy had been murdered until he visited the bluesman's apartment; he was expecting to have another harmonica lesson. He had to make a phone call to Club Georgia, one of Sonny Boy's regular venues, to verify his death. "In fact when I first heard he got killed I couldn't quite believe it, so I called Club Georgia, y'know, and said, 'What time does Sonny Boy start?' And the man said, 'He got killed.' You know I couldn't really believe that it was really true, y'know, the way it happened."[64]

The fact that the murder case of Sonny Boy Williamson did not make the front page of the *Chicago Defender* is astounding to our modern sensibilities. After all, he was a popular artist on RCA Victor and its subsidiary Bluebird Records who had nationwide distribution. "Sonny Boy was real, real famous but he was burned some [*sic*: burned out], because he'd been there quite a spell before I went [to Chicago]," remembered Henry Townsend.[65] Even though he might have appeared burned out to Townsend, Sonny Boy was still a famous local figure. Billy Boy Arnold also recalled: "If you saw him on the street, you could ask him to sing and play. Homesick James said if he would be on the bus, he would play [for passengers]. People who knew his music would say, 'Oh that's Sonny Boy.' He was so popular."[66] Sonny Boy's club dates appeared many times in the *Defender*, and his records were always listed in the mail-order service ads. His "Shake the Boogie" was positively reviewed in the January 11, 1947, issue, even though the editors of the *Defender* rarely reviewed blues records. Was Sonny Boy's death not sensational enough for the *Defender* to report?

Sonny Boy Williamson was not the only blues artist who received such raw treatment. A close reading of the *Chicago Defender* files shows that the editors of its entertainment section treated blues musicians with what only can be called disdain. As seen in Jeff Todd Titon's *Early Down Home Blues*, a considerable area of the entertainment pages of each issue was occupied with the advertisements of records and performance announcements. On the other hand, blues artists—especially those who performed down home blues—hardly ever made the columns, as opposed to hundreds of articles about swing bands, be-bop artists, female jazz singers, cocktail trios, and vocal harmony groups. For instance, there were no articles about Muddy Waters until 1955.

The *Defender* rarely reviewed blues records and performances by blues musicians but also did not even print obituaries of blues artists until the late 1960s. Blind Lemon Jefferson's death was not covered in the *Defender*. Jefferson was the best-known down home blues singer before the Depression, as his record ads constantly appeared in the entertainment pages. He migrated from Texas to Chicago in 1929. Reportedly in December of the same year, after he performed for a house party, he lost his way in a storm and froze to death on the street. [67]

Ironically, many blues history books describe the *Chicago Defender* as one of the strongest cultural forces by which the country blues developed into the urban blues, since the *Defender* made efforts to encourage African Americans in the South to migrate to the northern cities, and many musicians who later contributed to the formulation and the maturation of Chicago blues joined the exodus. On the other hand, the *Defender* usually ignored the "lowbrow" [68] blues artists frequented by poorer, less educated, working-class African Americans, while they eagerly promoted music with "higher taste" that suited the middle-class blacks.

Over the decades, the cultural attitude of the *Defender* did not change much. The commercially successful "lowbrow" blues artists whose deaths did not appear in the *Defender* obituaries include Leroy Carr (d. 1935), Gertrude "Ma" Rainey (d. 1939), Elmore James (d. 1963), and Sonny Boy Williamson II (Rice Miller, d. 1965). Some artists such as Bessie Smith (d. 1937), though, were simply too famous to ignore. By the time Little Walter died in 1968, the editors' attitudes had changed a little: his death warranted a headline on the entertainment page.

* * *

The lack of media reports contributed to various theories regarding Sonny Boy's death. The most prevalent was that he was stabbed six times with an ice pick. Big Joe Williams recorded this story for the album *Piney Woods Blues* in 1958, but the album was not released until 1969. [69] According to the story, Sonny Boy got into some trouble at a "hop joint" that he went to after he received his check. Williams said, "It didn't look like a man. It had to be a woman that killed him . . . never found a killer." [70] Reports of the murder weapon being an ice pick likely came from Sonny Boy's recording in 1940, "I Been Dealing with the Devil": "I've got the meanest woman, the meanest woman you most ever seen, she sleep with an ice pick in her hand." It appears that the "stabbed by an ice pick" story had been circulated before 1958. Jazz historian Hugues Panassié referred to it in Sonny Boy's biographical article for the April 1955 issue of *Jazz Journal* and a jazz dictionary *Guide to Jazz* in 1956.[71] After that the "ice pick" theory would be accepted as the standard cause of Sonny Boy's death, at least for a while. For the liner notes of Rice Miller's (Sonny Boy #2) album *Down and Out Blues* in 1959, Studs Terkel wrote, "It was a wayward ice pick that did in Sonny Boy at the Plantation Club in Chicago."[72]

In the April/May 1964 issue of *Blues Unlimited*, Little Brother Montgomery gave his version of Sonny Boy's death. During his visit to England, Montgomery was interviewed by blues researchers Francis Smith and Bob Dixon. "The same day he got killed, we was together—me an' him and Sunnyland Slim and—er [*sic*] who else was there. . . . He had just got a cheque [*sic*] from royalties that he had got—be bought er [*sic*], he had with him a new hat and a blue jumper, and we was all on 29th drinking and up at Sunnyland's house—he got killed that same night."[73] According to Montgomery, Sonny Boy was a victim of "country boys"— those who came to Chicago to exact revenge for the hard agricultural labor they experienced in the South and the cold shoulder they received after arriving up north.

Montgomery continued the story. The wife of a club customer paid Sonny Boy fifty cents to play a tune, while her husband was shooting pool with his friend. "They ran him down and beat him with the butt end of those cue-sticks, y'know."[74] Montgomery even mentioned three men were arrested—one was sent to the electric chair and the other two were sentenced for life.

In the same issue of *Blues Unlimited*, Smith asked if any readers in Chicago could verify Montgomery's story. Smith also wrote, "it is more than probable that it was well reported in the *Chicago Defender*."[75] In 1967, Smith himself obtained a report from the Chicago Police Department and the Cook County Coroner's Office. His article "Study in Violence" appeared in the November/December 1967 issue of *Blues Unlimited*. Eighteen years later, the story behind Sonny Boy's murder was published for the first time.

But not everybody read *Blues Unlimited*, or they did not believe Francis Smith's article. In 1977, Sonny Boy's pianist partner Eddie Boyd told

Living Blues a story that he claimed to have heard from Lacey Belle herself. According to Boyd, after somebody hit Sonny Boy in the head with a piece of cement from the sidewalk and cracked his skull, he barely made it home and rang the bell. Lacey Belle, however, thought he came home drunk, as he had done several times before. She left him there alone. When she finally opened the door, he fell and said his last words, "Lacey, they got me, baby."[76] Ultimately, Boyd thought the incident was triggered by alcohol. "That show you what alcohol or narcotics can do to people. 'Cause normally, man, he would have died soon as that person, whoever it was, hit him in the head like that. . . . She say he stayed on that bell for at least 35 minutes. 'Cause she was kinda angry with him, you know, he stayed out all night, and she figured he was coming home broke and drunk, and she got to worry with him like always."[77]

In the same year, Blind John Davis, another of Sonny Boy's pianist partners, told his story to *Cadence*. Sonny Boy, he said, was stabbed by a lesbian with an ice pick, who assumed her lover had a relationship with him. Davis said:

> So she called Sonny Boy, he was playing at the Club Joyce [*sic*: supposedly Georgia] at 45th and State, she thought this woman (her lover) had gone to St. Louis on business. And she called Sonny Boy to come up over to her house, and when Sonny Boy got there this woman done come back and she was there when Sonny Boy rang the bell she opened the door and stabbed him in the head with an ice pick. Punctuated his brain, he died on the way to the hospital.[78]

In 1984, in a nationally syndicated radio show from Chicago, *Blues before Sunrise*, Yank Rachell shared the story that he had heard from his stepfather who was a preacher in Jackson, Tennessee. According to what Yank was told, after Sonny Boy won money gambling, he caught a cab. Wearing sharp clothing and displaying a diamond ring, he foolishly shared the taxi with someone who must have suspected he had money. Yank said:

> He got in the cab and they got in the cab with him. He got out; they got out. When they got out, they knocked him down and jumped on his chest. They took his ring and his money. And he staggered up to the door, rung the doorbell, and told his wife. . . . "I made more money tonight than I ever made in my life. But I'm hurt, I'm sick." She ran

out and called an ambulance. It came and he died before he got in the hospital.[79]

Like Eddie Boyd, Rachell also thought the ultimate cause of Sonny Boy's death was alcohol. While he certainly showed sympathy toward his ex-music partner, he was also relieved that he was not the victim. "So I said [to my father-in-law], 'Well I didn't go with Sonny Boy to Chicago and I'm glad I didn't.' 'Cause he drinks too heavy. He get to playin', he get to drinkin'."[80]

In the interview for the same radio show, *Blues before Sunrise*, in 1985, guitarist Little Hudson claimed he was playing with Sonny Boy at the Plantation Club on the night he was killed—possibly true. After they played together until midnight, Sonny Boy left the club. Hudson heard the news the next morning. "And I just couldn't believe it. I say, 'Well, me and the guy was together about four or five hours ago.'"[81]

Hudson had noticed that Sonny Boy's careless behavior toward club customers—his tendency to suddenly stop playing to hug female patrons, for example—would likely lead to trouble. Hudson gave Sonny Boy a warning, "Man, let me tell you one thing. You don't do that, 'cause you don't know who the old lady's husband or boyfriend. They might get other thoughts about what you doing."[82]

In fact, Hudson had trouble with customers on the same night he warned Sonny Boy. A couple approached Hudson on the bandstand. The woman told her husband that Hudson was trying to flirt with her before— he did not even know her. She later told her husband she was joking to make him jealous. Sonny Boy was killed the next night. He assumed Sonny Boy's death was the result of his reckless behavior: "If he would have listened to what I had to tell him about them women, he probably be living today."[83]

The wildest story came from Emma Bruce Ross, Sonny Boy's elementary schoolteacher who later became a family member. In the oral history interview by Union University student Steve Baker in 1992, Ross carefully suggested that Rice Miller "Sonny Boy" had something to do with the crime. She told Baker that on the night John Lee "Sonny Boy" was killed, there was a rumor—"he took his name and went by Sonny Boy. . . . He had a gold and diamond harmonica and a fine ring and he took that, too. That's what they say."[84] Ross concluded:

It proved out pretty much I'm sure like they said, because he played and something bothered him so, until he became just helpless almost as an alcoholic for twelve years. And after twelve years he couldn't take it any longer, so he came home and committed suicide. They had a little grave out there, kind of bring him up, so that's what happened. That's all I can tell you what happened. [85]

* * *

Most of the recent work published about the cause of Sonny Boy's death relies on Francis Smith's 1967 article in *Blues Unlimited*. In *Encyclopedia of the Blues* (2006), Sonny Boy's entry reads, "Early on the morning of June 1, 1948, Williamson left the Chicago nightclub and was beaten and stabbed to death," [86] but the article does not specify the weapon. On the other hand, the "ice pick" theory still surfaces occasionally. [87] And even today various hypotheses about the circumstances of the murder are offered, more or less because the crime has been a cold case. In 1998, Billy Boy Arnold told Scott Dirks, one of the authors of Little Walter's biography: "Sonny Boy, when he got paid that night, he liked to hang out and gamble. That's the bad sign, fooling around in those gambling joints, dangerous places. You go there, win all the money, then they want something back . . . and they wanna fight. Well, Sonny Boy had probably been drinking, there was more than one [of them], somebody picked up a piece of concrete and hit him in the head." [88]

Although there were no audio recordings, Sonny Boy's final year is full of stories of the man rather than the famous recording artist—reuniting with a former schoolteacher, spending time in the neighborhood, and teaching a young, earnest fan how to play the instrument.

The death of Sonny Boy Williamson raises a number of issues. It not only gives an opportunity to revisit the public documents but also to reflect on the cultural attitude of mainstream black media at the time. We have observed the result of the lack of proper reporting and the tradition of storytelling. That also makes us wonder what brought Sonny Boy and Lacey Belle to the Plantation Club on the day he was not scheduled to perform.

6

EPILOGUE: SONNY BOY'S LEGACY

1948–Present

Sonny Boy had been forgotten for many years, until staff members of the Jackson-Madison County Library helped stimulate recognition from his own community.

* * *

After Sonny Boy's tragic death on June 1, 1948, RCA Victor continued to release his records, as if nothing had occurred. "Rub a Dub" coupled with "Stop Breaking Down" was listed in "Advance Race Record Releases" in the July 31, 1948, issue of *Billboard*.[1] RCA also released "Better Cut That Out" with "The Big Boat" in December 1948 and "Wonderful Time" with "Blues about My Baby" in February 1949.[2] In an RCA Victor advertisement, "Now the New Ones Are on 45 RPM!,"[3] Sonny Boy's portrait is featured as well as other artists on the label, including Freddy Martin and Jim Boyd. In this same advertisement, "Bring another Half a Pint" with "Little Girl" is introduced as "This Week's Release!"[4] No statement of his death appears in any issue of *Billboard*.

European jazz enthusiasts who respected blues music as the root of jazz noticed Sonny Boy's artistry quite early on. In 1955, French jazz historian Hugues Panassié wrote for *Jazz Journal* about Sonny Boy's performing style—"At first one would think that it couldn't be the same man doing both; but on realizing that never a note of harmonica can be heard at the same time as the singing, one is forced to the conclusion that

Sonny Boy is actually doing both singing and playing the harmonica."[5]
Panassié also talked about Sonny Boy's lisping singing style. He quoted
what Big Bill Broonzy stated about Sonny Boy, "You've got to be
tongue-tied to sing the blues. That's why Sonny Boy was such a great
singer."[6]

Panassié held Sonny Boy in high esteem. He constructed a brief biography of Sonny Boy just by listening to records and compiled a nearly
complete discography. Since he had collected only a little more than half
of Sonny Boy's entire recordings after seven years of constant purchas-
ing, he concluded the article with a petition to HMV, the distributor of
RCA Records in the United Kingdom, to reissue Sonny Boy's recordings.[7] He even wrote an entry on Sonny Boy for *Guide to Jazz* in 1956—
"One of the greatest blues singers on records," he called him.[8]

Before the Panassié article, an anonymous writer for the *Guardian*
wrote about Sonny Boy's performing style. As to what he heard from a
"colleague" of Sonny Boy (probably Big Bill Broonzy), the writer wrote
that such a technique—switching voice and harmonica quickly—was accomplished by a unique feature of his body: "his mouth was of such
proportions that he could retain the harmonica in one half while singing
out of the other."[9]

In 1965, RCA Victor issued a compilation album, *Big Bill & Sonny
Boy*. Derrick Stewart-Baxter, writer for *Jazz Journal*, called the release
"[t]he most important event of the month for blues enthusiasts."[10] His
article implies that Sonny Boy's records had been out of print for a long
time: "Now that the younger readers of this column are able to hear
Williamson at some length for the first time."[11] While critics and historians remembered the historical importance and the magnitude of his
influence, RCA, for which he recorded his whole career, dropped him
from the catalog during the 1970s. His music was available only from an
independent label, Chris Strachwitz's Blues Classics, which made many
other old blues treasures available as well.

* * *

In 1951, three years after Sonny Boy's death, Billy Boy Arnold ran
into Lacey Belle in Chicago. When he recognized her, he told his friend
that she looked familiar. The man with Lacey Belle, overhearing their
conversation, said to her, "That boy knows you." Billy Boy stated, "She
was very surprised to see me and asked if I was still playing. So I pulled a
harp out and started playing for her. She said she knew Sonny Boy would

have been proud of me."[12] They kept in touch with each other. In the interview for *Melody Maker* in the November 27, 1971, issue, Billy Boy mentioned that he talked to Lacey Belle on the phone two years before—1969.[13] He was informed that she remarried and had two children. She died around 1972—we don't know the exact date—from cancer.[14]

* * *

When Sonny Boy Williamson was murdered in June 1948, Rice Miller "Sonny Boy" became known as "the original and only Sonny Boy."[15] In 1951, he was signed to Trumpet Records, and in 1955, his contract was sold to Chess Records—his records were issued by Chess's subsidiary Checker label. As well as Muddy Waters and Howlin' Wolf, Rice Miller "Sonny Boy" represented the company's down home blues catalog, and he was also one of the most popular acts on the American Folk Blues Festival—a blues package tour in European countries that started in 1962. He tried to immigrate to the United Kingdom but died on May 25, 1965, soon after he returned to Helena, Arkansas, where he hosted *King Biscuit Time*, a radio show on KFFA.

The relationship between John Lee "Sonny Boy" and Rice Miller "Sonny Boy" developed in a strange way. Some of John Lee's compositions are copyrighted as Rice Miller's. According to the BMI website—this is not an official database—39 out of 222 work titles registered by Sonny Boy Williamson/Willie Williamson/Willie "Sonny Boy" Williamson through ARC Music (Chess Records' music publishing division) are the same titles that John Lee "Sonny Boy" Williamson recorded (see table 6.1).[16] This is about a third of John Lee's total recordings.

Of the listed titles, Rice Miller "Sonny Boy" recorded only "Check Up on My Baby"—released as "Checkin' Up on My Baby" (1960)—and "Decoration Day" (1963). As indicated above, some of the compositions are not John Lee's originals, for example, "Sloppy Drunk Blues" by Lucille Bogan (1930) and "Sugar Mama [Blues]" by Tampa Red (1934). In this sense, John Lee's ownership of these songs is debatable.[17] In addition, it is possible that some of the songs may just share the same titles with different lyrics—actually "Check Up on My Baby" is such a case. However, there are too many overlaps to say these songs coincidentally have the same titles. Furthermore, beyond such quibbling, songs like "Sonny Boy's Jump" and "Sonny Boy's Cold Chills" obviously belong to John Lee "Sonny Boy." In fact, Rice Miller's "Decoration Day," which was released by Chess/Checker in 1963, is an obvious adaptation of John

Table 6.1.   John Lee "Sonny Boy" Williamson's Compositions Registered as Rice Miller "Sonny Boy" Williamson's Compositions

Registered title by Rice Miller	Original title by John Lee Williamson (if different)	Notes
Better Cut That Out		
Big Boat		
Black Panther Blues		
Bluebird Blues	Blue Bird Blues	
Blues about My Baby		
Bring another Half a Pint		A variation of "Sloppy Drunk Blues" by Sonny Boy himself on 7/2/1941. The composition was first recorded by Lucille Bogan in 1930. Sonny Boy referred to "Sloppy Drunk Blues" by Leroy Carr (v, p) with Scrapper Blackwell (g) (1930).
Broken Heart Blues		A variation of "Broken Hearted, Ragged, and Dirty Too" by Sleepy John Estes (v, g) (1929).
Buenos Dias Pequena Nina (Legal Title) Alternate Titles: Good Morning Little School Gir [*sic*] Buenos Dias Colegia Good Morning Little Mutant [*sic*]	Good Morning, School Girl	The vocal melody is loosely borrowed from "Back and Slide Blues" by Son Bonds (v, g) with Hammie Nixon (h) (1934).
Check Up on My Baby		
Coal and Iceman Blues		
Dealing with the Devil		
Decoration Day	Decoration Blues Decoration Day Blues No.2	
Desperado Woman		
Drink on Little Girl		
Elevator Woman		
G M and O	G. M. & O. Blues	The vocal melody is borrowed from "How Long How Long Blues" by Leroy Carr (v, p) with Scrapper Blackwell (g) (1928).

Ground Hog Blues		
I Have Got to Go		
I Love You for Myself		
I'm Gonna Catch You Soon		The melodic pattern is borrowed from "Hittin' the Bottom Stomp" by Mississippi Jook Band aka Blind Roosevelt Graves and Brother in 1936.
Joe Louis and John Henry	Joe Louis and John Henry Blues	
Love Me Baby		
Mattie Mae Blues		
Mean Old Highway		
Million Years Blues		
My Baby Made a Change		A variation of "Somebody Done Changed the Lock on My Door" by Casey Bill Weldon (v, g) (1935).
My Black Name Blues		
Polly Put Your Kettle On Registered also as "Polly Put the Kettle On"	Polly Put Your Kettle On	
Rub a Dub		
Shady Lane Blues	Shady Grove Blues	
Shake the Boogie		Borrowed the fast couplet/refrain pattern in "Bottle Up and Go" by Will Shade's Memphis Jug Band (1934). Sonny Boy used the pattern for "Got the Bottle Up and Gone" (5/5/1937), You've Been Foolin' Round Town (6/17/1938), Susie-Q (12/17/1938), Jivin' the Blues (5/17/1940), and "She Don't Love Me That Way" (12/11/1941).
She Don't Love Me That Way		Same as above
Shot Gun [sic] Blues	Shotgun Blues	
Sloppy Drunk Blues		The composition was first recorded by Lucille Bogan in 1930. Sonny Boy referred to "Sloppy Drunk Blues" by Leroy Carr (v, p) with Scrapper Blackwell (g) (1930).

Sonny Boy S [*sic*] Cold Chills	Sonny Boy's Cold Chill	
Sonny Boy S [*sic*] Jump	Sonny Boy's Jump	Adaptation from "Shotgun Blues" by Sonny Boy himself (4/4/1941).
Southern Dream		A variation of "She Was a Dreamer" by Sonny Boy himself on 7/2/1941. The original source is "Little Laura Blues" by Sleepy John Estes on 9/24/1941.
Springtime Blues		The vocal melody is borrowed from "How Long How Long Blues" by Leroy Carr (v, p) with Scrapper Blackwell (g) (1928). The lyrics are borrowed from "Sail on Little Girl Sail On" by Amos Easton (Bumble Bee Slim) (v, poss. g) (1934).
Stop Breaking Down		Loosely related to Robert Johnson's song.
Sugar Mama Registered also as "Sugar Mama Blues"		A variation of "Sugar Mama Blues" by Tampa Red (v, g) (1934). Tampa's recording is based on "Sugar Farm Blues" by Yank Rachell with Dan Smith in 1934.

Lee's "Decoration Blues" and "Decoration Day Blues No. 2." Rice Miller's first verse is almost exactly taken from the first verse of the former, and the third verse is a derivative of the third verse of the latter, while Rice Miller's second verse is his own. In addition, Rice Miller's vocal melody clearly derives from the original.

The case of "Good Morning, School Girl" is noteworthy. As observed in table 6.1, the Spanish title "Buenos Dias Pequena Nina" is registered as the "legal title" with three "alternate titles"—including "Good Morning, School Gir [*sic*]." The way this song is handled appears to be what only can be called a shrewd trick.

* * *

"Good Morning, School Girl" is John Lee "Sonny Boy" Williamson's most frequently recorded composition to this day, including well-known versions by Muddy Waters, Mississippi Fred McDowell, Junior Wells, Rod Stewart, Johnny Winter, Grateful Dead, Johnny Lang, Van Morrison, the Derek Trucks Band, and Widespread Panic.

This song is also registered as "Good Morning School Gir [*sic*]" by Don M. Level Sr. and Bob Love, through ARC Music. Don and Bob, a duo from Wichita, Kansas, released this version under the title "Good Morning, Little Schoolgirl" in 1961, on the Chess subsidiary Argo label. Their co-composition is undeniably based on the 1937 recording by John Lee "Sonny Boy," since the first verse is exactly the same as the original first verse (the rest is their own work). Although their single did not go anywhere in the United States, its UK release from Pye Records became a hit in the British Mods youth subculture and inspired the Yardbirds, then a beat pop band, with a teenaged Eric Clapton. "Good Morning, Little Schoolgirl" was their first major hit single. It was also included on their albums *Five Live Yardbirds* (1964) and *For Your Love* (1965).

Regardless of the inspiration from Don and Bob, the Yardbirds' version was credited to "H. G. Demarais," though their later reissues were credited to John Lee "Sonny Boy" Williamson. According to Jim O'Neal's report that appeared in *Living Blues*, Demarais was probably Harding Guyon Des Marais (aka "Dee" Marais), a music publisher and one-time owner of Murco Records in Shreveport, Louisiana, and an associate of Jewel Records' Stan Lewis, who was very close to the Chess family.[18] Jewel Music was a publisher of "Good Morning, Little Schoolgirl" on the early UK releases. Des Marais is still registered in BMI today, but "Good Morning, Little Schoolgirl" is not listed as his composition.

Whoever now collects songwriting royalties from "Good Morning, School Girl," John Lee's family members do not receive any share. T. W.'s daughter Linda Utley King tried to take legal action, but it never reached a resolution. She said, "There is a song royalty written to the family but it is not coming here. So where are they going?"[19] Sometime in the 1990s, the family contacted Willie Dixon's Blues Heaven Foundation, which helped blues songwriters retrieve their lost copyrights and collect unpaid fees, but they still could not resolve the issue.

Besides "Good Morning, School Girl," no songs are currently registered under John Lee Williamson—neither through BMI nor ASCAP. Many artists who were affiliated with Lester Melrose's Wabash Music Publishing seem to have renounced their song copyrights early on, for example, Big Maceo (Maceo Merriweather), Memphis Minnie (Lizzie Douglas), and Tampa Red (Hudson Whittaker). Probably they sold songs to Melrose just to receive a flat rate payment after each session and did not particularly care about the income received from the copyright. But more than likely they probably had no idea what they were signing when they let their songs go—a classic and all-too-common story in the music publishing business. Some artists, including Big Bill Broonzy (registered as William Lee Conley Broonzy in BMI) and Sleepy John Estes (John Adam Estes), however, retrieved their songs.

Lester Melrose retired from the music business in the late 1950s. "He got drunk and had an auto accident. He couldn't keep the people after Sonny Boy died, and the scene was changing," remembered Bob Koester.[20] In the 1960s, Koester, the owner of Delmark Records, contacted Melrose from time to time when the artists on Delmark recorded songs owned by Melrose. But Koester surmised that Melrose even lost interest in collecting royalties. When Koester sent Melrose a check, he would say, "This is the last money I would get."[21] He died in Florida in 1968.

* * *

Sonny Boy's mother, Nancy, lived to be ninety-five years old. Reportedly, Sonny Boy's family put away his memorabilia, but Nancy kept some of his records in a cheese box and listened to them from time to time. T. W.'s daughter Linda Utley King remembered, "She [Nancy] would have me to get the cheese box out and a record player. . . . She would always say 'play this song.' . . . Then she would talk everything about Sonny Boy. . . . Then she starts crying so bad and getting so upset . . . but every occasion, like birthday. . . . Sonny Boy went to so and so whatever. . . . Then she would tell you like Lacey Belle."[22] Nancy's favorite song was "Welfare Store Blues" (1942).[23] When Nancy died in September 1985, her obituary was printed in the *Jackson Sun*, but it did not mention anything about her long lost son.

In 1980, Sonny Boy Williamson was inducted into the Blues Hall of Fame. In 1986, his first biography, *Bluebird Blues: Sonny Boy Williamson*, was published by Wolfgang Lorenz in West Germany. This book was a testimony to his popularity in Europe. In his own community, on the other hand, the rediscovery project started with a casual conversation of the Jackson-Madison County Library staff members in the summer of 1989. Audiovisual librarian Michael Baker heard that Sonny Boy Williamson had been buried somewhere in the county. He then shared the rumor with reference librarian and researcher Judy Pennel and historian and archivist Jack Wood. Being curious about the life of a legendary local hero, they soon found Sonny Boy's half brother T. W. and located a small, rusty, metal marker, which T. W. and other family members placed forty-one years earlier at the grave on Blair's Chapel Road. The librarians assembled a file on him, including two photographs obtained from his family and a video interview of T. W. and Sonny Boy's uncle Fred.

The librarians' project grew bigger than just locating family members and collecting files. They started publicity to raise funds for a gravestone that the artist truly deserved. Some famous local figures, such as radio deejay James "Super" Wolfe and his wife and rhythm and blues singer Denise LaSalle, were also involved in the fund-raising campaign.

The November 12, 1989, issue of the *Jackson Sun* featured a two-page article, "He Lived and Died the Blues: Jackson's Sonny Boy Took His Music to the Top," with hand-sketched portraits of Sonny Boy and T. W.'s photo. The article, complemented with blues historian David Evans's commentary—"He was the single most influential blues harmonica player of his day and possibly of all time"[24]—introduced Sonny Boy's life story to the community for the first time. Baker said to the *Jackson Sun*, "I'm glad Sonny Boy's going to get some local recognition. It's pretty long overdue."[25]

In the same issue, Curtis Coghlan, executive editor of the *Jackson Sun*, wrote an article, "Sonny Boy's Grave Tells a Tale of Jackson's Apathy." Here he discussed how unfairly their own local hero had been treated. "It [the obituary] never mentioned he was a musician. It didn't even list his name in the headline. It only said 'Colored Dead.'"[26] Coghlan compared the current status of the two Sonny Boys. "In Helena, Ark., where the second Sonny Boy lived and died, blues fans started a society in his memory and are trying to build a museum. They sponsor an annual blues festival that draws 5,000 people or more."[27]

The librarians' effort started to catch the attention of other community members. At the end of 1989, the *Metro Forum*, a weekly newsmagazine for Jackson's African American community, had an article "I Knew 'Sonny Boy,'" by Emma Bruce Ross. She shared her story of Sonny Boy being her relative and an elementary school student she had once taught.[28]

The most effective publicity was an article about the fund-raising that Pennel and Baker wrote for the November/December 1989 issue of *Living Blues*—"Blues News: Remembering Sonny Boy Number One."[29] They not only received donations from readers in and outside the United States, but also the article caught the eye of Billy Altman, executive producer of the RCA Heritage Series. "RCA and Billy Altman were the real movers behind the headstone," said Baker.[30]

> I was in my office at the library and got a call from Billy Altman. He said that he had read the article in *Living Blues* magazine and asked if he could be of any help. . . . I told him we were wanting to get Sonny Boy a headstone and he said he would talk to some folks at RCA. About a week later I got a call from a vice president asking about what we were doing. By the end of the call he said "go get him a headstone and we will pay for it."[31]

The March 25, 1990, issue of the *Jackson Sun* reported that the Tennessee Historical Commission was going to place a historical marker honoring Sonny Boy at Tennessee 18 and Caldwell Road in Malesus, and RCA Victor Records offered to pay the cost of the new headstone. The program of the ceremony, "John Lee 'Sonny Boy' Williamson Day," was announced in the May 18, 1990, issue. At 10:30 on the morning of June 1, the commission presented the marker, and community officials, friends, and family members dedicated the headstone later that day.[32]

The participants at the ceremony included Alex Leech, Madison County executive; Jackson mayor Charles Farmer; Billy Altman of RCA; David Evans, blues historian at the University of Memphis; Bruce Nemerov, special projects director and audio archivist from the Center for Popular Music at Middle Tennessee State University; Michael Baker, Judy Pennel, and Jack Wood, three librarians at Jackson-Madison County Library; and family members and friends, including T. W. Utley, Fred Utley, T. W's cousin James Utley, Emma Bruce Ross, and James Wolfe, among many others.

To open the ceremony, William Howse and Jack Pearson, a blues duo from Murfreesboro, Tennessee, played "Good Morning, School Girl." The performance was followed by an announcement by Jack Wood, the master of ceremonies. He introduced Baker, Pennel, and Sonny Boy's surviving family members. Then David Evans made a speech:

> It's a great thing when an artist can be recognized by his community. . . . Sonny Boy was a truly innovative musician on the harmonica as well as a unique vocalist and songwriter. . . . He had the mark of a great artist—others tried to imitate him. Like Carl Perkins—another

famous Madison County musician—Sonny Boy influenced many people that came after him and many of his songs became standards.[33]

Emma Bruce Ross followed:

Sonny Boy didn't have any formal education as a musician. None whatsoever. He'd decide what he wanted to sing about. He'd just get his harmonica and start tapping his feet and the song would just reel out of his head.[34]

Baker, Pennel, and Jana Lee Ellis from the Tennessee State Historical Commission removed the veil. The marker reads:

"Sonny Boy" Williamson (1914–1948), the music innovator responsible for the acceptance of the harmonica as an authentic blues tool, is buried in old Blair's Chapel CME Cemetery, 5 miles southwest. The most influential blues harmonica player of his day, he made a powerful contribution to American music and is recognized as a master of the blues genre. In his mouth and hands, the harmonica learned to wail and chirp, laugh and cry, in spanking new rhythms and to daring new beats.[35]

After unveiling the marker, local executives Leech and Farmer read a proclamation—June 1 would always be Sonny Boy Williamson Day in Madison County. Then T. W. delivered an address of thanks on behalf of the family. Subsequently, the attendees moved to Blair's Chapel. After they held a service and had lunch, they walked to see the beautiful marble headstone. "Judy Pennel and I went to Jackson Marble & Granite Works on Hollywood Drive and we picked out a headstone," said Michael Baker.[36] "I had them put a harmonica on it with the words 'Blues Harmonica Legend.' The family wanted to put Curtis in his name. That was the first time I had heard that Curtis was part of his name."[37]

Baker reflected, "Over the years, folks would want to see the gravesite and many times I would take them. Billy Boy Arnold went to the gravesite with T. W. and myself. When Charlie Musselwhite was in town, I took him to the grave and later to meet T. W. . . . Also I took John Sebastian and his band, which included Paul Rishell and Annie Raines, to the site. I remember Annie Raines wanted us all to go back to the road to our cars while she played a song just for Sonny Boy."[38]

* * *

"This is just a beginning of something," Emma Bruce Ross said about the first Sonny Boy Williamson Day.[39] The city of Jackson continued to celebrate the legacy of Sonny Boy. James Wolfe organized a music festival on September 1, 1990, with Bobby "Blue" Bland, Son Thomas, the Magi Band, and Denise LaSalle.[40] The Jackson Arts Council—Michael Baker was a committee member—organized the three-day Forked Deer Festival on September 9, 1990, featuring Waynell Jones; Jack Pearson and William Howse, who performed at the marker ceremony; the Last Chance Jug Band with David Evans; Johnny Shines; and Yank Rachell. Yank talked about the festival, "I'm proud to play. It'll bring back old memories. Me and him [Sonny Boy] were good friends. We were close, like brothers."[41] He also called Sonny Boy "the best harp player I've known. He played his own style. A lot of people tried to play like him, but couldn't."[42]

Yank Rachell was the sole survivor of the Brownsville-Jackson blues community after Sleepy John passed away in 1977 and Hammie Nixon in 1984. Though Yank suffered from arthritis, he kept performing. In 1997, just before he died, he made an album titled *Too Hot for the Devil.*[43]

Billy Boy Arnold was invited to perform for the festival in 1994 and 2002. He always included Sonny Boy's songs in his set list, including "You Can Lead Me" and "Mellow Chick Swing."

In addition to Yank and Billy Boy, many other blues artists have participated in the festival over the years—Slick Ballinger, Terry "Harmonica" Bean, Cary Bell, Eden Brent, Big George Brock, Kenny Brown, Michael Burks, R. L. Burnside, Sean Costello, Honeyboy Edwards, Anson Funderburgh, Guitar Shorty, Big Jack Johnson, Junior Kimbrough, Jimbo Mathus, Big Bill Morganfield, the North Mississippi Allstars, Bobby Parker, Lonnie Pitchford, and the Rockets with Sam Myers.

The city of Jackson still annually holds the music festival today, but the name was changed from Shannon Street Blues Festival to Shannon Street Music Festival in 2012. As observed in many blues festivals in the nation, the city incorporates more diverse artists rather than solely blues performers. Baker observed, "It is hard for a pure blues festival to draw an audience, but with the musical heritage of just this small part of West Tennessee, you can cover a lot of musical styles—Carl Perkins, Big Maybelle, Joe Hunter from the Funk Brothers of Motown, Eddy Arnold, Carl Mann, W. S. 'Fluke' Holland from Johnny Cash's band, Arthur

Adams from Medon, a 20 to 30 mile radius from Jackson, and not to mention Sonny Boy. A festival pulling all those musical styles together and presenting them in a loose historical context could bring in some folks."[44]

Baker kept in touch with T. W. and Fred. After T. W. lost his wife, Mary Lou, he spent more time with Fred. Fred lived to be 103 years old. He died on August 15, 2004. Baker remembered, "When Fred died, I think that took a lot out of T. W. But I would always run into him in the grocery store."[45] T. W. died on November 5, 2005.

In 2003, RCA Victor released a well-selected compilation of Sonny Boy's representative recordings, titled *Blue Bird Blues*, as a part of the *When the Sun Goes Down* series of blues and other African American roots music; David Evans was one of the compilers. The disc is currently out of print, but two volumes of four CD sets that cover Sonny Boy's complete recordings and all of his session work are available from JSP Records in the United Kingdom, under the titles *The Original Sonny Boy Williamson: Vol. 1* (2007) and *The Original Sonny Boy Williamson: The Later Years 1939–1947* (2008).

* * *

Although John Lee "Sonny Boy" Williamson died too soon, he left behind many legacies. First of all, he was the most influential for the next generation of Chicago blues harmonica players. Jimmy Rogers said, "Sonny Boy was 'the man' then. That was the style we were playin'. 'Good Mornin' Little Schoolgirl [*sic*]' and 'Black Gal' and all kind of stuff like that. That's the way we learned our licks on harmonica."[46] Sonny Boy's followers included Little Walter, Junior Wells, Forest City Joe, James Cotton, Billy Boy Arnold, and Snooky Pryor.[47]

Little Walter, of course, was not just Sonny Boy's follower; he became the next leading figure of the Chicago blues harmonica tradition. However, it should be emphasized that Walter's playing grew out of his experiences with Sonny Boy. "I Just Keep Loving Her (Take 1)" from Walter's 1947 session for the Ola Nell label is sheer proof that his licks developed from Sonny Boy's swing-like tunes "She Don't Love Me That Way" and "Jivin' the Blues." Also here Walter is trying to imitate Sonny Boy's vibrato-less, lisping vocal style. In "I Just Keep Loving Her (Take 2)," Walter plays chordally dominated phrases, which he also acquired from Sonny Boy's records. When Little Walter teamed up with Muddy Waters, they seem to have studied the duo performances of Sonny Boy and Big Joe Williams and/or Robert Lee McCoy (Robert Nighthawk). The earliest recordings of Muddy and Walter in 1950, for which Walter was still playing acoustic, such as "You're Gonna Need My Help I Said," "Sad Letter," and "Early Morning Blues," retain strong influence from their precursors. In "Early Morning Blues," Walter is actually playing Sonny Boy's cliché phrase in his medium-slow pattern.

Junior Wells was another harmonica player who was influenced by Sonny Boy. "Hoodoo Man Blues," an adaptation of Sonny Boy's "Hoodoo Hoodoo" in 1946, became Junior's signature side. Here Junior creates an impressive opening phrase with a tongue block technique, which he possibly learned from Sonny Boy's records, such as "New Early in the Morning" in 1940. Junior Wells recorded another of Sonny Boy's tunes, "Million Years Blues" with Buddy Guy.

Joe Filisko said Sonny Boy was a teacher even to contemporary harmonica players:

> I am a very curious person in nature. I work on harmonicas, and it puts me in a very unique position, because I know many of the best players in the world. When I was getting to know them, I would say to them— "Who are your favorite players? Who do you think I should listen to? What are your favorite songs?" I am just looking, because there has not been a tradition of people teaching how to play harmonica, which is what makes harmonica a perfect folk instrument. It is just an oral folk tradition. So just too many people would say to me Sonny Boy I was somebody to look into. He was the foundation. Who said that to me? Jerry Portnoy, Rick Estrin, Steve Geiger, Charlie Musselwhite, and certainly Billy Boy Arnold. It was a talk with Billy Boy some twelve years ago. He really explained to me his opinion of the significance of Sonny Boy I. When I talked to him about it, it really got me very curious to decipher about his whole playing style. And there's something about Sonny Boy's playing that is not, in my opinion, intuitive to many other important contemporary players. You have to really think differently to figure out what he is doing. [48]

Filisko emphasizes that the key to Sonny Boy's playing is his acoustic performance in a small ensemble:

> When I started to play music more in duo, I began to really see that the thinner tone style just didn't make it. If you play the harmonica like Sonny Boy I, when you play with the guitar player, you get the really

full, powerful sound—the guitar and harmonica blend together. Otherwise, the guitar is doing the work, and the harmonica is doing just little fills over the top, which any instruments can do that. But Sonny Boy I's playing is connected to the rhythm of the guitar, and the two drive together. I think he figured out how to play the coolest licks, playing to basically the blues scale, but he also figured out how to do it with a very big full sound. I think he brought out the essence of harmonica.

Listen to players like Junior Wells, James Cotton, Little Walter, and Big Walter. You will hear how he influenced them. You will notice that when those players play amplified, they tend to play more saxophone-like. But if they are put in a situation with playing more acoustically, then they tend to be more like Sonny Boy I's style.[49]

* * *

As stated in the introduction, my original intention was to explore the music of an unparalleled harmonica player whose performance on the harmonica originated in the blues traditions of Memphis and other areas of West Tennessee. But my work grew and expanded. A second-generation descendant of post-slavery with a harmonica and a creative mind became an influential wizard. Coming up from a southern town to Chicago, he represented the sound of the community—Bronzeville. He inspired many others. But here, in his adopted hometown, he was brutally murdered, and the mainstream African American media of the time did not seem to care.

This story is not just about the music. In my mind, it is a microcosm of American history. Without Sonny Boy Williamson, blues harmonica—a significant part of the African American musical practice—would be totally different. What he achieved in his short life changed the idea of harmonica performance: switching vocal and instrument seamlessly; developing the techniques to produce a fat and crunchy sound that determined the acoustic performance of blues; and giving a structure and speed to blues harmonica performance. He was one of the earliest harmonica players with amplification. In addition, his tongue-tied, lisping vocal style was widely imitated. Of equal importance, his songs are standard repertoire for many players today. As well as "Good Morning, School Girl," his songs that have been rerecorded by others include "Blue Bird Blues," "Decoration Blues," "Drink on Little Girl," "I Been Dealing with the Devil," "Mattie Mae," "Mellow Chick Swing," "My Black Name Blues," "My Little Machine," "Polly Put Your Kettle On," "Sonny

Boy's Jump," "Sugar Mama," "Western Union Man," and "Whiskey Headed Blues." Some of these songs may not be Sonny Boy's originals, but still many artists learned them from Sonny Boy's records.

I am still learning Sonny Boy's music; Joe Filisko, the harmonica player who has thoroughly studied Sonny Boy's style, is also a student of Sonny Boy.

> I was listening when I woke up this morning to his first recordings that he did. He just had such a nice way that he plays and goes into singing like he is really kind of telling a story with sincerity and kind of a confidence. He was in his early twenties when he recorded that stuff. He sounds like he's been doing it for twenty years. I can see how he would appeal to many people by that kind of laid-back vocal style, but he was not afraid to playfully cram a whole big bunch of words into a short amount of musical space. He did it in an unforgettable way. I like the way that comes across.
>
> I believe that Sonny Boy's style and licks became so synonymous with blues harmonica that it may have been difficult not to be taken seriously as a player if you couldn't sound like him. I do think that after amplification became commonplace, players were able to rely more on the amp than the aggressive driving full sounds associated with his style. The players who remained very true to his sound are mostly acoustic players like me. The general excitement of the big sounding harp is still there as we remember the lessons of copying him.[50]

APPENDIX

Discography

The sources for this appendix are *Blues and Gospel Records, 1890–1943* by Robert M. W. Dixon, John Godrich, and Howard Rye and *The Blues Discography 1943–1970* by Les Fancourt and Bob McGrath.

Abbreviations

acc	accompaniment
b	bass
d	drums
eg	electric guitar
g	guitar
h	harmonica
imb	imitation (oilcan or washtub) bass
p	piano
poss.	possibly
prob.	probably
v	vocal
wb	washboard

Sonny Boy Williamson's Leader Sessions from 1937 to 1938 (Aurora, Illinois)

Date, place, and personnel	Variations of the medium-slow blues pattern: Matrix/original release	Adaptations (based on preexisting compositions): Matrix/original release: Origins (sources)	Key
5/5 (Wed)/1937 **Leland Hotel, Aurora, IL** Sonny Boy Williamson, v; acc. own h Joe Williams, g Robert Lee McCoy, g/v-1		Good Morning, School Girl 07649-1/BB B7059 The vocal melody is loosely borrowed from "Back and Slide Blues" by Son Bonds (v, g) with Hammie Nixon (h) (1934).	C
	Blue Bird Blues 07650-1/BB B7098, MW M 7503		G
		Jackson Blues 07651-1/BB B7098, MW M7503 The vocal melody is borrowed from "Trouble in Mind" by Richard M. Jones (v, p) (1936).	A
		Got the Bottle Up and Gone-1 07652-1/BB B7012 Based on the traditional songs in the Memphis area: the earliest recording of the same melody pattern (the fast couplet/refrain pattern) is found in "Your Friends Gonna Use It, Part 1" and "Part 2" by Walter Vincent with the Mississippi Hot Footers, recorded in the Peabody Hotel in 1929. It is also found in "You Ought to Move Out of Town" and "Save Me Some" by Jed Davenport and His Beale Street Jug Band in 1930, followed by "You Got to Have That Thing" by the Picaninny Jug Band in 1932. Sonny Boy's version is based on "Bottle Up and Go" by Will Shade's Memphis Jug Band in 1934.	A
		Sugar Mama 07653-1/BB B7059 A variation of "Sugar Mama Blues" by Tampa Red (v, g) (1934). Tampa Red's recording is based on "Sugar Farm Blues" by Yank Rachell with Dan Smith in 1934.	A
		Skinny Woman 07654-1/BB B7012 A variation of "Gravel Road Woman" by Yank Rachell (v, g) in 1934. *The first verse is directly from Yank's version, while the rest is by Sonny Boy.	A

11/11 (Thu)/1937 **Leland Hotel**	Up the Country-1 016518-1/BB B7428		G
Aurora, IL Sonny Boy	Worried Me Blues-2 016519-1/BB B7404, MW M7502		F
Williamson, v; acc. own h Walter Davis, p-1 Unknown, g 2nd unknown, g-2		Black Gal Blues-2 016520-1/BB B7352, MW M 7502 A variation of "Crazy 'bout My Black Gal" by Charlie Pickett (1937).	F
According to the session log, three	Collector Man Blues-1 016251-1/BB B7428		G
guitarists were present for the	Frigidaire Blues-2 016522-1/BB B7404, MW M7502		F
session: Robert Lee McCoy, Henry Townsend, and Joe Williams.		Suzanna Blues-2 016523-1/BB B7352 A variation of "Louis Louis Blues" by Johnnie Temple (1936).	G
		Early in the Morning-2 016524-1/BB B7302 Based on the traditional: one of the earliest recordings is "Soon This Morning Blues" by Charlie Spand (v, p) (1929). Other early recordings include "Early This Morning—'bout Break of Day" Walter Roland (v, p) (1933), "At the Break of Day" by Big Bill Broonzy (v, g) (released under Big Bill in 1934), "Soon in the Morning" by Jimmie Gordon (v, p) (1935), and "'Bout the Break of the Day" by Bill Gaither (v, p) (1936).	A
	Project Highway-2 016525-1/BB B7302		G

3/13 (Sun)/1938 **Leland Hotel,** **Aurora, IL** Sonny Boy Williamson, v; acc. own h Yank Rachell, md- 1/g-2/poss. sp-4 Joe Williams, g- 3/poss. sp-5		My Little Cornelius-1, 3 020110-1/BB B7500, MW M7504 A variation of "Blue Bird Blues" by Sonny Boy himself on 5/5/1937.	G
	Decoration Day Blues-1, 3 020111-1/BB B 7665, MW M 7939 *Curtis Jones (p) claimed that he composed this song.		G
		You Can Lead Me-1, 3 020112-1/BB B7536, MW M7765 The vocal melody is borrowed from "Good Morning, School Girl" by Sonny Boy himself on 5/5/1937.	B
		Moonshine-1, 3 020113-1/BB B7603, MW M7765 A variation of "Need More Blues" by Sleepy John Estes (1937).	G
	Miss Louisa Blues-1, 3 020114-1, BB B7576		B
	Sunny Land-1, 3, 4, or 5 020115-1/BB B7500, MW M 7504		B
		I'm Tired Trucking My Blues Away- 2, 4, or 5 020116-1/BB B7536 The melodic pattern is borrowed from "Hittin' the Bottom Stomp" by Mississippi Jook Band, aka Blind Roosevelt Graves and Brother in 1936. *The melody pattern appeared in "They're Red Hot" by Robert Johnson (v, g) (1936).	C/B Poss. slow playb ack speed
	Down South-1, 3 020117-1/BB B7665, MW M7939 The introductory melody is loosely based on "Roll and Tumble Blues" by Hambone Willie Newbern (v/g) (1929).		G
	Beauty Parlor-1, 3 020118-1/BB B7603, MW M7766		G
		Until My Love Come Down-1, 3, 4, or 5 020119-1/BB B7576, MW M7766 A variation of "Lemon Squeezing Blues" by Bumble Bee Slim (1935) and "Let Me Squeeze Your Lemon" by Charlie Pickett (v, g) with Hammie Nixon (h) (1937).	A

6/17 (Fri)/1938 **Leland Hotel,** **Aurora, IL** Sonny Boy Williamson, v; acc. own h Walter Davis, p-1 Yank Rachell, g- 2/md-3/poss. sp-5 Joe Williams, g- 4/poss. sp-6	Honey Bee Blues-1, 2, 4 020842-1/BB B7707, MW M7940		A
	My Baby I've Been Your Slave-1, 2, 4, 5, or 6 020843-/BB B7805, MW M7592		A
	Whiskey Headed Blues-3, 4, 5, or 6 020844-1/BB B7707, MW M7940 * Tommy McClennan recorded as "Whiskey Head Woman" on 11/22/1939.		A
		Lord Oh, Lord Blues-3, 4 020845-1/BB B7847, MW M7589 The vocal melody is borrowed from "Roll and Tumble Blues" by Hambone Willie Newbern (v, g) (1929).	A
		You Give an Account-3, 4 020846-/BB B7756, MW M7941 The vocal melody is borrowed from "Sitting on the Top of the World" by Mississippi Sheiks (1930).	A
	Shannon Street Blues-3, 4 020847-1/BB B7847, MW M7589		A
		You've Been Foolin' Round Town-3, 4 020848-1/BB B7756, MW M7941 Borrowed the fast couplet/refrain pattern in "Bottle Up and Go" by Will Shade's Memphis Jug Band (1934) and its variation "Got the Bottle Up and Gone" by Sonny Boy himself on 5/5/1937.	A
		Deep Down in the Ground-2 020849-1/BB B7805, MW M7592 The melodic pattern is borrowed from "Good Morning, School Girl" by Sonny Boy himself on 5/5/1937.	A

12/17 (Sat)/1938 Leland Hotel, Aurora, IL Sonny Boy Williamson, v; acc. own h Speckled Red, p Willie Hatcher, md-1 Prob. Robert Lee McCoy, g	Number Five Blues-1 030848-1/BB B8010		F Poss. slow play-back speed
	Christmas Morning Blues-1 030849-1/BB B8094, MW M7945		G
		Susie-Q-1 030850-1/BB B7995, MW M7943 Borrowed the fast couplet/refrain pattern in "Bottle Up and Go" by Will Shade's Memphis Jug Band (1934) and its variation "Got the Bottle Up and Gone" by Sonny Boy himself on 5/5/1937.	G
		Blue Bird Blues—Part 2-1 030851-1/BB B7979, MW M7942 A variation of "Blue Bird Blues" by Sonny Boy himself on 5/5/1937.	G
	Little Girl Blues-1 030852-1/BB B8010		G
	Low Down Ways-1 030853-1/BB B7979, MW M7942 * Arranged in a faster tempo while the melodic structure follows the same mid-slow blues pattern.		G
		Goodbye Red 030854-1/BB B7995, MW M 7944 A variation of "Oh Red" by Harlem Hamfats (1936).	F
		The Right Kind of Life-1 030855-1/BB B8034, MW M7944 A variation of "Mistake in Life" by Roosevelt Sykes (v, p) (1938).	C
	Insurance Man Blues-1 030856-1/BB B8034, MW M7944 This song is similar to "Collector Man Blues" recorded by Sonny Boy himself on 11/11/1937.		F
	Rainy Day Blues-1 030857-1/BB B8094, MW M7945		F

Sonny Boy Williamson's Leader Sessions from 1939 to 1947 (Chicago)

Date, place, and personnel	Sonny Boy's own basics		Adaptations (based on preexisting compositions)	Key
	Variations of mid-slow blues compositions: Matrix/original release	**Other musical styles: Matrix/original release**	**Matrix/original release: Origins (sources)**	
7/21 (Fri)/1939 Chicago Sonny Boy Williamson, v; acc. own h Walter Davis, p-1 Big Bill Broonzy, eg	Bad Luck Blues-1 040525-1/BB B8265, MW M8575			G
			My Little Baby-1 040526-1/BB B8265, MW M8575 Based on "Good Morning, School Girl" by Sonny Boy himself on 5/5/1937—see 5/5 (Wed)/1937 for the original ("Back and Slide Blues" by Son Bonds).	C 1st positi on harp
	Doggin' My Love Around-1 040527-1/BB B8307, MW M8576			A
	Little Low Woman Blues-1 040528-1/BB B8307, MW M8576			B-flat 1st positi on harp
	Good for Nothing Blues-1 040529-1/BB B8237, MW M8574			F
	Sugar Mama Blues no. 2-1 040530-1/BB B8237, MW M8574			F
			Good Gravy 040531-1/BB B8333, MW M 8577 Based on "Hittin' the Bottom Stomp" by Mississippi Jook Band, aka Blind Roosevelt Graves and Brother (1936).	F
			T. B. Blues-1 040532-1/BB 8333, MW M8577 Traditional: The direct precursor of Sonny Boy's version is "T. B. Blues" by Victoria Spivey (v) (1927). Other recordings prior to Sonny Boy included "Dirty T. B. Blues" by Victoria Spivey (v) (1929), "T. B. Blues" by Jimmie Rodgers (v, g) (1931), and "T. B. Is Killing Me" by Buddy Moss (v, g) (1936). Except for Jimmie Rodgers's recording, all of them have a punch line "T. B. is killing me."	G

Something Goin' On Wrong-1 040533-1/BB B8357, MW M8578			A
Good Gal Blues-1 040534-1/BB B8357, MW M8578			F
		Joe Louis and Joe Henry Blues-1 040535-1/BB B8403, MW M8579 Traditional theme previously recorded as "Joe Louis Is the Man" by Joe Pullum (v) (1935), "Joe Louis Blues" by Carl Martin (v, g) (1935), "He's in the Ring (Doin' the Same Old Thing)" and "Joe Louis Strut" by Memphis Minnie (1935).	F
Thinking My Blues Away-1 040536-1/BB B8403, MW M8579			G
I'm Not Pleasing You-1 040537-1/BB B8383, MW M8580			F
		New "Jailhouse Blues"-1 040538-1/BB B8383, MW M8580 Traditional theme previously recorded as "Jail-House Blues" by Bessie Smith (v) (1927), "The Jail House Blues" by Crying Sam Collins (v, g) (1927), "In the Jail House Now" by Jimmie Rodgers (v, g) (1928), and "Jailhouse Blues" by Sleepy John Estes (v, g) with Robert Lee McCoy (h) (1940).	A
		Lifetime Blues-1 040539-1/BB B8439, MW M8581 A variation of "Viola Lee Blues" by Cannon's Jug Stompers (1928).	A
Miss Ida Lee-1 040540-1/BB B8439, MW M 8581			A
		Tell Me Baby-1 040541-1/BB B8474, MW M8582 A variation of "(Hey) Lawdy Mama" by Bumble Bee Slim (v, poss. g) (1935). ***Sonny Boy started to mix a swing feel with his recordings from this point on.**	A
		Honey Bee Blues-1 040542-1/BB B8474, MW M8582 (Different from the same title recorded on 6/17/1938)	G
		An adaptation from "Bumble Bee" by Memphis Minnie and Kansas Joe (1930) and "Honey Bee Blues" by Bumble Bee Slim (v, poss. g) (1931).	

5/17	I Been Dealing with			G
(Fri)/1940	the Devil			
Chicago	049196-1/BB B8580			
Sonny Boy	MW M8934			
Williamson, v;	***Fast swing feel in**			
acc. own h	**arrangement**			
Joshua	War Time Blues			G
Altheimer, p	049197-1/BB			
Fred Williams,	B8580, MW 8934			
d	Train Fare Blues			G
	049198-1/BBB8610,			
	MW 049198-1			
			Decoration Day Blues No. 2	G
			049199-1/BB34-0713, MW M8937	
			A variation of Sonny Boy's own	
			"Decoration Day Blues" on 3/13/1938.	
			New Early in the Morning	F
			053000-1/MW M8937	
			*Fast swing arrangement	
			Based on "Early in the Morning" by	
			Sonny Boy himself on 11/11/1937	
			(see above for the origins).	
			Welfare Store Blues	F
			05300-1/BB B8610, MW M8935	
			A variation of "Red Cross Blues" by	
			Walter Roland (v, p) (1939).	
	My Little Machine			G
	(Oh Yeah!)			
	053002-1, BB			
	B8674, MW M8936			
			Jivin' the Blues	G
			053003-1/BB B 8674, MW M8936	
			*Fast swing arrangement	
			Based on "Susie-Q" by Sonny Boy	
			himself on 12/17/1938. The original	
			"Susie-Q" is in the fast couplet/refrain	
			pattern seen in "Bottle Up and Go" by	
			Will Shade's Memphis Jug Band	
			(1934), and its variations by Sonny	
			Boy himself—"Got the Bottle Up and	
			Gone" (5/5/1937) and "You've Been	
			Foolin' Round Town" (6/17/1938).	

4/4 (Fri)/1941 Chicago Sonny Boy Williamson, v; acc. own h Big Bill Broonzy, g William Mitchell, imb			Western Union Man 064019-1/BB B8731 A variation of "Mailman Blues" by Sleepy John Estes (1940).	G
	Big Apple Blues 064020-1/BB B8766			G
			Springtime Blues 064021-1/BB B8955 The vocal melody is borrowed from "How Long How Long Blues" by Leroy Carr (v, p) with Scrapper Blackwell (g) (1928). The lyrics are borrowed from "Sail on Little Girl Sail On" by Amos Easton (Bumble Bee Slim) (v, poss. g) (1934).	C 1st p. harp
			My Baby's Made a Change 064022-1/BB B8766 A variation of "Somebody Done Changed the Lock on My Door" by Casey Bill Weldon (v, g) (1935).	G
		Shotgun Blues 064023-1 BB B8731 *Fast swing arrangement		G
	Coal and Iceman Blues 064024-1/BB B8797			G
	Drink on Little Girl 064025-1/BB B8955			G
	Mattie Mae Blues 064026-1/BB B8797			G

7/2 **(Wed)/1941** **Chicago** Sonny Boy Williamson, v; acc. own h Blind John Davis, p Ransom Knowling, b			I'm Gonna Catch You Soon 064490-1/BB B8866 ***Fast swing arrangement** The melodic pattern is borrowed from "Hittin' the Bottom Stomp" by Mississippi Jook Band, aka Blind Roosevelt Graves and Brother in 1936. Sonny Boy previously used the pattern for "I'm Tired Trucking My Blues Away" (3/13/1938) and "Good Gravy" (7/21/1939).	G
	Million Years Blues 064494-1/BB B8866			G
	Shady Grove Blues 064492-1/BB B8914			G
			Sloppy Drunk Blues 064493-1/BB B8822 Based on "Sloppy Drunk Blues" by Leroy Carr (v, p) (1930). The composition was first recorded by Lucille Bogan (v) in 1930.	C
			She Was a Dreamer 064494-1/BB B8914 ***Fast swing arrangement** Probably based on "Little Laura Blues" by Sleepy John Estes (v, g) (9/24/1941), though Sonny Boy recorded this composition prior to Sleepy John.	G
		You Got to Step Back 064495-1/BB B8822 ***Fast swing arrangement**		C

12/11 (Thu)/1941 Chicago	Ground Hog Blues-1 070143-1/BB B 9031			A
Sonny Boy Williamson, v; acc. own h Blind John	Black Panther Blues-1 070144-1/BB 34-0701			A
Davis, p Charlie McCoy, g Alfred Elkins, imb-1 Washboard Sam, wb-2		Broken Heart Blues-1 07145-1/BB B9031 A variation of "Broken-Hearted, Ragged, and Dirty Too" by Sleepy John Estes (v, g) (1929).		F
		She Don't Love Me That Way-2 07146-1/BB 34-0701 ***Fast swing arrangement** Borrowed the fast couplet/refrain pattern in "Bottle Up and Go" by Will Shade's Memphis Jug Band (1934), and its variations by Sonny Boy himself—"Got the Bottle Up and Gone" (5/5/1937).		F
		My Black Name Blues-2 07147-1/BB B 8992, Vi 20-2796 A variation of "Blues before Sunrise" by Leroy Carr (v, p) and Scrapper Blackwell (g) (1934).		F
		I Have Got to Go-2 07148-1, BB B8992, Vi 20-2796 ***Fast eight-beat arrangement**		A
7/30 (Thu)/1942 Chicago	Love Me, Baby 0746556-1/ BB 34-0713			A
Sonny Boy Williamson, v; acc. own h Blind John Davis, p Big Bill Broonzy, g Alfred Elkins, imb		What's Gettin' Wrong with You? 074657-1 BB unissued BB (F) PM42049 (LP) ***Fast eight-beat arrangement**		A
		Blues That Made Me Drunk 074658-1 BB unissued RCA(J) RA 5707, RCA (F) NL 90027(2) (LPs) ***Fast eight-beat arrangement**		A
		Come on Baby and Take a Walk 074659-1 BB unissued BB (F) PM42049 (LP) RCA (J) RA 5707		A
		(LPs) ***Fast swing arrangement**		

Musicians' Union Strike: 8/1/1942 to 11/11/1944

12/14 (Thu)/1944 Chicago Sonny Boy Williamson, v; acc. own h Blind John Davis, p Ted Summit, eg Jump Jackson, d	Miss Stella Brown Blues D4AB 324/Bb 34-0736			F
	Desperado Woman D4AB 325/Bb 34-0736			F
	Win the War D4AB 326/Bb 34-0722			F
	Check Up on My Baby D4AB 327/Bb 34-0722			F
7/2 (Mon)/1945 Chicago Sonny Boy Williamson, v; acc. own h Eddie Boyd, p Big Sid Cox, g Ransom Knowling, b			G. M. & O. Blues D5AB 339/Vic 20-2369 The vocal melody is borrowed from "How Long How Long Blues" by Leroy Carr (v, p) with Scrapper Blackwell (g) (1928).	C 1st p. harp
	We Got to Win D5AB 340/RCA Int(E) 5099			G
			Sonny Boy's Jump D5AB 341/Bb34-0744 Adaptation from "Shotgun Blues" by Sonny Boy himself (4/4/1941). ***Fast swing arrangement**	
	Elevator Woman D5AB 342/Bb34-0744 * Willie Dixon claimed that he played the bass for this recording.			G
10/19 (Fri)/1945 Chicago Sonny Boy Williamson, v; acc. own h Big Maceo, p Tampa Red, g Charles Sanders, d			Early in the Morning D5AB 396/Vic20-1875 ***Fast swing arrangement** A variation of "Soon This Morning Blues" by Charlie Spand (v, p) (1929). Sonny Boy previously recorded this song as "Early in the Morning" (11/11/1937) and "New Early in the Morning" (5/17/1940).	G
	The Big Boat D5AB 397/Vic 20-3218			G
	Stop Breaking Down D5AB 398/Vic 20-3047 * Loosely related to Robert Johnson's song.			
		You're an Old Lady D5AB 399/Vic 20-1875 ***Fast swing arrangement**		G

8/6 (Tue)/1946 **Chicago** Sonny Boy Williamson, v; acc. own h Blind John Davis, p Willie Lacey, eg Ransom Knowling, b	Sonny Boy's Cold Chills D6VB 1917/Vic 20- 2154			G
	Mean Old Highway D6VB 1918/Vic 20- 2056			G
	Hoodoo Hoodoo D6VB 1919/Vic 20- 2154 Later recorded as "Hoodoo Man Blues" by Junior Wells (1953).			G
			Shake the Boogie D6VB 1920/Vic 20-2056 ***Fast swing arrangement** Borrowed the fast couplet/refrain pattern in "Bottle Up and Go" by Will Shade's Memphis Jug Band (1934). Sonny Boy used the pattern for "Got the Bottle Up and Gone" (5/5/1937), "You've Been Foolin' Round Town" (6/17/1938), "Susie-Q" (12/17/1938), "Jivin' the Blues" (5/17/1940), and "She Don't Love Me That Way" (12/11/1941).	G
3/28 **(Fri)/1947** **Chicago** Sonny Boy Williamson, v; acc. own h Blind John Davis, p Big Bill Broonzy, eg Willie Dixon, b Charles Sanders, d		Mellow Chick Swing D7VB 374/Vic 2369 ***Fast swing arrangement**		G
		Polly Put Your Kettle On D7VB 375/Vic 2521 ***Fast swing arrangement**		G
	Lacey Belle D7VB 376/Vic 2521			G
		Apple Tree Swing D7VB 377/Vic 2893 ***Fast swing arrangement**		G

9/19 (Fri)/1947 Chicago Sonny Boy Williamson, v; acc. own h Eddie Boyd, p Willie Lacey, eg Ransom Knowling, b Judge Riley, d			Wonderful Time D7VB 1036/Vic 22-0001 *Fast swing arrangement The melodic pattern is borrowed from "Hittin' the Bottom Stomp" by Mississippi Jook Band, aka Blind Roosevelt Graves and Brother in 1936. Sonny Boy previously borrowed the pattern for I'm Tired Trucking My Blues Away" (3/13/1938), "Good Gravy" (7/21/1939), "I'm Gonna Catch You Soon" (7/2/1941).	G
			Sugar Gal D7VB 1037/Vic 22-2623 *Fast swing arrangement A variation of "Sugar Mama" (5/5/1937). Also borrowed the musical idea for soloing from "Caldonia" by Louis Jordan and His Tympany Five (1945).	G
	Willow Tree Blues D7VB 1038/Vic 22-2623			G
			Alcohol Blues D7VB 1039/Vic 22-2893 A variation of "Shannon Street Blues" by Sonny Boy himself (6/17/38).	G

11/12 (Wed)/1947 Chicago Sonny Boy Williamson, v; acc. own h Blind John Davis, p Big Bill Broonzy, g Ransom Knowling, b Judge Riley, d	Little Girl D7VB 1149/Vic 22-0021, 50-0005			G
	Blues about My Baby D7VB 11 1150/Vic 22-0001			
			No Friend Blues D7VB 1151/RCA (F) NL 90027 Based on the well-circulated melody that appeared in "Four O'clock Blues" by Johnny Dunn's Original Jazz Hounds (1922),"Four O'clock Blues" by Original Memphis Five (1923), "Four O'clock Blues" by Skip James (v, g) (1931), "Georgia Bound" by Blind Blake (v, g) (1929), "Midnight Hour Blues" by Leroy Carr (v, p) (1932), "From Four until Late" by Robert Johnson (v, g) (1937).	G
	I Love You for Myself D7VB 1152/Vic 22-0046, 50-0030			G
			Bring another Half a Pint D7VB 1153/Vic 22-0021, 50-0005 ***Fast swing arrangement** A variation of "Sloppy Drunk Blues" by Sonny Boy himself on 7/2/1941. The composition was first recorded by Lucille Bogan in 1930. Sonny Boy referred to "Sloppy Drunk Blues" by Leroy Carr (v, p) with Scrapper Blackwell (g) (1930).	G
			Southern Dream D7VB 1154/Vic 22-0046, 50-0030 ***Fast swing arrangement** A variation of "She Was a Dreamer" by Sonny Boy himself on 7/2/1941. The original source is "Little Laura Blues" by Sleepy John Estes on 9/24/1941.	G
		Rub a Dub D7VB 1155, Vic 20-347 **Hokum influence**		G
			Better Cut That Out D7VB 1156/Vic 20-3218 ***Fast swing arrangement** A cover of Big Bill Broonzy's record in 1940.	G

John Lee "Sonny Boy" Williamson's Session Work from 1937 to 1947

Date, place, and personnel	Matrix	Song titles (notes)	Original release
5/5 (Wed)/1937 **Leland Hotel, Aurora, IL** **Robert Lee McCoy, v/g** Sonny Boy Williamson, h Joe Williams, g	 07655-1	*Sonny Boy had a leader session prior to McCoy on the same date: 07649-1 – 07654-1. Tough Luck	 BB B7115
	- - -	*McCoy recorded three songs without Sonny Boy for this session.	- - -
	07659-1 07660-1	Prowling Night-Hawk Sweet Pepper Mama	BB B6995 BB B7090
Joe Williams as Big Joe, **v/g** Sonny Boy Williamson, h Robert Lee McCoy, g	07661-1 07662-1 07663-1 07664-1	I Know You Gonna Miss Me Rootin' Ground Hog Brother James I Won't Be in Hard Luck No More	BB B7022 BB B7065 BB B7022 BB B7065
11/11 (Thu)/1937 **Leland Hotel, Aurora, IL** **Robert Lee McCoy, v/g** Poss. Walter Davis, p-1 Henry Townsend, g-2 Joe Williams, g Sonny Boy Williamson, h	 016526-1 016527-1 016528-1 016529-1 016530-1 016531-1 016532-1 016533-1	*Sonny Boy had a leader session prior to McCoy on the same date: 016518-1 – 016525-1. Danger Blues-1 My Friend Has Forsaken Me-1 Mean Black Cat-1 Brickyard-1 Mamie Lee-1 Take It Easy Baby I Have Spent My Bonus-2 CNA-2	 BB unissued BB B7416 BB B7303 BB B7416 BB B7386 BB B7386 BB B7303 BB B7440, MW M7499
Henry Townsend, v/g Poss. Walter Davis, p Robert Lee McCoy, g Sonny Boy Williamson, h	016534-1 016535-1 016536-1 016537-1	Lose Your Man All I've Got's Gone A Ramblin' Mind Now I Stay Away	BB B7453 BB B7474 BB B7474 BB B7453
3/13 (Sun)/1938 **Leland Hotel, Aurora, IL** **Elijah Jones, v/g** Sonny Boy Williamson, h Yank Rachell, md/v/interjections-1	 - -	*Sonny Boy had a leader session prior to Jones on the same date: 020110-1 – 020119-1. Jones recorded two songs without Sonny Boy.	 - -
	020122-1 020123-1 020124-1 020125-1	Only Boy Child Lonesome Man Mean Actin' Mama Stuff Stomp-1	BB B7565 BB B7655 BB B7616 BB B7526, MW M7500
Yank Rachell, v/md-1, g-2 Elijah Jones, g-3 Sonny Boy Williamson, h Unknown, 2nd v-4	020126-1 020127-1 020128-1 020129-1	J. L. Dairy Blues-1, 3 Rachel Blues-1 Lake Michigan Blues-1, 3 I'm Wild and Crazy as Can Be-2, 4	BB 7525 BB 7525 BB 7602 BB 7602, MW M7498

6/17 (Fri)/1938 Leland Hotel, Aurora, IL Yank Rachell, v/md Sonny Boy Williamson, h		*Sonny Boy had a leader session prior to Rachell on the same date: 020842-1 – 020849-1.	
Joe Williams, g	020850-1 020851-1 020852-1 020853-1	When You Feel Down and Out Texas Tommy It's All Over My Mind Got Bad	BB B7731 BB B7731 BB B7694 BB B7694
Joe Williams, v/g Sonny Boy Williamson, h Yank Rachell, md/sp	-	Williams recorded two songs without Sonny Boy for this session.	-
	020855-1 020856-1 -	Peach Orchard Mama Haven't Seen No Whiskey	BB B7770 BB B7719 -
12/17 (Sat)/1938 Leland Hotel, Aurora, IL Speckled Red, v/p Sonny Boy Williamson, h Willie Hatcher, md Robert Lee McCoy, g	030847-1	*Speckled Red recorded nine songs without Sonny Boy: 030838-1 – 030846-1. You Got to Fix It *Followed by Sonny Boy's leader session: 030848-1 – 030857-1.	BB B8036, MW M7917
Robert Lee McCoy as Rambling Bob, v/g Sonny Boy Williamson, h/sp-1 Speckled Red, p		*McCoy recorded four songs without Sonny Boy prior to the following cuts: 030858-1 – 030861-1.	
	030862-1	Next Door Neighbor-1	BB B8059, MW M7908
	030863-1	Big Apple Blues	BB B7987, MW M7910
	030864-1	Freight Train Blues	BB B8067, MW M7907
	030865-1	Good Gamblin'	BB B8059, MW M7908

4/3 (Thu)/1941 Chicago Yank Rachell, v/g Sonny Boy Williamson, h/sp-1/v-2 William Mitchell, imb Washboard Sam, wb Unknown, sp-3	064104-1 064105-1 064106-1 064107-1 064108-1 064109-1 064110-1 064111-1	Hobo Blues-1 It Seems Like a Dream-2 Army Man Blues 38 Pistol Blues-1, 3 Worried Blues Biscuit Baking Woman Insurance Man Blues Up North Blues (There's a Reason)-1	BB B8768 BB B8732 BB B8840 BB B8732, Vi 20-2995 BB B8440 BB B8768 BB B8796 BB B8796
		*Sonny Boy's leader session was held on the following day (4/4/1941): 064019-1 – 064026-1.	
12/11 (Thu)/1941 Chicago Yank Rachell, v/g Sonny Boy Williamson, h/sp-1 Alfred Elkins, imb Washboard Sam, wb	070470-1 070471-1 070472-1 070473-1 070474-1 070475-1 070476-1 070477-1	Yellow Yam Blues Tappin' That Thing Rainy Day Blues Peach Tree Blues She Loves Who She Please Bye Bye Blues Loudella Blues-1 Katy Lee Blues	BB B8951 BB B8951, Vi 20-2955 BB B8993 BB B9033 BB B9033 BB 34-0715 BB B8993 BB 34-0715
		* Sonny Boy had his leader session on the same date: 070143-1 – 070148-1.	
12/12 (Fri)/1941 Chicago Big Joe Williams, v/g Sonny Boy Williamson, h Alfred Elkins, imb	070482-1 070483-1 070484-1 070485-1 070486-1 070487-1	Throw a Boogie Woogie North Wind Blues Please Don't Go Highway 49 Someday Baby Break 'Em On Down	BB unissued BB (Eu) NL90302 (LP) BB unissued BB (Eu) NL90302 (LP) BB B8969 BB B9025 BB B9025 BB B8969

Musicians' Union Strike: 8/1/1942 to 11/11/1944

7/12 (Thu)/1945	DA AB 354	Drop Down Blues	RCA (F) FXM1 7323
Chicago			
Big Joe Williams, v/g	DA AB 355	Somebody's Been Worryin'	Bb 34-0739
Sonny Boy Williamson, h			
Armand "Jump" Jackson, d	DA AB 356	Wanita	RCA (F) FXM1 7323
	DA AB 357	Vitamin A	Bb 34-0739
7/22 (Tue)/1947	CCO 4833	Baby Please Don't Go	Co 37945, 30099
Chicago	CCO 4833-NG	Baby Please Don't Go	CO CK 47911 [CD]
Big Joe Williams, v/g			
Sonny Boy Williamson, h	CCO 4834	Stack of Dollars	Co 38055, 30107
Ransom Knowling, b	CCO 4835	Mellow Apples	Co 38055, 30107
Judge Riley, d	CCO 4836	Wild Cow Moan	Co 37945, 30099
12/18 (Thu)/1947	CCO 4942	P Vine Blues	Co 30191
Big Joe Williams, v/g	CCO 4943	Bad and Weak-Hearted Blues	Epic EG 37318
Sonny Boy Williamson, h	CCO 4944	King Biscuit Stomp	Co 30129
Ransom Knowling, b	CCO 4945	I'm a Highway Man	Co 30191
Judge Riley, d	CCO 4946	Banta Rooster Blues	Co 38190, 30119
	CCO 4947	Mean Stepfather Blues	Epic EG 37318
	CCO 4948	House Lady Blues	Co 38190, 30119
	CCO 4949	Don't You Leave Me Here	Co C 46215

NOTES

INTRODUCTION

1. Bob Koester, interview by the author, Chicago, July 11, 2011.

2. Lawrence Hoffman, "The Blues Harp," *Living Blues*, no. 99 (September/October 1991): 31.

3. http://us.playhohner.com/news/video-series-hohner-masters-of-the-har-monica (accessed January 29, 2014).

4. Bob Koester was born in Wichita, Kansas, in 1932. He grew up in the midst of the swing jazz craze. He collected and traded jazz records when he was a high school student. While studying at St. Louis University, he started a mail-order record sales service from his dormitory room. He soon opened a record store in St. Louis with his record collector friend Ron Fister. After splitting from his partner, Koester founded Delmar Records (which later changed to Delmark Records) and recorded traditional jazz and blues musicians. In 1958, Koester moved to Chicago. The next year he purchased Seymour's Jazz Mart in the Roosevelt University Building and named it Jazz Record Mart. The store was located at 27 East Illinois Street for a long time, but it was closed in February 2016.

I. LEARNING THE BLUES

1. Department of Commerce, Bureau of the Census, Thirteenth Census of the United States Taken in the Year 1910: Vol. III, Population 1910, Nebraska-Wyoming, Alaska, Hawaii, and Porto Rico, reports by States, with Statistics for

Counties, Cities and Other Civil Divisions, director E. Dana Durand, Wm. J. Harris (Washington, DC: Department of Commerce, 1913), 755.

2. Interstate Directory Co., *Jackson and Bemis, Tennessee City Directory 1939–1940*, 1st ed. (Parsons, KS: Interstate Directory Co., 1939), 2.

3. According to the social security index, her name is spelled "Nancie," while most other sources including the headstone of her grave and marriage licenses read "Nancy."

4. Emma Bruce Ross, "Society/Entertainment—around the Town: 'I Knew "Sonny Boy,"'" *Metro Forum*, December 20–27, 1990–January 2, 1991, 6. Ross later became Nancy's family member. Willie Utley, Nancys second husband, died in the service during World War II. Nancy remarried Mack Reid, who was Ross's relative. Through this connection, as a preteen Emma got to know Nancy.

5. Ibid.

6. State of Tennessee, Madison County, marriage license, Rafe Williamson and Nancy Utley, June 21, 1913.

7. Mary S. Reed, "He Lived and Died the Blues: Jackson's Sonny Boy Took His Music to the Top," *Jackson Sun*, November 12, 1989, 1C.

8. State of Tennessee, Madison County, marriage license, Willie Utley and Nancy Williamson, June 10, 1918.

9. Thomas W. Utley, Fred Utley, Mary Lou Utley, Linda Utley King, and Michael Baker, interview by Jim O'Neal, Jackson, Tennessee, January 30, 1997.

10. Ross, "Society/Entertainment," 6.

11. Thomas W. Utley and Fred Utley, interview by Michael Baker, Jackson, Tennessee, January 19, 1992.

12. Thomas W. Utley, Fred Utley, Mary Lou Utley, Linda Utley King, and Michael Baker, interview by Jim O'Neal, January 30, 1997.

13. Lawrence Hoffman, "The Blues Harp," *Living Blues*, no. 99 (September/October 1991): 24.

14. Kotez and Mie Senoo, *Blues Harmonica Yokubari Guide* [Blues Harmonica Greedy Guide] (Tokyo: P-Vine Books, 2012), 3.

15. Aaron F. Tatum, "'Sonny Boy' Lived, Played the Blues with Harmonica," *Independent Appeal*, November 8, 1990, 3A.

16. Ibid.

17. Linda T. Wynn. "John Lee 'Sonny Boy' Williamson: Blues Innovator," *Courier* 29, no. 2 (February 1991): 4.

18. Thomas W. Utley and Fred Utley, interview by Michael Baker, January 19, 1992.

19. Thomas W. Utley, Fred Utley, Mary Lou Utley, Linda Utley King, and Michael Baker, interview by Jim O'Neal, January 30, 1997.

20. Ibid.

21. Thomas W. Utley, Fred Utley, Mary Lou Utley, Linda Utley King, and Michael Baker, interview by Jim O'Neal, January 30, 1997.

22. Ibid. The name of Sonny Boy's guitarist friend is unidentifiable.

23. Ross, "Society/Entertainment," 6.

24. Thomas W. Utley and Fred Utley, interview by Michael Baker, January 19, 1992.

25. Chris Millar and Mike Rainsford, "We Were Bad to the Bone! Homesick James Interviewed," *Blues and Rhythm, the Gospel Truth*, no. 95 (January 1995): 6.

26. Thomas W. Utley, Fred Utley, Mary Lou Utley, Linda Utley King, and Michael Baker, interview by Jim O'Neal, January 30, 1997.

27. According to the headstone of his grave, Estes was born in 1899, but his birth year varies in different sources. One source says 1900, and another says 1904.

28. Yank Rachell claimed he wrote "Divin' Duck Blues," but he preferred not to sing: "I'd write songs and give them to John 'cause I usually didn't like to sing." Steve Cushing, Pete Crawford, and Rich DelGrosso, "James 'Yank' Rachell," *Living Blues*, no. 79 (March/April 1988): 16.

29. Barry Lee Pearson, "Sleepy John Estes," in *All Music Guide to the Blues: The Expert's Guide to the Best Blues Recordings*, ed. Michael Erlewine, Vladimir Bogdanov, Chris Woodstra, and Cub Koda (San Francisco: Miller Freeman, 1996), 137. Another source says he got this nickname because of his propensity to take naps. Robert Santelli, *The Big Book of Blues: A Biographical Encyclopedia* (New York: Penguin, 1993; rep. 2001), 160. Citation is from the 2001 edition.

30. Richard Congress, *Blues Mandolin Man: The Life and Music of Yank Rachell* (Jackson: University Press of Mississippi, 2001), 17–20.

31. Barry Lee Pearson and Bill McCulloch, *Robert Johnson: Lost and Found* (Urbana: University of Illinois Press, 2003), 75. Newbern also mentored Sleepy John Estes. Jason Ankeny, "Hambone Willie Newbern," in *All Music Guide to the Blues: The Expert's Guide to the Best Blues Recordings*, ed. Michael Erlewine, Vladimir Bogdanov, Chris Woodstra, and Cub Koda (San Francisco: Miller Freeman, 1996), 336.

32. Congress, *Blues Mandolin Man*, 25.

33. Steve Cushing, *Blues before Sunrise: The Radio Interviews* (Urbana: University of Illinois Press, 2010), 9.

34. Congress, *Blues Mandolin Man*, 41.

35. T. W. said, "He [Sonny Boy] farmed until he moved from Jackson." Thomas W. Utley, Fred Utley, Mary Lou Utley, Linda Utley King, and Michael Baker, interview by Jim O'Neal, January 30, 1997.

36. Their first session is dated July 9, 1935, in Chicago, and they had another session about a week after, July 17. For these sessions, they made "Down South Blues," "Someday Baby," "Drop Down Mama," and three other cuts. Robert M. W. Dixon, John Godrich, and Howard Rye, *Blues and Gospel Records, 1890–1943*, 4th ed. (Oxford: Clarendon Press, 1997), 247.

37. Congress, *Blues Mandolin Man*, 43.

38. Ibid., 43.

39. Ibid.

40. Ibid., 42.

41. Cushing, Crawford, and DelGrosso, "James 'Yank' Rachell," 16.

42. Thomas W. Utley, Fred Utley, Mary Lou Utley, Linda Utley King, and Michael Baker, interview by Jim O'Neal, January 30, 1997. Sleepy John recorded as early as 1929.

43. David Evans, *Big Road Blues: Tradition and Creativity in Folk Blues* (Berkeley: University of California Press, 1982), 131.

44. Other biographical songs by Sleepy John are built around, for example, a local bootlegger ("Liquor Store Blues," 1938), fire department ("Fire Department Blues," 1938), and lawyer ("Lawyer Clark Blues," 1941).

45. Bob Riesman, *I Feel So Good: The Life and Times of Big Bill Broonzy* (Chicago: University of Chicago Press, 2011), 143.

46. Thomas W. Utley and Fred Utley, interview by Michael Baker, January 19, 1992.

47. Evans, *Big Road Blues*, 131.

48. Thomas W. Utley, Fred Utley, Mary Lou Utley, Linda Utley King, and Michael Baker, interview by Jim O'Neal, January 30, 1997.

49. "Blues in the Mississippi Night," *American Folk-Blues Train: Alan Lomax Field and Studio Recordings* [CD], notes by Neil Slaven (London: Castle Music/Sanctuary Records, CMETD 648, 2003). Chris Smith, "A Memory of Sonny Boy," *Folk Roots*, no. 60 (June 1988): 31.

50. Dave Helland, "A Naptown Blues Party," *Living Blues*, no. 13 (Summer 1973): 7.

51. Cushing, Crawford, and DelGrosso, "James 'Yank' Rachell," 16.

52. Thomas W. Utley, Fred Utley, Mary Lou Utley, Linda Utley King, and Michael Baker, interview by Jim O'Neal, January 30, 1997. T. W. meant "He wrote or made."

53. Hoffman, "The Blues Harp," 27–28. Hoffman included Jaybird Coleman in this list, but there is no evidence that Coleman performed in Memphis.

54. Thomas W. Utley, Fred Utley, Mary Lou Utley, Linda Utley King, and Michael Baker, interview by Jim O'Neal, January 30, 1997.

55. Ibid.

56. It seems that cross harp became a common technique by 1928 in the blues community. In 1927, Jaybird Coleman from Gainesville, Alabama, recorded six-teen sides, including "Mill Log Blues," "Boll Weevil," "Man Trouble Blues," and "My Jelly Blues" (accompaniment for vocalist Bertha Ross), on all of which he plays in cross harp position. In the following years, more players used cross harp technique—"Just It" by William McCoy (1928), "Lost Boy Blues" by Palmer McAbee (1928), "Touch Me Light Mama" by George "Bullet" Williams (1928), "Davidson County Blues" by Deford Bailey (1928), "Medley of Blues" by Freeman Stowers (1929), "The Old Folks Started It (Take 1 and 2)" by Minnie Wallace and Will Shade (1929), "How Long How Long" by Jed Daven-port (1929), "Don't Mistreat Your Good Boy Friend" by the Bubbling Over Five (1929), "Chicksaw Special" by Noah Lewis (1929), and "Pennsylvania Woman Blues (Part 1)" by Six Cylinder Smith (1929).

57. Kip Lornell and Jim O'Neal, "Sleepy John Estes and Hammie Nixon," in *The Voice of the Blues*, ed. Jim O'Neal and Amy van Singel (New York: Rout-ledge, 2002), 50. Originally published as "*Living Blues* Interview: Hammie Nix-on and Sleepy John Estes," *Living Blues*, no. 19 (January/February 1975): 13–19. Citations are from the Routledge edition. By choking, the instrument can pro-duce pitches that are not regularly available in certain ranges. The third hole draw can produce the deepest bend, one and a half steps below; for example, "B" on a C harmonica can be bent to A-flat.

58. Hoffman, "The Blues Harp," 29.

59. Joe Filisko, interview by the author, Chicago, July 11, 2011.

2. REACHING NEW HEIGHTS

1. Alistair Findlay, "The Real St. Louis Blues," *Jazz Journal International* 36, no. 5 (1983): 13.

2. Robert Santelli, *The Big Book of Blues: A Biographical Encyclopedia* (New York: Penguin, 1993), 248–49.

3. *St. Louis 1927–1933* [CD], notes by Paul Garon (Vienna, Austria: Docu-ment Records, DOCD-5181), n.p.

4. Blues mandolin player Al Miller was also from St. Louis.

5. Findlay, "The Real St. Louis Blues," 13.

6. Robert Palmer, *Deep Blues* (New York: Viking, 1981; reprint New York: Penguin, 1982), 135. Citations are from the Penguin edition.

7. Bob Koester, the owner of Chicago-based Delmark Records and Jazz Record Mart, talked about Lester Melrose's music publishing operation. "Most of his [Melrose's] artists, he gave one-third of the money, instead of half the money from royalties. A lot of people criticize that. The recent book on Big Bill

[Broonzy] said Big Bill only got a fourth (25%). When I found out, I could hardly believe it, because Big Bill wasn't an idiot. . . . People have accused Melrose of being such a bastard and everything. But how much money did a thirty-five-cent record pay in royalties? I am convinced they did not pay two cents per side, 'cause a thirty-five-cent record was sold to a retail store for twenty-two cents, something like that. And it's gonna cost about a dime or so to press it. With a label, maybe another penny or two. You don't have enough room [for royalties]. And you do pay the artists something—I think with a union scale probably in those days." Bob Koester, interview by the author, Chicago, July 11, 2011. Blues historian David Evans has different insights: "The 25% figure is derived as follows. The royalty is split 50/50 between the publisher and the songwriter(s), as was standard practice of the time. If the writer was musically illiterate (as were most blues and country music songwriters), the publisher would 'write down' the song (or more often, pay a scribe to do so) for the purpose of creating a lead sheet for copyright registration (as required by law). For this service the publisher could claim to be a co-author and claim half of the songwriter's share. Thus Melrose would get 75% of the royalty. This was standard practice at the time." David Evans, notes for Mitsutoshi Inaba's manuscript, 2015.

8. Inaba Mitsutoshi, *Willie Dixon: Preacher of the Blues* (Lanham, MD: Scarecrow Press, 2011), 28.

9. Walter Davis, *M&O Blues* [CD], notes by Hitoshi Koide (Tokyo: P-Vine Records, PCD 20083, 2011).

10. Steve Cushing, *Blues before Sunrise: The Radio Interviews* (Urbana: University of Illinois Press, 2010), 9.

11. Thomas Moon, "The Verdict on Big Joe Williams," *Blues Access*, no. 33 (Spring 1998): 26.

12. "Oberstein, Eli and Maurice," *Welcome to Donald Clarke's Music Box: Donald's Encyclopedia of Popular Music*, www.donaldclarkemusicbox.com/encyclopedia/detail.php?s=2735 (accessed December 19, 2013).

13. Ibid.

14. Billy Boy Arnold, interview by the author, Chicago, June 24, 2011. Billy Boy's meeting with Sonny Boy is detailed in chapter 5.

15. *Okeh Chicago Blues* [CD], notes by Jim O'Neal (New York: Epic/Columbia Records, EG 37318, 1982), 16.

16. State of Tennessee, Madison County, marriage license, John Lee Williamson and Sallie Lee Hunt, June 14, 1933.

17. Thomas W. Utley, Mary Lou Utley, Fred Utley, Linda Utley King, and Michael Baker, interview by Jim O'Neal, Jackson, Tennessee, January 30, 1997.

18. State of Tennessee, Madison County, Chancery Court Minute Book, 40 (1937–1938), minutes December term, January 21, 1937, 23. The record contin-

ues: "It is therefore ordered, adjudged and decreed by the Court, that the bonds of matrimony now subsisting between the complainant and defendant, be and the same are hereby perpetually dissolved and for nothing held, and the complainant granted an absolute divorce from the defendant as prayed for in his bill, and restored to all the rights and privileges of an unmarried person." Ibid.

19. Thomas W. Utley, Mary Lou Utley, Fred Utley, Linda Utley King, and Michael Baker, interview by Jim O'Neal, January 30, 1997.

20. Richard Congress, *Blues Mandolin Man: The Life and Music of Yank Rachell* (Jackson: University Press of Mississippi, 2001), 98.

21. Cushing, *Blues before Sunrise*, 9. In his biography, Yank said, "Nineteen thirty-eight I went to Chicago to record. Lester Melrose used to have Walter Davis come down to the country and pick us up, we music boys, and we'd go and record for him. Him, Sonny Boy, Big Joe Williams, and I would go record together." Congress, *Blues Mandolin Man*, 46.

22. Steve Cushing, Pete Crawford, and Rich DelGrosso, "James 'Yank' Rachell," *Living Blues*, no. 79 (March/April 1988): 18.

23. Mary S. Reed, "He Lived and Died the Blues: Jackson's Sonny Boy Took His Music to the Top," *Jackson Sun*, November 12, 1989, 2C.

24. Dave Clark, "Green Dumps Band to Produce Show," *DownBeat*, November 15, 1941, 13. This article is another proof that Sonny Boy was likely to have a base in Jackson until the early 1940s. The Clark article will be discussed later in the chapter.

25. Eric Schwartz, "Aurora Happy about Its Blues History," *Beacon News*, February 22, 1997, n.p. Currently this building is Fox Island Place Apartments.

26. Robert M. W. Dixon, John Godrich, and Howard Rye, *Blues and Gospel Records, 1890–1943*, 4th ed. (Oxford: Clarendon Press, 1997), 888–89, 1005.

27. Olivia Wu, "'Nice Little Festival' to Celebrate Aurora's Place in Blues History," *Metro*, February 12, 1997, 14. Wu also wrote that possibly the RCA studios in Chicago were booked, but this theory is unlikely, because Sonny Boy had four other sessions at the Leland Hotel until 1938. In addition, there were other studios in Chicago even if the RCA studios were booked.

28. Dixon, Godrich, and Rye, *Blues and Gospel Records, 1890–1943*, 1044.

29. Cushing, Crawford, and DelGrosso, "James 'Yank' Rachell," 18.

30. Not much is known about Alfred Lewis, except he recorded "Mississippi Swamp Moan" and "Friday Moan Blues" in Chicago on May 5, 1930, for Vocalion label. He also recorded "Easy Rider's Blues" in the same session, but this side was unissued. It is assumed that Lewis was from Mississippi because of the song title.

31. Sonny Terry was born in Greensboro, Georgia, in 1911, and died in Mineola, New York, in 1986. He became blind from separate accidents when he was a teen. He played harmonica on the streets and teamed up with Blind Boy Fuller,

Piedmont blues guitarist/vocalist. They made their first recordings in 1937 for Vocalion. In Sonny Terry's first solo recording "Mountain Blues," made in 1938, he switches harmonica and "whoopin'" (a vocal style with high shrill sounds). Sonny Boy's half brother T. W. told Jim O'Neal that Terry was one of the artists Sonny Boy was listening to. Thomas W. Utley, Mary Lou Utley, Fred Utley, Linda Utley King, and Michael Baker, interview by Jim O'Neal, January 30, 1997.

32. Lawrence Hoffman, "The Blues Harp," *Living Blues*, no. 99 (September/October 1991): 29. Hoffman also writes, "He [Sonny Boy Williamson] used formula like fills and cadence figures to frame his lines, and switched freely from a chordally dominated style to a predominantly single-note style with all possible graduations" (Ibid., 31).

33. Joe Filisko, interview by the author, Chicago, July 11, 2011.

34. Cushing, *Blues before Sunrise*, 73.

35. Bob Riesman, *I Feel So Good: The Life and Times of Big Bill Broonzy* (Chicago: University of Chicago Press, 2011), 143.

36. Kim Field writes, "he [Sonny Boy] could turn a catchy phrase; his warm, personable singing . . . was absolutely credible." Kim Field, *Harmonicas, Harps, and Heavy Breathers: The Evolution of the People's Instrument* (New York: Fireside/Simon & Schuster, 1993), 166.

37. David Evans, "John Lee 'Sonny Boy' Williamson," in *Creating Traditions, Expanding Horizons: A History of Tennessee Arts*, ed. C. Van West and M. D. Binnicker (Knoxville: University of Tennessee Press, 2004), 424.

38. Jim O'Neal and Amy van Singel, "Jimmy Reed," in *The Voice of the Blues: Classic Interviews from* Living Blues *Magazine*, ed. Jim O'Neal and Amy van Singel (New York; London: Routledge, 2002), 308.

39. For "Blue Bird Blues," Derrick Stewart-Baxter writes, "Williamson pulls out all the stops, cutting short words, or running them into the next line, producing tremendous rhythmic excitement." Derrick Stewart-Baxter, "Blues and News from *Blues Unlimited*: The Two Sonny Boy Williamsons: Part 1," *Jazz Journal* 18, no. 5 (May 1965): 17.

40. Filisko, interview by the author, July 11, 2011.

41. Thomas W. Utley and Fred Utley, interview by Michael Baker, Jackson, Tennessee, January 19, 1992.

42. Not much is known about Jed Davenport, since nobody remembers him, and he was not listed in the Memphis area directories from 1925 to 1940. Blues historian Bengt Olsson wrote that Davenport probably came from northern Mississippi and started his band around the time when the popularity of jug band music reached its peak in 1930. He was a friend of Will Shade. Davenport's band, the Beale Street Jug Band, consisted of violin, guitar, and jug, with Jed himself supposedly on harmonica. One of their recordings also featured a man-

dolin player. Davenport seems to have been a multi-instrumentalist—he played jug and trumpet as well as harmonica, but it is not confirmed that Davenport played any of these instruments. Possibly his name is a pseudonym. Davenport and Sonny Boy were acquaintances through their common friend, "Jackson" Joe Williams from Jackson or Big Joe Williams from Crawford, Mississippi. Bengt Olsson, *Memphis Blues and Jug Bands* (London: Studio Vista, 1970), 50–51.

43. Yank Rachell's "Sugar Farm Blues" was released under Poor Jim with Dan Jackson. Yank recorded "Sweet Mama" during Sleepy John Estes's leader session on May 30, 1930. Yank took a lead vocal for this cut. Tampa Red recorded "Sugar Mama Blues 1" and "Sugar Mama Blues 2" on March 23, 1934.

44. Willie Dixon, with Don Snowden, *I Am the Blues: The Willie Dixon Story* (New York: Da Capo, 1989), 62.

45. Field, *Harmonicas, Harps, and Heavy Breathers*, 166.

46. "Similarity to previous hits ensures another hit" was, for example, an important formula for Motown Records in the 1960s—as heard in "I Can't Help Myself (Sugar Pie Honey Bunch)" and "It's the Same Old Song" by the Four Tops. Even the Beatles relied on the same formula in their early days as heard in the similarities between "Please Please Me" and "From Me to You."

47. One may be able to find lyrical association among each stanza of "Jackson Blues" and "Skinny Woman," respectively, on a deep structural level, but they do not appear to be cohesive at least on the visible level.

48. Henry Townsend, as told to Bill Greensmith, *A Blues Life* (Urbana: University of Illinois Press, 1999), 81.

49. Ibid., 86.

50. Charlie Pickett participated as a side guitarist in Sleepy John Estes's sessions in August 1937 and April 1938. In the August 1937 session, he cut his own records "Crazy 'bout My Gal Blues," "Trembling Blues," and "Down the Highway" as well as "Let Me Squeeze Your Lemon" (a variation of "Lemon Squeezing Blues," recorded by Bumble Bee Slim on July 11, 1935, with Hammie Nixon and pianist Lee Brown). Pickett has a very characteristic nasal voice. Dixon, Godrich, and Rye, *Blues and Gospel Records, 1890–1943*, 248, 720.

51. Thomas W. Utley, Fred Utley, Mary Lou Utley, Linda Utley King, and Michael Baker, interview by Jim O'Neal, January 30, 1997.

52. Ibid.

53. Filisko, interview by the author.

54. Ibid.

55. In 1937 (the year of this recording), the Ford line of cars was updated with a major change—the introduction of an entry-level 136 CID V-8 in addition to the popular 212 CID flathead V-8. The model was the company's main product. "1937 Ford," *Wikipedia: The Free Encyclopedia*, http://en.wikipedia.org/wiki/1937_Ford (accessed May 28, 2014).

56. Guido van Rijn writes, "A total of $4.4 billion was spent on highways, roads and streets under the WPA, 38.9 percent of the total outlay, by far the highest percentage. The result of all this work was six hundred thousand miles of roads, 'enough to circle the world twenty-four times,' according to WPA historian Donald S. Howard." Guido van Rijn, *Roosevelt's Blues: African-American Blues and Gospel Songs on FDR* (Jackson: University Press of Mississippi, 1997), 85.

57. State of Tennessee, Madison County, marriage license, John Lee Williamson and Lacey Belle Davidson, November 13, 1937.

58. Billy Boy Arnold said, "She also told me she was 15 years old when Sonny Boy married her." Billy Boy Arnold, "The Last Time I Saw Sonny Boy," *Melody Maker*, November 27, 1971, 28.

59. A third position harp is playing the diatonic harmonica in a key a second above its intended key, for example, playing a C harmonica in the key of D. By doing so, a performer can create a minor chord, such as D-F-A (holes 4, 5, and 6, all draw), a tonic chord of D minor. Sonny Boy plays a B-flat harp in the key of C for "Brickyard" and "Mamie Lee" by McCoy and "CAN" by Henry Townsend, and an F harmonica in the key of G for "Lose Your Man" by Townsend.

60. In *Blues and Gospel Records, 1890–1943*, Joe Williams is listed as the recording personnel for this session instead of Elijah Jones. Dixon, Godrich, and Rye, *Blues and Gospel Records, 1890–1943*, 1044.

61. Thomas W. Utley, Mary Lou Utley, Fred Utley, Linda Utley King, and Michael Baker, interview by Jim O'Neal, January 30, 1997. Sonny Boy sometimes sounds like "Cornelia." Sonny Boy's biographer Wolfgang Lorenz writes, "The name Cornelius Bond is understood not unequivocally but acoustically. The last name could be called even Brnes or Bonds. Also the name of the place where the Miss Cornelius lived could be different." Wolfgang Lorenz, *Bluebird Blues* (Bonn: Moonshine Blues Books, 1986), 144 (translation by the author).

62. Stewart-Baxter, "Blues and News from *Blues Unlimited*: The Two Sonny Boy Williamsons: Part 1," 16.

63. "Kro Ken Know curl" is the name of certain lady hairdo of the day, according to Billy Boy Arnold. Lorenz, *Bluebird Blues*, 93.

64. It has been pointed out that Robert Johnson's "They're Red Hot" is based on "Hittin' the Bottom Stomp" by the Mississippi Juke Band in 1936, but they have nothing in common except for the similar musical structure. Hence, neither of these songs inspired Sonny Boy's "I'm Tired Trucking My Blues Away."

65. Sonny Boy recorded two compositions with the same title "Honey Bee Blues" on June 17, 1938, and July 21, 1939, but they are different songs. As discussed later in the chapter, the 1939 version is a variation of "Bumble Bee" by Memphis Minnie and Kansas Joe in 1930 and "Honey Bee Blues" by Bumble Bee Slim in 1931.

66. Congress, *Blues Mandolin Man*, 43.

67. Ibid., 46.

68. Ibid.

69. Sonny Boy probably means the 1939 Chevrolet Master 85 or Master Deluxe. Both were very popular models along with the Ford V-8, which Sonny Boy sings of in "Project Highway," recorded on November 11, 1937.

70. Congress, *Blues Mandolin Man*, 37.

71. Ron Wynn, "Speckled Red," in *All Music Guide to the Blues: The Definitive Guide to the Blues*, ed. Vladimir Bogdanov, Chris Woodstra, and Stephan Thomas Erlewine, 3rd ed. (San Francisco: Backbeat Books, 2003), 411.

3. WINDY CITY BLUES

1. Interstate Directory Co., *Jackson and Bemis, Tennessee City Directory 1939–1940*, 1st ed. (Parsons, KS: Interstate Directory Co., 1939), 355.

2. Thomas W. Utley and Fred Utley, interview by Michael Baker, Jackson, Tennessee, January 19, 1992.

3. Bob Corritore, Bill Ferris, and Jim O'Neal, "Willie Dixon (Part 1)," *Living Blues*, no. 81 (July–August 1988): 20.

4. The Original Sonny Boy Williamson, *The Original Sonny Boy Williamson: Vol. 1*, notes by Neil Slaven (London: JSP, 7797, 2007), n.p.

5. Thomas W. Utley, Fred Utley, Mary Lou Utley, Linda Utley King, and Michael Baker, interview by Jim O'Neal, Jackson, Tennessee, January 30, 1997.

6. Spivey sings, "When I's [*sic*] upon my feet, I could not walk down the street, for the men lookin' at me from my head to my feet," in her "T. B. Blues" in 1927. The idea of burial is sung in "T. B. Is Killing Me" by Buddy Moss in 1936: "T. B. is Killing me, / And it won't be long before some lonely graveyard I'll be."

7. Paul Oliver writes, "For the blues singer, the singular inspiration of a man who had within his achievements all the drama, the appeal and the invincibility of the traditional Negro ballad hero." Paul Oliver, *Screening the Blues: Aspects of the Blues Tradition*, 1st ed. (London: Cassell, 1968; reprint, New York: Da Capo, 1989), 149. Citations are from the reprint edition.

8. "Jailhouse" (jail house) is one of the oldest subject matters for popular music recordings. Prior to Sonny Boy Williamson, some well-known recordings include "Jail-House Blues" by Bessie Smith (1923), "The Jail House Blues" by Crying Sam Collins (1927), and "In the Jail House Now" by Jimmie Rodgers (1928). After Sonny Boy, Sleepy John Estes with Hammie Nixon recorded "Jailhouse Blues" in 1940, and Lightnin' Hopkins recorded "Jailhouse Blues" in 1962.

9. Thomas W. Utley, Fred Utley, Mary Lou Utley, Linda Utley King, and Michael Baker, interview by Jim O'Neal, January 30, 1997.

10. Other artists who recorded "(Hey) Lawdy Mama" included Bumble Bee Slim in 1935, Count Basie in 1938, and Louis Armstrong and His Hot Seven in 1941. One of the most popular versions was by Andy Kirk and His Twelve Clouds of Joy, featuring the vocalist June Richmond, in 1943.

11. Joe Filisko, interview by the author, Chicago, July 11, 2011.

12. Walter Davis sat out for "Good Gravy," and he offers only quiet comping for "Tell Me Baby." Apparently Big Bill Broonzy is leading the ensemble in these tracks.

13. Thomas W. Utley, Fred Utley, Mary Lou Utley, Linda Utley King, and Michael Baker, interview by Jim O'Neal, January 30, 1997.

14. Ibid.

15. M. H. Orodenker, "Part 3—The *Billboard* Music Popularity Chart, Week Ending May 11, 1944: Folk Record Reviews," *Billboard*, May 20, 1944, 21.

16. Guido van Rijn, *Roosevelt's Blues: African-American Blues and Gospel Songs on FDR* (Jackson: University Press of Mississippi, 1997), 54.

17. Department of Commerce–Bureau of the Census, "The Sixteenth Census of the United States: 1940: Population Schedule, Beloit City, Rock County, Wisconsin" (Washington, DC: Department of Commerce–Bureau of the Census, 1940), sheet number 61-A.

18. Ibid.

19. Dave Clark, "Green Dumps Band to Produce Show," *DownBeat*, November 15, 1941, 13. Dave Clark was also a leader of the musical group Dave Clark's Memphis Band. Big Maybelle (Mabel Louise Smith), who was from Jackson, Tennessee, joined Dave Clark's Memphis Band in 1936 and toured with the all-female International Sweethearts of Rhythm. She then joined Christine Chatman's orchestra as a vocalist and made her first recordings, including "Naptown Boogie," for Decca in 1944.

20. Sonny Boy also recorded "Got the Bottle Up and Gone" in 1937.

21. Filisko, interview by the author, July 11, 2011.

22. Blind John Davis said in an interview, "I arranged so many numbers for the original Sonny Boy, and Lonnie Johnson and Doctor Clayton. I even played piano for Sunnyland Slim." Bob Rusch, "Blind John Davis: Interview," *Cadence*, June 1978, 18. However, it is not clear to what extent Davis had an input for Sonny Boy's recordings. While he has his own distinctive piano style compared to other players'—such as Walter Davis, Speckled Red, and Joshua Altheimer, there is not much difference in arrangement with or without Davis.

23. Rusch, "Blind John Davis," 18.

24. The compositions that Yank Rachell recorded a day before are also in the key of G. "Hobo Blues" and "Biscuit Baking Woman" sound like they are in F-

sharp major in the available CD, but more likely the playback speed is too slow. Probably Sonny Boy only had a C harmonica for these dates.

25. This "Big Apple Blues" has no relation to the song with the same title recorded by Rambling Bob (Robert Lee McCoy) with Sonny Boy on harmonica and Speckled Red on piano in Aurora on December 18, 1939.

26. Sonny Boy's "Mattie Mae Blues" has nothing to do with "Black Mattie Blues" by Sleepy John Estes in 1929.

27. In this song, Sonny Boy uses the first position harmonica (straight harp)— a C instrument for the key of C. He exclusively uses a higher range to produce the chirping sounds of birds.

28. For example, "She Caught the Katy (And Left Me a Mule to Ride)" cowritten by Taj Mahal and Yank Rachell in 1968 and "My Baby She Left Me (She Left Me a Mule to Ride)" by Buddy Guy and Junior Wells in 1970 include the expression, as their titles indicate. The former is included in Taj's album *The Natch'l Blues* (1968), and the latter is in *Buddy Guy and Junior Wells Play the Blues* (1970).

29. "Sloppy Drunk Blues" was premiered by Lucille Bogan in March 1930. Sonny Boy referred to Leroy Carr's version. Both recordings have the similar eight-beat feel.

30. In Sleepy John's version, "now my baby" in the first line is replaced with "little Laura," and "she was a dreamer" in the third line is changed to "little Laura was a dreamer." The rest is almost identical.

31. "She Don't Love Me That Way" and "I'm Tired Trucking My Blues Away" have a verse structure, rhythm, and tempo similar to "You Gotta Have That Thing" by the Picaninny Jug Band. But the lyrics of both songs are Sonny Boy's original.

32. Billy Boy Arnold, "The Last Time I Saw Sonny Boy," *Melody Maker*, November 27, 1971, 28. Tony Glover, Scott Dirks, and Ward Gaines, biographers of Little Walter, write: "[Little] Walter was exposed to more blues harp players than he'd heard before, both firsthand and through the jukeboxes in the local joints. He'd derived much of his early inspiration from the records of John Lee 'Sonny Boy' Williamson, who was hugely popular and influential both in Chicago and throughout the blues-rich southern states from the time of his first recordings in 1937." Tony Glover, Scott Dirks, and Ward Gaines, *Blues with a Feeling: The Little Walter Story* (New York: Routledge, 2002), 16.

33. By the age of eleven or twelve, Walter's harmonica technique was good enough for him to support himself financially. He left Louisiana for Helena, Arkansas, but he soon moved to Memphis. Around 1944, he moved to Chicago and made it his base town. Therefore, his meeting with Sonny Boy probably took place sometime in his Helena or Memphis period.

34. Thomas W. Utley, Fred Utley, Mary Lou Utley, Linda Utley King, and Michael Baker, interview by Jim O'Neal, January 30, 1997.

35. Ibid.

36. All the songs are performed in the key of G. Sonny Boy uses a C harmonica in the second position (cross harp).

37. M. H. Orodenker, "Part 3—The *Billboard* Music Popularity Chart, Week Ending June 29, 1944: Folk Record Reviews," *Billboard*, July 8, 1944, 23. The review continues: "[P]articular emphasis on shouting, even to such an extent where it sometimes becomes impossible to distinguish the wordage. . . . Guitars and harmonicas [*sic*] create raucous rhythmic backgrounds."

38. This recording sounds B-flat probably due to slow playback speed.

4. THE SOUND OF BRONZEVILLE

1. Thomas W. Utley, Fred Utley, Mary Lou Utley, Linda Utley King, and Michael Baker, interview by Jim O'Neal, Jackson, Tennessee, January 30, 1997.

2. Ibid. For example, Tom Fisher writes, "In 1934, Williamson moved to Chicago and was active in the growing blues scene there." Tom Fisher, "Williamson, Sonny Boy I (John Lee Williamson)," in *Encyclopedia of the Blues*, ed. Edward M. Komara (New York: Routledge, 2006), 2:1086.

3. Maren Stange, *Bronzeville: Black Chicago in Pictures, 1941–1943* (New York: New Press, 2003), xiii.

4. Ibid.

5. The remnants of entertainment places exist to this day. Meyers Ace Hardware on East Thirty-Fifth Street is now a Chicago landmark; its building used to be home to the Sunset Café, where artists such as Louis Armstrong, Benny Goodman, and Earl Hines regularly played.

6. Thomas W. Utley, Fred Utley, Mary Lou Utley, Linda Utley King, and Michael Baker, interview by Jim O'Neal, January 30, 1997.

7. "Come on Baby and Take a Walk" is also about drinking. A line in the third verse, "Every morning before breakfast I drink a lil' whiskey from nine to ten," describes serious alcoholism.

8. Derrick Stewart-Baxter points out the same vocal characteristic in his article for *Jazz Journal*. Derrick Stewart-Baxter, "Blues and News from *Blues Unlimited*: The Two Sonny Boy Williamsons: Part 1," *Jazz Journal* 18, no. 5 (May 1965): 16.

9. Wolfgang Lorenz, *Bluebird Blues* (Bonn: Moonshine Blues Books, 1986), 101.

10. "Gulf, Mobile and Ohio Railroad," *Wikipedia: The Free Encyclopedia*, http://en.wikipedia.org/wiki/Gulf,_Mobile_and_Ohio_Railroad (accessed May 1, 2013).

11. All of these patriotic songs are built upon the medium-slow blues pattern.

12. Willie Dixon, with Don Snowden, *I Am the Blues: The Willie Dixon Story* (New York: Da Capo, 1989), 61.

13. Eddie Boyd said, "I played with Sonny Boy from 1941 until he got killed." The Original Sonny Boy Williamson, *The Original Sonny Boy Williamson: The Later Years* [CD], notes by Neil Slaven (London: JSP, 77101, 2008), n.p.

14. Jim O'Neal and Amy van Singel, "Eddie Boyd," in *The Voice of the Blues: Classic Interviews from* Living Blues *Magazine*, ed. Jim O'Neal and Amy van Singel (New York; London: Routledge, 2002), 239.

15. Ibid. This statement supports the theory that Sonny Boy came up with a chordally dominated, loud playing style to fill up musical spaces himself and to compete with a loud instrument of the ensemble.

16. Ibid.

17. Ibid.

18. Ibid.

19. Ibid.

20. Henry Townsend, as told to Bill Greensmith, *A Blues Life* (Urbana: University of Illinois Press, 1999), 90.

21. Ibid., 91. Sonny Boy had an address on 3226 Giles Avenue. He might have had a different address when he united with Henry Townsend. Townsend also said, "I was also living around the corner from Bowtie—Eddie Boyd—and I got acquainted with him." Ibid.

22. Dawayne Gilley and Brenda Haskins, "Henry Townsend," *Living Blues*, no. 164 (July/August 2008): 25.

23. Sonny Boy's "Stop Breaking Down" is loosely related to Robert Johnson's recording with the same title in 1937. The refrain "Stop breaking down, baby please stop breaking down" in Sonny Boy's version sounds similar to Johnson's refrain, though there are no similarities in other sections.

24. M. H. Orodenker, "Part 4—The *Billboard* Music Popularity Chart, Week Ending May 23, 1946: Reviews of New Records," *Billboard*, June 15, 1946, 32.

25. Eddie Boyd said in an interview for *Living Blues*, "The first day I went to school, Muddy and I went to school the same day, and we was going to school together until I left home, and we would play together mostly every day and fight every day!" O'Neal and van Singel, "Eddie Boyd," 229.

26. Ibid., 183.

27. Ibid., 177.

28. Ibid., 178.

29. Ibid., 177.

30. Ibid., 172.

31. Tom Wheeler, "Muddy Waters and Johnny Winter," in *Rollin' and Tumblin': The Postwar Blues Guitarists*, ed. Jas Obrecht (San Francisco: Miller Freeman, 2000), 411.

32. Within a few weeks, Barnes also played electric guitar on sessions with Hattie Bolton, Blind John Davis, Jazz Gillum, Merline Johnson, and others.

33. On the same day (December 16, 1938), Casey Bill Weldon recorded four songs, including "I Believe You Are Cheatin' on Me," with an amplified steel guitar. From the successive matrix numbers—from 03084-1 through 030811—it is certain that they had an amplifier in the room they used as a studio. Robert M. W. Dixon, John Godrich, and Howard Rye, *Blues and Gospel Records, 1890–1943*, 4th ed. (Oxford: Clarendon Press, 1997), 889, 1005. Sleepy John Estes once said, "Me and Hammie (Nixon) were going down the street here at 51st and State, and we were drunk, and we hadn't been used to no electric guitar then. And he [Tampa Red] opened that thing up!" Vincent Cortese, "Tampa Red: Long Live the Guitar Wizard," *Blues Revue Quarterly*, no. 6 (Fall 1992): 22.

34. Larry Hoffman, "Robert Lockwood Jr. Interview," *Living Blues*, no. 121 (1995): 18.

35. Jim O'Neal and Amy van Singel, "Muddy Waters," in *The Voice of the Blues: Classic Interviews from* Living Blues *Magazine*, ed. Jim O'Neal and Amy van Singel (New York; London: Routledge, 2002), 172.

36. Ibid., 171.

37. Jim O'Neal, Steve Wisner, and David Nelson, "Snooky Pryor: I Started the Big Noise around Chicago," *Living Blues*, no. 123 (September/October 1995): 13.

38. Townsend, *A Blues Life*, 91. "Jew Town"/Maxwell Street Market was located from Halsted Street to Sixteenth Street in Bronzeville, the South Side of Chicago. The area was famous for blues musicians—including Big Bill Broonzy, Muddy Waters, Howlin' Wolf, and Bo Diddley, as well as others mentioned in the text—performing in the open-air flea market.

39. Ibid., 81.

40. Dixon, with Snowden, *I Am the Blues*, 62.

41. Bob Koester, interview by the author, Chicago, July 11, 2011.

42. Joe Filisko, interview by the author, Chicago, July 11, 2011.

43. Thomas W. Utley, Fred Utley, Mary Lou Utley, Linda Utley King, and Michael Baker, interview by Jim O'Neal, January 30, 1997.

44. Ibid.

45. When the union had a strike, Sonny Boy could not record because his sidemen were union members, even though he did not belong to the union.

46. Williamson, *The Later Years*, n.p. Eddie Boyd also said, "Sonny Boy was a harmonica player and the Union didn't consider him to be a musician, so he wasn't in the Union. So I played behind Sonny Boy and at that time he was playing the Triangle Inn on 14th and Blues Island. . . . It was much better than any job in the city, and at the time I was making $60 a week and so was Sonny Boy." Ibid.

47. "Wright Music Shoppe," *Chicago Defender*, February 23, 1946, 26.

48. *Chicago Defender*, March 2, 1946, 26. Snooky Pryor said, "Purple Cat" was Sonny Boy's regular venue. "Yeah, Sonny Boy was here then. . . . But when I came from overseas . . . in 1945, I was stationed up here at Fort Sheridan, and Sonny Boy, he was playin' at this place called the Purple Cat." O'Neal, Wisner, and Nelson, "Snooky Pryor," 10. Therefore, this "Sonny Boy Williams" is more likely not Enoch Williams, known as "Sonny Boy" Williams on Decca Records.

49. The soloist for "Mean Old Highway" is Big Bill Broonzy.

50. *Billboard*, "Record Reviews," *Billboard*, April 5, 1947, 122.

51. *Chicago Defender*, January 14, 1947, 26. The flip side of "Shake the Boogie" was "Mean Old Highway." The review reads: "It's sad, sad story of 'That Mean Old Highway' where Sonny Boy is looking for his lost love, on the flipover [*sic*]. The sentiments are bitterly tearful and the rhythm has all that irresistible Sonny Boy swing." Ibid.

52. Joel Whitburn, Billboard *Top R&B Singles 1942–1999* (Menomonee Falls, WI: Record Research Inc., 2000), 483.

53. Alan Lomax, *The Land Where the Blues Began* (New York: Pantheon, 1993), 459.

54. Ibid.

55. "Blues in the Mississippi Night," *American Folk-Blues Train: Alan Lomax Field and Studio Recordings* [CD], notes by Neil Slaven (London: Castle Music/Sanctuary Records, CMETD 648, 2003).

56. Ibid. Lomax, *The Land Where the Blues Began*, 461.

57. "Blues in the Mississippi Night."

58. Ibid.

59. Lomax, *The Land Where the Blues Began*, 473.

60. Memphis Slim (as "Leroy"), Sonny Boy Williamson (as "Sib"), Big Bill Broonzy (as "Natchez"). *Blues in the Mississippi Night: The Real Story of the Blues*, recorded by Alan Lomax, March 2, 1947 (New York: United Artists, UAL 4027, 1959).

61. *Billboard*, "Record Reviews," *Billboard*, August 9, 1947, 136.

62. Filisko, interview by the author, July 11, 2011.

63. *Billboard*, "Record Reviews," *Billboard*, May 29, 1948, 136. *Billboard* introduced the rating system in this year. According to the ratings, "Alcohol Blues" is overall 76; disk jockey 75; dealer 75; and operator 78. "Apple Tree

Swing" is overall 60; disk jockey 57; dealer 58; and operator 63. Some reviewers still preferred Sonny Boy's slow blues songs to swing-influenced tunes. Ibid.

64. Big Joe Williams recorded "Baby Please Don't Go" in 1935 and 1941. The 1941 version is titled "Please Don't Go." Sonny Boy played the harmonica for this version.

65. *Chicago Defender*, January 25, 1947, 29.

66. *Anniston Alabama Star*, March 23, 1947.

67. Bill Dahl, "Billy Boy Arnold: Back Where He Belongs," *Blues Revue*, no. 12 (June/July 2008): 21.

68. Dahl, "Billy Boy Arnold," 28.

69. *Chicago Defender*, August 9, 1947, 25.

70. *Chicago Defender*, September 13, 1947, 29. Jimmie Boyd is possibly Eddie Boyd.

71. Lorenz, *Bluebird Blues*, 176.

72. The third-round solo is by guitarist Willie Lacey.

73. Filisko, interview by the author, July 11, 2011.

74. Steve Cushing, *Blues before Sunrise: The Radio Interviews* (Urbana: University of Illinois Press, 2010), 149–50.

75. *Billboard*, "Record Reviews," *Billboard*, February 12, 1949, 109.

76. This song has no relation to Jazz Gillum's "No Friend Blues." They only share the same title.

77. As pointed out in chapter 3, "Sloppy Drunk Blues" was first recorded by Lucille Bogan in March 1930. Sonny Boy covered Leroy Carr's version.

78. *Billboard*, "The *Billboard* Music Popularity Charts, Part VI Race Records, Week Ending July 23: Advance Race Record Releases," *Billboard*, July 31, 1948, 33.

79. *Billboard*, "Record Reviews," *Billboard*, September 25, 1948, 129.

80. Ibid. According to the ratings, "Stop Breaking Down" is overall 70; disk jockey 68; dealer 70; and operator 72. "Rub a Dub" is overall 72; disk jockey 78; dealer 70; and operator 78. Ibid.

81. *Billboard*, "Record Reviews," *Billboard*, December 18, 1948, 112. According to the ratings, "The Big Boat" is overall 67; disk jockey 66; dealer 68; and operator 68. "Better Cut That Out" is overall 69; disk jockey 68; dealer 70; and operator 70. Ibid.

82. The number of sides Big Joe recorded implies that the forthcoming recording ban by the musicians' union was predicted, as Sonny Boy likewise recorded more songs than usual for his last leader session on November 12, 1947.

83. Filisko, interview by the author, July 11, 2011.

84. O'Neal, Wisner, and Nelson, "Snooky Pryor," 10.

85. *Okeh Chicago Blues*, notes by Jim O'Neal (New York: Columbia/Epic, EG 37318, 1982), 17. Rice Miller later recorded the theme for *King Biscuit Time* as "Good Evening Everybody" for Chess Records on August 12, 1955. It was released under "Sonny Boy Williamson."

86. Little Brother Montgomery claims that his "Vicksburg Blues" was the source for Sykes's "Forty-Four Blues," although Sykes recorded it in 1929, a year earlier than Montgomery, who recorded in 1930. Karl Bert zur Heide, *Deep South Piano: The Story of Little Brother Montgomery* (London: Studio Vista, 1970), 19–21. "Forty-Four Blues" is thoroughly discussed in Paul Oliver, "The Forty-Four," in *Screening the Blues: Aspects of the Blues Tradition*, 1st ed. (New York: Da Capo, 1989), 90–127. "Vicksburg Blues" is known as the hardest barrelhouse piano blues of any blues in history to play because of the double-time meter. In "Vicksburg Blues" and its variation "44 Blues," on the basis of the pulse of four-four time (1-and-2-and-3-and-4-and-, instead of simply 1-2-3-4), a right hand plays a fast shuffle pattern, while a left hand plays a slow blues pattern accentuated by quick arpeggio figures.

87. Stewart-Baxter, "Blues and News from *Blues Unlimited*: The Two Sonny Boy Williamsons: Part 1," 16–17.

88. Mike Rowe, "I Was Really Dedicated: An Interview with Billy Boy Arnold, Part 1: A Memory of Sonny Boy," *Blues Unlimited*, no. 126 (1977): 5.

5. THE FINAL DAYS

1. Billy Boy Arnold, "The Last Time I Saw Sonny Boy," *Melody Maker*, November 27, 1971, 28.

2. David Evans, "From Bumble Bee Slim to Black Boy Shine: Nicknames of Blues Singers," in *Ramblin' on My Mind*, ed. David Evans (Urbana: University of Illinois Press, 2008), 207.

3. Les Fancourt and Bob McGrath, *The Blues Discography 1943–1970* (West Vancouver, BC: Eyeball Productions, 2006), 593.

4. Jim O'Neal and Amy van Singel, "Houston Stackhouse," in *The Voice of the Blues: Classic Interviews from* Living Blues *Magazine*, ed. Jim O'Neal and Amy van Singel (New York; London: Routledge, 2002), 113.

5. Robert M. W. Dixon, John Godrich, and Howard Rye, *Blues and Gospel Records, 1890–1943*, 4th ed. (Oxford: Clarendon Press, 1997), 1043. Fancourt and McGrath, *The Blues Discography 1943–1970*, 589.

6. "Sonny Boy Williams: this artist's real name is Enoch Williams; his records are more jazz than blues." Dixon, Godrich, and Rye, *Blues and Gospel Records, 1890–1943*, 1043.

7. There were also other "Sonny Boys" after the death of John Lee "Sonny Boy" Williamson, but they possibly nicknamed themselves after Rice Miller "Sonny Boy." One-man band Joe Hill Louis recorded as Chicago Sunny Boy in 1953. There were Little Sonny (recorded in 1958) and Sugar Boy Williams (recorded in 1960). Fancourt and McGrath, *The Blues Discography 1943–1970*, 345, 338, 589. Alan Lomax mentioned he met Sonny Boy Rogers, who was Forest City Joe's favorite guitar player, in 1959. Alan Lomax, *The Land Where the Blues Began* (New York: Pantheon, 1993), 475.

8. Steve Cushing, *Blues before Sunrise: The Radio Interviews* (Urbana: University of Illinois Press, 2010), 76.

9. Bob Koester, interview by the author, Chicago, July 11, 2011.

10. Arnold, "The Last Time I Saw Sonny Boy," 28.

11. Thomas W. Utley, Fred Utley, Mary Lou Utley, Linda Utley King, and Michael Baker, interview by Jim O'Neal, Jackson, Tennessee, January 30, 1997.

12. Snooky Pryor said, "And I remember when Sonny Boy [John Lee] went from [Chicago] down to Helena, and pulled him off the air. Yeah." Jim O'Neal, Steve Wisner, and David Nelson, "Snooky Pryor: I Started the Big Noise around Chicago," *Living Blues*, no. 123 (September/October 1995): 11.

13. Larry Hoffman, "Robert Lockwood Jr.," in *Rollin' and Tumblin': The Postwar Blues Guitarists*, ed. Jas Obrecht (San Francisco: Miller Freeman, 2000), 172–73.

14. Thomas W. Utley, Fred Utley, Mary Lou Utley, Linda Utley King, and Michael Baker, interview by Jim O'Neal, January 30, 1997.

15. Ibid.

16. Koester, interview by the author, July 11, 2011.

17. Emma Bruce Ross, "Society/Entertainment—around the Town: 'I Knew "Sonny Boy,"'" *Metro Forum*, December 20–27, 1990–January 2, 1991, 6.

18. Ibid.

19. Steve Baker, "'What Makes Johnny Run'—an Interview with Mrs. Emma Bruce Ross," March 5, 1992 (Oral History Collection, Union University, 1992), 40.

20. Ibid., 41.

21. Ibid., 40.

22. Ibid.

23. Ross, "Society/Entertainment," 6.

24. Henry Townsend, as told to Bill Greensmith, *A Blues Life* (Urbana: University of Illinois Press, 1999), 81.

25. Big Bill Broonzy, *Big Bill Blues: William Broonzy's Story as Told to Yannick Bruynoghe* (London: Cassel & Company, 1955), 95.

26. Mike Rowe, "I Was Really Dedicated: An Interview with Billy Boy Arnold, Part 1: A Memory of Sonny Boy," *Blues Unlimited*, no. 126 (1977): 5.

27. Billy Boy Arnold, "The Last Time I Saw Sonny Boy," *Melody Maker*, November 27, 1971, 28.

28. Gary Erwin, "The Strange Case of the Two Sonny Boys," *Poor William's Omnibus* 3, no. 4 (January 1988): 14.

29. John Anthony Brisbin, "Jimmy Rogers," in *Rollin' and Tumblin': The Postwar Blues Guitarists*, ed. Jas Obrecht (San Francisco: Miller Freeman, 2000), 128.

30. Billy Boy Arnold, interview by the author, Chicago, June 24, 2011.

31. Ibid.

32. Ibid.

33. Ibid. "G. M. & O. Blues" coupled with "Mellow Chick Swing" was released as RCA Victor 20-2369 in 1947. "Wow wow wow" is heard in the solo section of "Mellow Chick Swing."

34. Ibid.

35. Billy Boy Arnold said in the interview, "He had his own trio. I heard Eddie Boyd played with them. And when I went to his house, Johnny Jones was playing the piano." Ibid.

36. Ibid.

37. Ibid. Billy Boy talked about the price of records then. "Some of them were on Bluebird label. It was a subsidiary of RCA Victor. Some were on RCA Victor. Ones on RCA Victor came out in 1945. That's the first time blues were on RCA Victor Records and they deleted Bluebird Records. But the Bluebird Records were still in the record shops all over Chicago. Bluebird sold for 40 cents, while RCA Victor records sold for 79 cents." Ibid.

38. Ibid.

39. Ibid. Billy Boy later on found that "Bill" was Lazy Bill Lucas.

40. Ibid.

41. Ibid.

42. Ibid.

43. Ibid.

44. Ibid.

45. I. A. L. Brodie, Coroner of Cook County, "Inquest upon the Body of John Lee Williamson" (Cook County, Illinois, 1948), 19, 38.

46. Ibid., 3.

47. Little Hudson's statement is detailed later in the chapter.

48. Brodie, "Inquest upon the Body of John Lee Williamson," 31–32.

49. Thomas W. Utley and Fred Utley, interview by Michael Baker, Jackson, Tennessee, January 19, 1992. In the interview with Jim O'Neal, T. W. said, "Lacey called me about 5 o'clock in the morning when I got here. . . . [She said] 'Sonny Boy got killed. Died. [clear throat] He was attacked . . . with some kind of sharp instrument. And he had been dragged quite a bit and hemorrhaged . . .

died on an operating table." Thomas W. Utley, Fred Utley, Mary Lou Utley, Linda Utley King, and Michael Baker, interview by Jim O'Neal, January 30, 1997.

50. Mary S. Reed, "He Lived and Died the Blues: Jackson's Sonny Boy Took His Music to the Top," *Jackson Sun*, November 12, 1989, 2C.

51. Thomas W. Utley and Fred Utley, interview by Michael Baker, January 19, 1992.

52. Ibid.

53. Richard Congress, *Blues Mandolin Man: The Life and Music of Yank Rachell* (Jackson: University Press of Mississippi, 2001), 68.

54. Reed, "He Lived and Died the Blues," 2C.

55. Arnold, interview by the author, June 24, 2011.

56. Brodie, "Inquest upon the Body of John Lee Williamson," 30.

57. Rowe, "I Was Really Dedicated," 7.

58. Reed, "He Lived and Died the Blues," 2C.

59. Theo R. Hawes, "Metropolitan Funeral Parlors: Funerals Held May 29, 1948 to and Including June 4, 1948," *Chicago Defender*, June 12, 1948, 30.

60. "Jackson News," *Chicago Defender*, June 26, 1948, 19.

61. *Jackson Sun*, June 6, 1948, section two, 15.

62. See chapter 2.

63. Dave Clark, "Windy City Chatter," Associated Negro Press News Releases, Claude A. Barnett Collection, June 16, 1948, 11.

64. Rowe, "I Was Really Dedicated," 5.

65. Townsend, *A Blues Life*, 93.

66. Arnold, interview by the author, June 24, 2011.

67. Mark K. Dolan writes, "Bluesmen were outsiders, and the *Defender* covered none of their performances, not even printing an obituary for Chicago resident Blind Lemon Jefferson, who froze to death on a city street in 1929 after migrating from Texas. . . . It underscored the role of the *Defender* as vehicle for the music and at the same time its lack of editorial attention to artists such as Jefferson, whose country blues songs were too lowbrow to discuss in its entertainment news, despite the prevalence of ads for him." "Extra! *Chicago Defender* Race Records Ads Show South Afar," *Southern Cultures* 13, no. 3 (2007): 114–15.

68. Ibid.

69. Big Joe Williams, *Piney Woods Blues* [Phonograph], notes by Bob Koester (Chicago: Delmark Records, DS-602, 1969; CD reissue, DD-602, 1997).

70. Ibid.

71. Hugues Panassié and Madeleine Gautier, "Sonny Boy Williamson," *Jazz Journal* 8, no. 4 (April 1955): 1. Hugues Panassié and Madeleine Gautier,

"Williamson, John Lee 'Sonny Boy,'" *Guide to Jazz* (Boston: Houghton Mifflin, 1956), 299.

72. Sonny Boy Williamson [Rice Miller], *Down and Out Blues* [LP record], liner notes by Studs Terkel (Chicago: Chess Records/Checker LP 1437, 1959; reissue [CD], Tokyo: Chess Records/Universal Music Japan, UICY-93205, 2001).

73. Francis Smith, "Study in Violence: The Death of Sonny Boy Williamson," in *Nothing but the Blues*, ed. Mike Leadbitter (London: Hanover Books, 1971), 3. The article originally appeared as "The Death of Sonny Boy Williamson: Told for the First Time," *Blues Unlimited*, no. 48 (November/December 1967): 14–15.

74. Ibid., 4.

75. Ibid., 5.

76. Jim O'Neal and Amy van Singel, *The Voice of the Blues: Classic Interviews from* Living Blues *Magazine*, ed. Jim O'Neal and Amy van Singel (New York, London: Routledge, 2002), 241.

77. Ibid., 242.

78. Bob Rusch, "Blind John Davis: Interview," *Cadence*, June 1978, 21.

79. Cushing, *Blues before Sunrise*, 11. Yank Rachell shared the same story on other occasions. See his *Living Blues* interview, Steve Cushing, Pete Crawford, and Rich DelGrosso, "James 'Yank' Rachell," *Living Blues*, no. 79 (March/April 1988): 17; and his biography, Congress, *Blues Mandolin Man*, 67.

80. Congress, *Blues Mandolin Man*, 67.

81. Cushing, *Blues before Sunrise*, 150.

82. Ibid. Yank Rachell remembered a similar incident. See chapter 2.

83. Cushing, *Blues before Sunrise*, 150.

84. Baker, "'What Makes Johnny Run,'" 41.

85. Ibid., 43.

86. Tom Fisher, "Williamson, Sonny Boy I (John Lee Williamson)," in *Encyclopedia of the Blues*, ed. Edward M. Komara (New York: Routledge, 2006), 2:1087.

87. For example, Kim Field wrote, "Half an hour later his wife found him struggling to open the door of their apartment and bleeding heavily from a head wound and a gash near his left eye; someone had attacked him with an ice pick." Kim Field, *Harmonicas, Harps, and Heavy Breathers: The Evolution of the People's Instrument* (New York: Fireside, Simon & Schuster, 1993), 167. See also the Internet encyclopedia, *Fact Monster*, http://www.factmonster.com/ipka/A0780961.html (accessed August 14, 2013).

88. Tony Glover, Scott Dirks, and Ward Gaines, *Blues with a Feeling: The Little Walter Story* (New York: Routledge, 2002), 48. In other interviews, Billy Boy implied that some famous musicians were involved in this incident.

6. EPILOGUE: SONNY BOY'S LEGACY

1. *Billboard*, "The *Billboard* Music Popularity Charts, Part VI Race Records, Week Ending July 23: Advance Race Record Releases," *Billboard*, July 31, 1948, 33.

2. Advance Race Record Releases, *Billboard*, February 19, 1949, 32.

3. "Now the New Ones Are on 45RPM!" *Billboard*, May 14, 1949, 23.

4. Ibid.

5. Hugues Panassié and Madeleine Gautier, "Sonny Boy Williamson," *Jazz Journal* 8, no. 4 (April 1955): 1.

6. Ibid.

7. Ibid.

8. Hugues Panassié and Madeleine Gautier, "Williamson, John Lee 'Sonny Boy,'" in *Guide to Jazz* (Boston: Houghton Mifflin, 1956), 299.

9. "Miscellany: One Mouth, Two Voices," *Manchester Guardian*, January 23, 1954, 3. Big Bill Broonzy was the first blues artist who performed in Europe, in 1951. He performed numerous times in the United Kingdom during the 1950s.

10. Derrick Stewart-Baxter, "Blues and News from *Blues Unlimited*: The Two Sonny Boy Williamsons: Part 1," *Jazz Journal* 18, no. 5 (May 1965): 16.

11. Ibid.

12. Billy Boy Arnold, "The Last Time I Saw Sonny Boy," *Melody Maker*, November 27, 1971, 28.

13. Ibid.

14. Billy Boy Arnold, interview by the author, Chicago, June 24, 2011.

15. In the liner notes for the album *Down and Out Blues* by Rice Miller "Sonny Boy," Studs Terkel wrote, "In Tuscaloosa, Alabama, lived another Williamson. He, too, sang the blues. And when the original died, this one became Sonny Boy." Sonny Boy Williamson [Rice Miller], *Down and Out Blues*, liner notes by Studs Terkel (Chicago: Chess Records/Checker LP 1437, 1959).

16. http://repertoire.bmi.com/writer.asp?page=1&blnWriter=True& blnPublisher=True&blnArtist=True&fromrow=1&torow=25&affiliation=BMI& cae=63518677&keyID=371989&keyname= WILLIAMSON%20SONNY%20BOY&querytype=WriterID (accessed September 16, 2013).

17. As discussed in chapter 2, reworking existing songs was a common technique in blues composition. There are numerous instances where writers copyrighted reworked songs as their original compositions throughout history.

18. Jim O'Neal, "BluEsoterica: Good Morning, Little School Girl," *Living Blues* 36, no. 6 (January/February 2006): 181.

19. Thomas W. Utley, Fred Utley, Mary Lou Utley, Linda Utley King, and Michael Baker, interview by Jim O'Neal, Jackson, Tennessee, January 30, 1997.

20. Bob Koester, interview by the author, Chicago, July 11, 2011.

21. Ibid.

22. Ibid.

23. Ibid.

24. Mary S. Reed, "He Lived and Died the Blues: Jackson's Sonny Boy Took His Music to the Top," *Jackson Sun*, November 12, 1989, 1C.

25. Ibid.

26. Curtis Coghlan, "Sonny Boy's Grave Tells Tale of Jackson's Apathy: Blues Great Virtually Unknown in His Own Hometown," *Jackson Sun*, November 12, 1989, 3E.

27. Ibid.

28. Emma Bruce Ross, "Society/Entertainment—around the Town: 'I Knew "Sonny Boy,"'" *Metro Forum*, December 20–27, 1990–January 2, 1991, 6.

29. Judy Pennel and Michael Baker, "Blues News: Remembering Sonny Boy Number One," *Living Blues*, no. 89 (November/December 1989): 4.

30. Michael Baker, e-mail correspondence with the author, October 3, 2013.

31. Ibid.

32. Mary S. Reed, "Madison to Honor Musician: Marker to Go Up for Blues Legend," *Jackson Sun*, May 18, 1990, 1B.

33. Linda T. Wynn, "John Lee 'Sonny Boy' Williamson: Blues Innovator," *Courier* 29, no. 2 (February 1991): 4–5.

34. Linda Zettler, "Singing Sonny Boy's Praises: Jackson Legend's Fame Cast in Stone—at Last," *Jackson Sun*, June 2, 1990, 2A.

35. *John Lee "Sonny Boy" Williamson: June 1, 1990* [video recording] (Jackson: Jackson-Madison County Library, 1990).

36. Baker, e-mail correspondence with the author, October 3, 2013.

37. Ibid.

38. Baker, e-mail correspondence with the author, October 7, 2013.

39. Zettler, "Singing Sonny Boy's Praises," 2A.

40. The announcement appeared in the *Commercial Appeal*, June 27, 1990, issue. The article introduced Sonny Boy's well-known songs as "Don't Start Me Talkin'," "One Way Out," and "Nine below Zero," all of which were actually part of Rice Miller's repertoire. "Two Hometown Festivals to Honor Blues Legend," stated the *Commercial Appeal* article (June 27, 1990, 13). The article was corrected in the June 30 issue: "Corrections and Amplifications," *Commercial Appeal*, June 30, 1990, 2.

41. Mary S. Reed, "Old Blues Ways Followed," *Jackson Sun*, September 4, 1990, 2A.

42. Ibid.

43. Yank's three of four children became musicians. He called his son the best gospel singer in town, and his granddaughter played in Yank's band. Yank

had moved to Indianapolis, where his youngest daughter lived. Sleepy John Estes and Hammie Nixon performed as a duo. They played in Japan in 1974. They were some of the first blues artists who performed in Japan, as well as B. B. King (1971 and 1972) and Robert Lockwood Jr. (1974).

44. Baker, e-mail correspondence with the author, October 7, 2013.

45. Ibid.

46. John Anthony Brisbin, "Jimmy Rogers," in *Rollin' and Tumblin': The Postwar Blues Guitarists*, ed. Jas Obrecht (San Francisco: Miller Freeman, 2000), 119.

47. Snooky Pryor said, "Well, I listened to Ma Rainey, Blind Lemon—Blind Jefferson, Charley Patton, and then on up to Sonny Boy number two, which is Rice Miller, and then Sonny Boy number one [John Lee Williamson] started to makin' records, and I started to listen to him much." Jim O'Neal, Steve Wisner, and David Nelson, "Snooky Pryor: I Started the Big Noise around Chicago," *Living Blues*, no. 123 (September/October 1995): 10. Snooky's December 1948 recording, "Fine Boogie," shows strong influence from Sonny Boy's playing style.

48. Joe Filisko, interview by the author, Chicago, July 11, 2011.

49. Ibid.

50. Ibid.

BIBLIOGRAPHY

INTERVIEWS

Arnold, Billy Boy. Interview by the author. Chicago, June 24, 2011.
Filisko, Joe. Interview by the author. Chicago, July 11, 2011.
Koester, Bob. Interview by the author. Chicago, July 11, 2011.
Utley, Thomas W., and Fred Utley. Interview by Michael Baker. Jackson, Tennessee, January 19, 1992.
Utley, Thomas W., Fred Utley, Mary Lou Utley, Linda Utley King, and Michael Baker. Interview by Jim O'Neal. Jackson, Tennessee, January 30, 1997.

E-MAIL CORRESPONDENCE

Baker, Michael. E-mail correspondence with the author, October 3, 2013.
———. E-mail correspondence with the author, October 7, 2013.

WRITTEN SOURCES

Ankeny, Jason. "Hambone Willie Newbern." In *All Music Guide to the Blues: The Expert's Guide to the Best Blues Recordings*, edited by Michael Erlewine, Vladimir Bogdanov, Chris Woodstra, and Cub Koda. San Francisco: Miller Freeman, 1996.
Anon. "Aurora's Blues." *Aurora History*, January–February–March 1997, 5.
Anon. "Colored Dead [obituary]." *Jackson Sun*, June 6, 1948, 15.
Anon. "Jackson News." *Chicago Defender*, June 26, 1948, 19.
Anon. "Marker Is Fitting Tribute." *Jackson Sun*, May 30, 1990, 6A.
Anon. "Miscellany: One Mouth, Two Voices." *Manchester Guardian*, January 23, 1954, 3.
Anon. "Nancie Jane Taylor [obituary]." *Jackson Sun*, September 20, 1985, 10B.
Anon. Proclamation for John Lee "Sonny Boy" Williamson Day [certificate]. City of Jackson, Tennessee, County of Madison, Tennessee, June 1990.
Anon. "Two Hometown Festivals to Honor Blues Legend." *Commercial Appeal*, June 27, 1990, C4. Reprinted in *Blues & Rhythm*, no. 54 (August 1990): 17.

Anon. "Urban Street Beat . . . Blues Great Honored." *Urban Network: Information Update.* (Page from unidentified publication, possibly *Urban Network*, ca. June 1990.)

Arnold, Billy Boy. "In Search of Sonny." *Melody Maker*, November 20, 1971, 22.

———. "The Last Time I Saw Sonny Boy." *Melody Maker*, November 27, 1971, 28.

Baker, Steve. "'What Makes Johnny Run'—an Interview with Mrs. Emma Bruce Ross," March 5, 1992. Oral History Collection, Union University, 1992.

Beauchamp, Lincoln T., Jr. *Blues Speak: The Best of the Original Chicago Blues Annual.* Urbana: University of Illinois Press, 2010.

Beers, D. G., and J. Lanagan. *State of Tennessee* [map]. Philadelphia, 1877.

Billboard. "The *Billboard* Music Popularity Charts, Part VI Race Records, Week Ending July 23: Advance Race Record Releases." *Billboard*, July 31, 1948, 33.

———. "Now the New Ones Are on 45RPM!" *Billboard*, May 14, 1949, 23.

———. "Part 4—The *Billboard* Music Popularity Chart, Week Ending May 23, 1946: Reviews of New Records." *Billboard*, June 15, 1946, 32.

———. "Record Reviews." *Billboard*, April 5, 1947, 122.

———. "Record Reviews." *Billboard*, August 9, 1947, 136.

———. "Record Reviews." *Billboard*, May 29, 1948, 136.

———. "Record Reviews." *Billboard*, September 25, 1948, 129.

———. "Record Reviews." *Billboard*, December 18, 1948, 112.

———. "Record Reviews." *Billboard*, February 12, 1949, 109.

Boatfield, Graham. "Four Blues Men." *Jazz Journal* 11, no. 4 (April 1958): 3–4, 6.

Bogdanov, Vladimir, Chris Woodstra, and Stephan Thomas Erlewine, eds. *All Music Guide to the Blues: The Definitive Guide to the Blues.* 3rd ed. San Francisco: Backbeat Books, 2003.

Brisbin, John Anthony. "Jimmy Rogers." In *Rollin' and Tumblin': The Postwar Blues Guitarists*, edited by Jas Obrecht, 115–52. San Francisco: Miller Freeman, 2000.

Broonzy, Big Bill. *Big Bill Blues: William Broonzy's Story as Told to Yannick Bruynoghe.* London: Cassel & Company, 1955.

Clark, Dave. "Green Dumps Band to Produce Show." *DownBeat*, November 15, 1941, 13.

———. "Windy City Chatter." Associated Negro Press News Releases. Claude A. Barnett Collection, June 16, 1948, 11.

Coghlan, Curtis. "Sonny Boy's Grave Tells Tale of Jackson's Apathy: Blues Great Virtually Unknown in His Own Hometown." *Jackson Sun*, November 12, 1989, 3E.

Cohn, Lawrence, ed. *Nothing but the Blues: The Music and the Musicians.* New York: Abbeville Press, 1993.

Congress, Richard. *Blues Mandolin Man: The Life and Music of Yank Rachell.* Jackson: University Press of Mississippi, 2001.

Corritore, Bob, Bill Ferris, and Jim O'Neal. "Willie Dixon (Part 1)." *Living Blues*, no. 81 (July–August 1988): 20.

Cortese, Vincent. "Tampa Red: Long Live the Guitar Wizard." *Blues Revue Quarterly*, no. 6 (Fall 1992): 22.

Cushing, Steve. *Blues before Sunrise: The Radio Interviews.* Urbana: University of Illinois Press, 2010.

Cushing, Steve, Pete Crawford, and Rich DelGrosso. "James 'Yank' Rachell." *Living Blues*, no. 79 (March/April 1988): 12–21.

———. "Sonny Boy Williamson [I]." In *All Music Guide to the Blues*, edited by Vladimir Bogdanov, Chris Woodstra, and Stephan Thomas Erlewine, 485–86. San Francisco: Backbeat Books, 2003.

Dahl, Bill. "Billy Boy Arnold: Back Where He Belongs." *Blues Revue*, no. 12 (June/July 2008): 21.

Davis, Francis. *The History of the Blues: The Roots, the Music, the People from Charley Patton to Robert Cray.* New York: Hyperion, 1995.

Davis, Frank Marshall. "Rating Hot Records." Associated Negro Press News Releases. Claude A. Barnett Collection, June 30, 1948, 10.

———. "Rating Hot Records." Associated Negro Press News Releases. Claude A. Barnett Collection, September 15, 1948, 13.

————. "Rating Hot Records." Associated Negro Press News Releases. Claude A. Barnett Collection, December 1, 1948, 13.

DeKoster, Jim. "Sonny Boy Williamson: The Bluebird Recordings, 1937–1938." *Living Blues*, no. 134 (July/August 1997): 101–2.

Dicaire, David. "John Lee 'Sonny Boy' Williamson (1914–1948): The Bluebird Blues." In *Blues Singers*, 74–78. Jefferson, NC: McFarland, 1999.

Dixon, Robert M. W., John Godrich, and Howard Rye. *Blues and Gospel Records, 1890–1943*. 4th ed. Oxford: Clarendon Press, 1997.

Dixon, Willie. "'I Am the Blues.'" *Living Blues*, no. 33 (July/August 1977): 9–10.

Dixon, Willie, with Don Snowden. *I Am the Blues: The Willie Dixon Story*. New York: Da Capo, 1989.

Dolan, Mark K. "Extra! *Chicago Defender* Race Records Ads Show South Afar." *Southern Cultures* 13, no. 3 (2007): 114–15.

Erlewine, Michael, Vladimir Bogdanov, Chris Woodstra, and Cub Koda, eds. *All Music Guide to the Blues: The Expert's Guide to the Best Blues Recordings*. San Francisco: Miller Freeman, 1996.

Erwin, Gary. "The Strange Case of the Two Sonny Boys." *Poor William's Omnibus* 3, no. 4 (January 1988): 1, 14–16.

Evans, David. *Big Road Blues: Tradition and Creativity in Folk Blues*. Berkeley: University of California Press, 1982.

————. "From Bumble Bee Slim to Black Boy Shine: Nicknames of Blues Singers." In *Ramblin' on My Mind*, edited by David Evans. Urbana: University of Illinois Press, 2008.

————. "Goin' up the Country: Blues in Texas and the Deep South." In *Nothing but the Blues: The Music and the Musicians*, edited by Lawrence Cohn, 33–86. New York: Abbeville Press, 1993.

————. "John Lee 'Sonny Boy' Williamson." In *Creating Traditions, Expanding Horizons: A History of Tennessee Arts*, edited by C. Van West and M. D. Binnicker, 424. Knoxville: University of Tennessee Press, 2004.

————. "Notes for Mitsutoshi Inaba's Manuscript." 2015.

Fancourt, Les, and Bob McGrath. *The Blues Discography 1943–1970*. West Vancouver, BC: Eyeball Productions, 2006.

Field, Kim. *Harmonicas, Harps, and Heavy Breathers: The Evolution of the People's Instrument*. New York: Fireside/Simon & Schuster, 1993.

Findlay, Alistair. "The Real St. Louis Blues." *Jazz Journal International* 36, no. 5 (1983): 13–14.

Fisher, Tom. "Williamson, Sonny Boy I (John Lee Williamson)." In *Encyclopedia of the Blues*, edited by Edward M. Komara, 2:1086–87. New York: Routledge, 2006.

Gilley, Dawayne, and Brenda Haskins. "Henry Townsend." *Living Blues*, no. 164 (July/August 2008): 18–25.

Glaze, John. "Sonny Boy Williamson." *Metro Forum*, June 6–12, 1990, 1.

Glover, Tony, Scott Dirks, and Ward Gaines. *Blues with a Feeling: The Little Walter Story*. New York: Routledge, 2002.

Hawes, Theo R. "Metropolitan Funeral Parlors: Funerals Held May 29, 1948 to and Including June 4, 1948." *Chicago Defender*, June 12, 1948, 30.

Heide, Karl Bert zur. *Deep South Piano: The Story of Little Brother Montgomery*. London: Studio Vista, 1970.

Helland, Dave. "A Naptown Blues Party." *Living Blues*, no. 13 (Summer 1973): 7–8.

Herzhaft, Gerard. *Encyclopedia of the Blues*. 2nd ed. Translated by Brigitte Debora. Fayetteville: University of Arkansas Press, 1997.

Hoffman, Larry. "John Lee 'Sonny Boy' Williamson: The Bluebird Recordings 1938." *Living Blues*, no. 136 (November/December 1997): 85–86.

————. "Robert Lockwood Jr." In *Rollin' and Tumblin': The Postwar Blues Guitarists*, edited by Jas Obrecht, 172–73. San Francisco: Miller Freeman, 2000.

————. "Robert Lockwood Jr. Interview." *Living Blues*, no. 121 (June 1995): 12–29.

Hoffman, Lawrence. "The Blues Harp." *Living Blues*, no. 99 (September/October 1991): 24–31.

———. "The Blues Harp, Part Two." *Living Blues*, no. 100 (November/December 1991): 43–48.
———. "The Blues Harp." *Living Blues*, no. 167 (March/April/May 2003): 111–23 [reprint of "The Blues Harp" (*Living Blues*, no. 99) and "The Blues Harp, Part Two" (no. 100)].
Huggins, Cilla. "Billy Boy, Neal Pattman and a Prisoner's Plea." *Juke Blues*, no. 33 (Summer 1995): 30–31.
Inaba, Mitsutoshi. *Willie Dixon: Preacher of the Blues*. Lanham, MD: Scarecrow Press, 2011.
Interstate Directory Co. *Jackson and Bemis, Tennessee City Directory 1939–1940*. 1st ed. Parsons, KS: Interstate Directory Co., 1939.
Kindlon, Skip. "Sonny Boy's Blues." *Fox Valley Blues Society Newsletter*, n.d., 2–3.
Komara, Edward M. *Encyclopedia of the Blues*. New York: Routledge, 2006.
Kotez and Mie Senoo. *Blues Harmonica Yokubari Guide* [Blues Harmonica Greedy Guide]. Tokyo: P-Vine Books, 2012.
Lee, Peter, and David Nelson. "Willie Foster: Right Out the Cotton Field." *Living Blues*, no. 106 (November/December 1992): 33–38.
Lomax, Alan. *The Land Where the Blues Began*. New York: Pantheon, 1993.
Lorenz, Wolfgang. *Bluebird Blues*. Bonn: Moonshine Blues Books, 1986.
Lornell, Kip, and Jim O'Neal. "Sleepy John Estes and Hammie Nixon." In *The Voice of the Blues*, edited by Jim O'Neal and Amy van Singel. New York: Routledge, 2002. Originally published as "*Living Blues* Interview: Hammie Nixon and Sleepy John Estes." *Living Blues*, no. 19 (January/February 1975): 13–19.
Memphis Commercial Appeal, with David Evans and Jim O'Neal. "Hammie Nixon [obituary]." *Living Blues*, no. 62 (Winter 1984): 43–44.
Millar, Chris, and Mike Rainsford. "We Were Bad to the Bone! Homesick James Interviewed." *Blues and Rhythm, the Gospel Truth*, no. 95 (January 1995): 4–8.
Moon, Thomas. "The Verdict on Big Joe Williams." *Blues Access*, no. 33 (Spring 1998): 20–28.
"Oberstein, Eli and Maurice." *Welcome to Donald Clarke's Music Box: Donald's Encyclopedia of Popular Music*. www.donaldclarkemusicbox.com/encyclopedia/detail.php?s=2735. Accessed December 19, 2013.
Oliver, Paul. *Blues Off the Record: Thirty Years of Blues Commentary*. Tunbridge Wells, UK: Baton Press, 1984. Reprint, New York: Da Capo, 1984. Citations are from the Da Capo edition.
———. *Conversation with the Blues*. 2nd ed. Cambridge: Cambridge University Press, 1997.
———. *Screening the Blues: Aspects of the Blues Tradition*. 1st ed. London: Cassell, 1968. Reprint, New York: Da Capo, 1989.
———. *The Story of the Blues*. Philadelphia: Chilton, 1969. Reprint, Boston: Northeastern University Press, 1997. Citations are from the Northeastern University edition.
Olsson, Bengt. *Memphis Blues and Jug Bands*. London: Studio Vista, 1970.
O'Neal, Jim. "Big Bill Opening the Door to the Blues." *Living Blues*, no. 55 (Winter 1982/1983): 4–5.
———. "BluEsoterica: Good Morning, Little School Girl." *Living Blues*, no. 181 (November/December 2005): 96.
———. "Sonny Boy 'John Lee' Williamson." *DownBeat* 41, no. 15 (September 12, 1974): 26.
O'Neal, Jim, and Amy van Singel, eds. *The Voice of the Blues: Classic Interviews from Living Blues Magazine*. New York; London: Routledge, 2002.
O'Neal, Jim, Steve Wisner, and David Nelson. "Snooky Pryor: I Started the Big Noise around Chicago." *Living Blues*, no. 123 (September/October 1995): 8–21.
Orodenker, M. H. "Part 3—The *Billboard* Music Popularity Chart, Week Ending May 11, 1944: Folk Record Reviews." *Billboard*, May 20, 1944, 21.
———. "Part 3—The *Billboard* Music Popularity Chart, Week Ending June 29, 1944: Folk Record Reviews." *Billboard*, July 8, 1944, 23.
———. "Part 4—The *Billboard* Music Popularity Chart, Week Ending May 23, 1946: Reviews of New Records." *Billboard*, June 15, 1946, 32.
Palmer, Robert. *Deep Blues*. New York: Viking, 1981. Reprint, New York: Penguin, 1982. Citations are from the Penguin edition.

Panassié, Hugues. "The Blues Singers." *Melody Maker*, May 24, 1952, 9.

Panassié, Hugues, and Madeleine Gautier. "Sonny Boy Williamson." *Jazz Journal* 8, no. 4 (April 1955): 1–2. (Note: Includes discography.)

———. "Williamson, John Lee 'Sonny Boy.'" In *Guide to Jazz*. Boston: Houghton Mifflin, 1956.

Pearson, Barry Lee. "Sleepy John Estes." In *All Music Guide to the Blues: The Expert's Guide to the Best Blues Recordings*, edited by Michael Erlewine, Vladimir Bogdanov, Chris Woodstra, and Cub Koda. San Francisco: Miller Freeman, 1996.

Pearson, Barry Lee, and Bill McCulloch. *Robert Johnson: Lost and Found*. Urbana: University of Illinois Press, 2003.

Pennel, Judy, and Michael Baker. "Blues News: Remembering Sonny Boy Number One." *Living Blues*, no. 89 (November/December 1989): 4.

Pierson, Leroy. "St. Louis Blues." *Living Blues*, no. 3 (Autumn 1970): 20–21.

Reed, Mary S. "Blues Great Finally Recognized: Historical Marker to Honor Madison County Harmonica Genius." *Jackson Sun*, May 31, 1990, 1B, 2B.

———. "He Lived and Died the Blues: Jackson's Sonny Boy Took His Music to the Top." *Jackson Sun*, November 12, 1989, 1C, 2C.

———. "Jackson's First Bluesfest to Honor Sonny Boy." *Jackson Sun*, June 19, 1990, 1A.

———. "Local Blues Artist to Receive Marker 4 Decades after Death." *Jackson Sun*, March 25, 1990, 1A.

———. "Madison Countians Honor Native Blues Master." *Commercial Appeal*, June 10, 1990, G8.

———. "Madison to Honor Musician: Marker to Go Up for Blues Legend." *Jackson Sun*, May 18, 1990, 1B.

———. "Old Blues Ways Followed." *Jackson Sun*, September 4, 1990, 1A, 2A.

———. "'Something Going on Wrong': As Madison County Honors Sonny Boy No. 1, Everybody Wants to Get In on the Act." *Blues and Rhythm, the Gospel Truth*, no. 54 (August 1990): 17.

Riesman, Bob. *I Feel So Good: The Life and Times of Big Bill Broonzy*. Chicago: University of Chicago Press, 2011.

Rijn, Guido van. *Roosevelt's Blues: African-American Blues and Gospel Songs on FDR*. Jackson: University Press of Mississippi, 1997.

Ross, Emma Bruce. "Society/Entertainment—around the Town: 'I Knew "Sonny Boy."'" *Metro Forum*, December 20–27, 1990–January 2, 1990, 6.

Rowe, Mike. "I Was Really Dedicated: An Interview with Billy Boy Arnold, Part 1: A Memory of Sonny Boy." *Blues Unlimited*, no. 126 (1977): 5.

Rowland, Mary Pat. "West Tennessee Diary: Blues Legend Reaches Out." *Jackson Sun*, November 13, 1991, 10A.

Rusch, Bob. "Blind John Davis: Interview." *Cadence*, June 1978, 18–22.

Santelli, Robert. *The Big Book of Blues: A Biographical Encyclopedia*. New York: Penguin, 1993. Reprinted 2001.

Schwartz, Eric. "Aurora Happy about Its Blues History." *Beacon News*, February 22, 1997, n.p.

Smith, Chris. "A Memory of Sonny Boy." *Folk Roots*, no. 60 (June 1988): 31, 33.

———. "100 Years of Big Bill Broonzy." *Juke Blues*, no. 41 (Summer 1998): 41–44.

———. "Yank Rachell [obituary]." *Blues and Rhythm, the Gospel Truth*, no. 119 (May 1997): 10–11.

Smith, Francis. "Study in Violence: The Death of Sonny Boy Williamson." In *Nothing but the Blues*, edited by Mike Leadbitter, 3–6. London: Hanover Books, 1971. Originally published as "The Death of Sonny Boy Williamson: Told for the First Time." *Blues Unlimited*, no. 48 (November/December 1967): 14–15.

Stange, Maren, compiler. *Bronzeville: Black Chicago in Pictures, 1941–1943*. New York: New Press, 2003.

Stewart-Baxter, Derrick. "Blues and News from *Blues Unlimited*: The Two Sonny Boy Williamsons: Part 1." *Jazz Journal* 18, no. 5 (May 1965): 16–17.

Tatum, Aaron F. "'Sonny Boy' Lived, Played the Blues with Harmonica." *Independent Appeal*, November 8, 1990, 3A.

Townsend, Henry, as told to Bill Greensmith. *A Blues Life*. Urbana: University of Illinois Press, 1999.

Wheeler, Tom. "Muddy Waters and Johnny Winter." In *Rollin' and Tumblin': The Postwar Blues Guitarists*, edited by Jas Obrecht. San Francisco: Miller Freeman, 2000.

Whitburn, Joel. Billboard *Top R&B Singles 1942–1999*. Menomonee Falls, WI: Record Research Inc., 2000.

Wu, Olivia. "'Nice Little Festival' to Celebrate Aurora's Place in Blues History." *Metro*, February 12, 1997, 14.

Wynn, Linda T. "John Lee 'Sonny Boy' Williamson: Blues Innovator." *Courier* 29, no. 2 (February 1991): 4–5.

Wynn, Ron. "Speckled Red." In *All Music Guide to the Blues: The Definitive Guide to the Blues*, edited by Vladimir Bogdanov, Chris Woodstra, and Stephan Thomas Erlewine, 3rd ed. San Francisco: Backbeat Books, 2003.

Zettler, Linda. "Singing Sonny Boy's Praises: Jackson Legend's Fame Cast in Stone—at Last." *Jackson Sun*, June 2, 1990, 1A–2A.

LEGAL DOCUMENTS AND PUBLIC RECORDS

Brodie, I. A. L. Coroner of Cook County. "Inquest upon the Body of John Lee Williamson." Cook County, Illinois, 1948.

Coroner's Certificate of Death: John Lee Williamson. Chicago: State of Illinois, Department of Public Health, Division of Statistics and Records, 1948.

Coroner's Verdict about the Murder Case of John Lee Williamson. July 2, 1948.

Department of Commerce–Bureau of the Census. "The Sixteenth Census of the United States: 1940: Population Schedule, Beloit City, Rock County, Wisconsin." Washington, DC: Department of Commerce–Bureau of the Census, 1940.

Department of Police, Chicago. "Homicide Record about the Murder Case of John Lee Williamson on June 1, 1948." July 7, 1948.

People of the State of Illinois versus "Unknown Slayer: For the Fatal Assault of John Lee Williamson: Which occurred on June 1st, 1948 at about 2:30 A.M., the exact place of occurrence is unknown [police record]." June 2, 1948.

"Schedule 2—Slave Inhabitants in District No. 3 in the County of Madison of Tennessee, enumerated by me, on the 6th day of July 1860."

Social Security Death Index. Nancie Taylor, born February 15, 1894, died September 17, 1985. The Generations Network, Inc., 2012.

Social Security Death Index. Thomas William Utley, born February 15, 1919, died November 5, 2005. The Generations Network, Inc., 2012.

State of Tennessee, Madison County. Chancery Court Minute Book, 40 (1937–1938). Minutes December Term, January 21, 1937, 23.

———. Marriage License: Rafe Williamson and Nancy Utley, June 21, 1913.

———. Marriage License: Willie Utley and Nancy Williamson, June 10, 1918.

———. Marriage License: John Lee Williamson and Sallie Lee Hunt, June 14, 1933.

———. Marriage License: John Lee Williamson and Lacey Belle Davidson, November 13, 1937.

ELECTRONIC SOURCES

http://repertoire.bmi.com/writer.asp?page=1&blnWriter=True&blnPublisher=True&blnArtist=True&fromrow=1&torow=25&affiliation=BMI&cae=63518677&keyID=371989&keyname=WILLIAMSON%20SONNY%20BOY&querytype=WriterID. Accessed September 16, 2013.

http://us.playhohner.com/news/video-series-hohner-masters-of-the-harmonica. Accessed January 29, 2014.

AUDIO RECORDINGS

Compilations

"Blues in the Mississippi Night." *American Folk-Blues Train: Alan Lomax Field and Studio Recordings* [CD]. Notes by Neil Slaven. London: Castle Music/Sanctuary Records, CMETD 648, 2003.
Blues in the Mississippi Night: The Real Story of the Blues. Recorded by Alan Lomax, March 2, 1947. New York: United Artists, UAL 4027, 1959.
Harmonica Blues: Great Harmonica Performances of the 1920s and '30s. Notes by Steve Calt. New Town, NJ: Shanachie/Yazoo, 1053, 1991.
Okeh Chicago Blues. Notes by Jim O'Neal. New York: Columbia/Epic, EG 37318, 1982.
Tribute to Sonny Boy Williamson I & II. Notes by Akiyoshi Yasuda. Tokyo: P-Vine, PCD-5839/40.

Individual Artists

Arnold, Billy Boy. *Sings Sonny Boy.* Notes by Billy Boy Arnold. New York: Electro-Fi Records, 3405, 2008.
Davis, Walter. *M&O Blues* [CD]. Notes by Hitoshi Koide. Tokyo: P-Vine Records, PCD 20083, 2011.
Williams, Big Joe. *Piney Woods Blues.* Notes by Bob Koester. Chicago: Delmark Records, DD-602, 1997.
Williamson, John Lee "Sonny Boy." *The Bluebird Recordings 1938.* Notes by Jim O'Neal. New York: RCA, 07863 66796-2, 1997.
Williamson, Sonny Boy. *Blues Classics* [LP]. n.p., BC-3, 1964.
———. *The Bluebird Recordings 1937–1938.* Notes by Mark Humphrey. New York: RCA/BMG, 07863-66723-2, 1997.
———. *When the Sun Goes Down: Bluebird Blues.* Notes by Colin Escott and David Evans. New York: BMG Music, 82876-55156-2, 2003.
Williamson, Sonny Boy [Rice Miller]. *Down and Out Blues* [LP record]. Liner notes by Studs Terkel. Chicago: Chess Records/Checker LP 1437, 1959. Reissue [CD], Tokyo: Chess Records/Universal Music Japan, UICY-93205, 2001.
Williamson, the Original Sonny Boy. *The Original Sonny Boy Williamson: The Later Years.* Notes by Neil Slaven. London: JSP, 77101, 2008.
———. *The Original Sonny Boy Williamson: Vol. 1.* Notes by Neil Slaven. London: JSP, 7797, 2007.

GENERAL INDEX

SONG INDEX

ABOUT THE AUTHOR

Mitsutoshi Inaba was born in Hiroshima, Japan. He earned a PhD in music history and ethnomusicology from the University of Oregon and is the author of *Willie Dixon: Preacher of the Blues* (2011, Scarecrow Press). Dr. Inaba is assistant professor of African American studies in the Department of Languages and Literature at Austin Peay State University in Clarksville, Tennessee.